The Finest View in England

JERI BAPASOLA

The Finest View in England

THE LANDSCAPE AND GARDENS
AT
BLENHEIM PALACE

PUBLISHED BY BLENHEIM PALACE
© 2009 His Grace, The Duke of Marlborough

The Finest View in England: The Landscape and Gardens at Blenheim Palace

First published in the UK in 2009 by
Blenheim Palace
Woodstock, Oxfordshire OX20 1PP
United Kingdom

The right of Jeri Bapasola to be identified as the author of this work
has been asserted in accordance with the Copyright, Designs and Patents Act 1988.

All plant names have been quoted or used as they appear in the documents of the period.
The reader should be aware that the Linnaean binomial system of nomenclature
has not been employed in every instance.

British Library Cataloguing-in-Publication Data
A catalogue record for this book is available from The British Library
ISBN 978-0-9502344-5-8 (hardback)
ISBN 978-0-9502344-6-5 (paperback)

Photography by Peter Smith of Newbery Smith Photography.
Design, reprographics, editorial: Kaarin Wall, Kevin Parker, Jane Bulmer.
Jarrold Publishing, Norfolk NR18 9RS
A-81710-1/09

Printed and bound in Great Britain.

Front cover and title page: *View of Blenheim*, courtesy of and © OAHS
Half title page: *Blenheim House*, the Seat of His Grace, the Duke of Marlborough,
from a drawing by the Rt. Hon. Lord Viscount Duncannon, 1787 © Private Collection.
Back cover: *Epidendrum ensifolium*, watercolour by Susan Blandford.

LIST OF SUBSCRIBERS

Judy Anderson

Hugh I. Axton

Yehu & Victoria Azaz

Lyttleton J. Barrett

Barbara & Brynley Baughan

Nigel A.G. Benford

Denis Bicknell

John Blair

Peter de Brant

Catherine Button

Blythe Campbell

Heather Carter

Gillian Chandler

James Chandler &
   Nicole Schragger

John E. Clarke, OBE

Peter Colville

Diana Collinge

Lara Colyer

Richard Andrew Connell

Maggie Cook

Tim & Tessa Cunningham

Mark Deakin

Jacqueline Desbaillets

Tom & Louise Digweed

John Driskell

Elizabeth M. Eatock

Peter & Paula Evans

Sean & Fiona Finn

Byron & Blake Franchi

Christine Gadsby

Lucy Galloway

Andrew Gosnell

Benjamin Gosnell

David & Marie Gosnell

Richard Gosnell

Thomas Gosnell

Sue Graham

Geoffrey Groves

Kay Hare

Margaret Hare

Brian Hook

Tracy Hoy

Liz Hunter

Carol Janes

Dennis & Enid Jerrams

Stuart & Susan Kemp

Angela & Graham Knox

Shesnath Lal

Allan & Isabel Lee

Dino & Mary Lemonofides

Peter Logan

Kathleen D.J. Love

Marion Mako

Angela & Tony Mann

Kate Marshall

Duncan & Kristina Matthews

The Paul Mellon Centre
   for Studies in British Art

Kevin & Janette Millson

Ken & Betty Norman

Rachel Parkin

John Phibbs

Alan & Judy Poole

John G. Potter

Roger Powell

Graham R. Price

Andrew James Regan

Milton Reid

Jean Roberts

William & Eileen Rose

G.R. & A.J. Routledge

Anissa Schlichting

Peter & Linda Schonthal

John Sheppard

Steffie Shields

Wendy Slater

Sumie Smith

Malcolm Soul

Neil Stafford

Alastair Steadman

Trevor & Elaine Stokes

Jacquie & Roger Stone

Paul Taylor

Gary & Jane Thomson

J.E. Turvey

Albert & Ivy Walton

Craig & Louise Walton

John H. Wells

Leonard White

Michael & Eileen Willemite

Jeffrey Williams

Alan Willoughby

James Winpenny

Jiawei Zhang

Wei Zhang

Contents

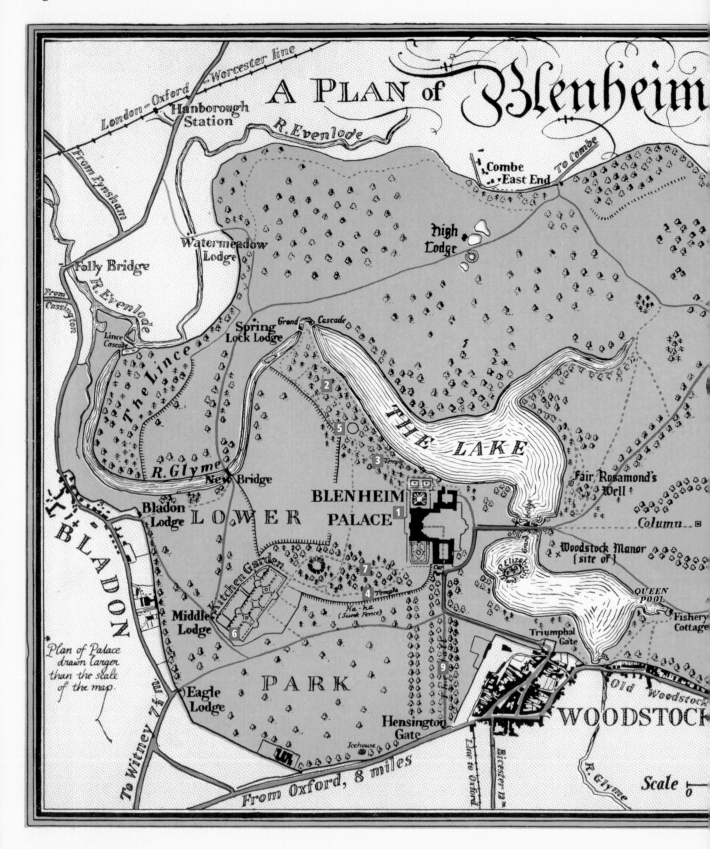

A PLAN of Blenheim

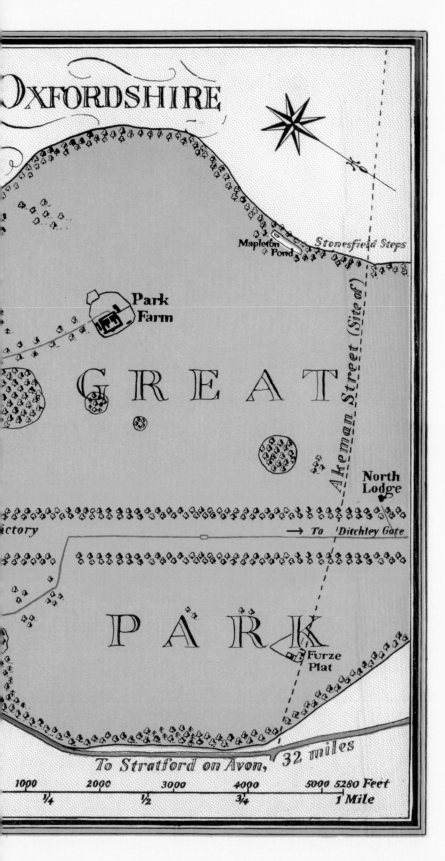

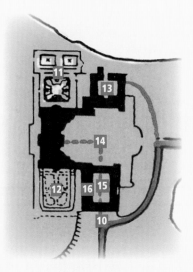

KEY TO MAIN PLAN

1 South lawn
2 Temple of Flora (relocated)
3 Temple of Diana
4 Temple of Health
5 Rose Garden
6 Maze
7 Secret Garden
8 North Avenue
9 East Avenue

BLENHEIM PALACE

10 East Gate (visitors' entrance)
11 Water Terraces
12 Italian Garden
13 Stable Court
14 North Court
15 Kitchen Court
16 Orangery

OXFORDSHIRE

Stonesfield Steps

Mapleton Pond

Park Farm

G R E A T

Akeman Street (Site of)

North Lodge

Rectory → To Ditchley Gate

P A R K

Furze Plat

To Stratford on Avon, 32 miles

| 1000 | 2000 | 3000 | 4000 | 5000 5280 Feet |
| ¼ | ½ | ¾ | 1 Mile |

Wigginton
Hokenorton   Milcombe   Ayno
                                        Clyfton
                  Borford   Deddington   Soulderne
      S. Neuncton   Hardw
Swerforde   Fritwell
            Wortons   N. Aston
      Twe mag   Somerton   Feuco
                    Ledwell
                                              Heyford
Rowleright mag   Buck
                    Stepleaston
e wright yua   Stepleborton   Ardley
                                              Heyfordpursell
      The Chapellonye heath   Middletonfto
ford   Westcolberton   Ronfim   Chefter
            Hethorp
                              Cydington
Chippingrton   Eynfton   Tade   Kirthington   Wen
                  Glympton   Wefto
      Dichley   Belchingto
esden Chadlingto Spelsburie   Wotton   Hamptongey
                              Chipton
            Woditok   in cheruel   Hamptonpoyle
            Cherlebury
Shorthampton   Stonsfeld   Kidlingto   Ifly
                              Baldo
            Logcombe   Begbrok
underwood Ascot   Wileot   Watercaton   Wode
                                        Yarnton
Langley Whichwood   N. Lee   Wuluercote   Mar
      forest   Longhanbora   Cafsenton
Siombrok   Minsterlonell Cogges   Anfham
                        S. Lee   OXFORD
Aftell   Wrightham
      Witney   Stannton   Both
Shilton   Laurence hinkey
      Caswell   Ducklington   S. Hnkfey
Nortonbrimere   Cunnor   Ifle
      Cockthorp   N. More   Kennyngton
Blakborton   Stanlake
      Yelford
      Shifford   Longworth   Newbridg
Bampton

1 *Before Blenheim*
THE ROYAL MANOR AT WOODSTOCK

Detail from a map of Oxfordshire by Saxton and Hole, 1637. ← **Woodstock is shown as an enclosed park. The earliest wall around it was reputed to be seven miles (11.2 km) long.**
© Private Collection

'As we passed through the entrance archway, and the lovely scenery burst upon me, Randolph said with pardonable pride, "this is the finest view in England". Looking at the lake, the bridge, the miles of magnificent park studded with old oaks, I found no adequate words to express my admiration, and when we reached the huge and stately palace, I confess I felt awed.'[1] Lady Randolph Churchill's description of her first arrival at Blenheim in 1874 reflects the sheer magnificence and beauty of the Palace and its landscape. The remarkable panorama that unfolds on entry to the grounds never fails to impress and inspire every visitor to Blenheim Palace. Yet the house and the bridge built three hundred years ago by the great architect John Vanbrugh for the 1st Duke of Marlborough, and the surrounding parkland designed by the renowned 'Capability' Brown in the 1760s for the 4th Duke, are relatively recent eighteenth-century transformations of the landscape which have almost completely effaced the memory of centuries of earlier parkland features.

Old Woodstock Manor was a sprawling complex of buildings with an imposing gatehouse. ↑
© Private Collection

The Romano-British once settled nearby, and Akeman Street (a principal Roman road) crossed through the northern boundary of the park. By the tenth century, this part of Oxfordshire had developed into a heavily wooded region on the edge of Wychwood forest where a medieval royal hunting manor was established at Woodstock (meaning 'a place in the woods').[2] The site was regularly visited by successive kings, predominantly for deer hunting and for the occasional tournament and the manor was haphazardly expanded to accommodate royal guests and their entourages, evolving over six centuries, from the Saxons to the Stuarts, into a rambling residence with several chapels and an imposing gatehouse.

In 1129, Woodstock Park was the first in the country to be enclosed, not, as is generally thought, to keep the deer in, but to stop more exotic animals from wandering out. King Henry I (1100–35) had established a menagerie here which included an ostrich (rare in England at the time), lions, leopards, porcupines, camels, and lynxes.[3] The rural retreat grew in importance when it became one of King Henry II's (1154–89) principal palaces in the 1170s during his romantic association with Jane Clifford,

commonly known as Fair Rosamund.[4] For Rosamund, Henry is reputed to have built an adjacent group of buildings with a labyrinth and gardens containing three rectangular pools fed by a natural spring.[5] This site was sometimes called the Everswell, after the stream of constant water that flowed through the garden. Many legends have accrued around Rosamund's life at Woodstock, including the common one that Henry's wife, Eleanor of Aquitaine, poisoned her rival here. The small spring of bubbling water, now called Rosamund's Well, is all that remains of this old medieval site within Blenheim Park today (see page 95).

In the Tudor period, the old palace was already in general decline and was used infrequently by King Henry VIII, but his daughter, the future Queen Elizabeth I, was imprisoned in the surviving east wing for almost eleven months in 1554–5, for her alleged part in the Wyatt plot.[6]

During the Civil War, King Charles I stayed briefly at Woodstock on his way to Oxford in October 1642. As a royalist stronghold it was subjected to parliamentary raids in 1646 and, after a brief siege, was surrendered in April of that year. Cromwell's forces took stone,

Jane Clifford, commonly known as Fair Rosamund, allegedly had a romantic association with King Henry II at Woodstock Manor. ←

A single stone memorial now marks the site of old Woodstock Manor. The inscription reads 'HERE STOOD THE ROYAL MANOR HOUSE OF WOODSTOCK FINALLY DEMOLISHED *c.*1720'. The four faces of the pedestal are carved with: the 1st Duke's armorial bearing; the Churchill motto 'Fiel Pero Desdichado' (Faithful but unfortunate); the Spencer motto 'Dieu defend le Droit'; and Anno Domini MDCCCCLXI. The commemorative stone was put up on 18 August 1961.

glass and other materials from the damaged building. On the restoration of the monarchy in 1660 the house was left unrepaired and rarely occupied. Subsequently, by Queen Anne's reign, royal visits to the decayed, uninhabitable palace had ceased.

When John Churchill, 1st Duke of Marlborough, returned to London in December 1704 as the triumphant victor of the Battle of Blenheim (fought on 13 August, a pivotal moment in the War of the Spanish Succession), addresses of thanks were made by both Houses of Parliament for his achievement against the hitherto unvanquished French King Louis XIV. In January 1705, Parliament resolved to take into consideration *'the great services that have been performed by His Grace … and to consider of some means to perpetuate the memory of them.'* [7] Queen Anne proposed the grant of the royal Manor of Woodstock, which included the deer park (roughly 2,000 acres/800 hectares) and, shortly afterwards, Parliament voted in favour of the public funding of a new building.[8] Never in the history of England had a gift of this magnitude been granted by a monarch to a subject.

John Churchill, 1st Duke of Marlborough (1650–1722). →

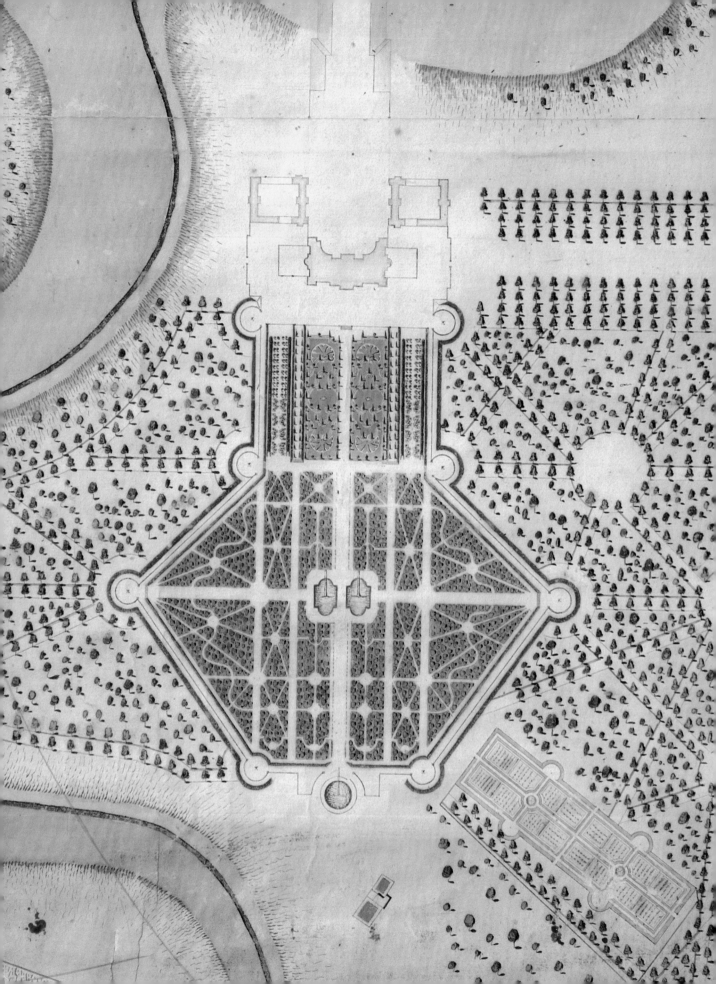

2 *Formal Parterres*

THE GARDENS OF JOHN VANBRUGH & HENRY WISE

Detail of Blenheim's Great Parterre Garden, from Bridgeman's plan dated 1709. ←
Note the scale of the garden compared to the house.

The Duke of Marlborough was shown several preliminary designs for his new house (originally known as Blenheim House or Blenheim Castle, after the battle he had won at Blindheim in Bavaria). By March 1705, he had visited Woodstock Park twice in the company of the architect, John Vanbrugh, then Comptroller of the Office of Works. Ground-clearing operations were begun by April and shortly afterwards construction of the building and the gardens was under way.[1]

Vanbrugh's decision to site the house almost directly facing the ruins of Woodstock Manor on the opposite bank of the valley, a wide but steep chasm, was to create many problems. The valley bottom was covered by water meadows and tracts of marshy land formed by the narrow stream of the Glyme as it wound its way to meet the Evenlode, a tributary of the Thames.[2] Leading across from the old manor were two

Engraving from *The Natural History of Oxfordshire* by Dr R. Plot, 1677. →
The old manor at Woodstock was an extensive royal residence sited on a mound (to give a better view of the surrounding hills and closely wooded country).
The Glyme is described as 'The Rivulet', over which two raised causeways provided a route to and from the building.
© Private Collection

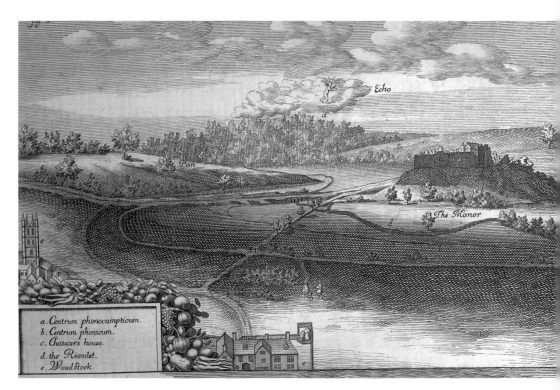

raised causeways offering a quick pedestrian route to the village of Woodstock, which had grown outside the gates of the royal hunting park.[3]

Although the position of the old manor was never crucial at the outset, Vanbrugh would later make a strong case for its preservation. Initially, great importance was attached to the majestic placing of the new building on a long north-south axis, leading from the intended entrance gateway at Ditchley in the north, to the church at Bladon in the south. This positioning would create the longest possible ceremonial approach avenue of almost two miles (3.2 km) within the park. The building would be in '*a very beautiful situation*', dramatically near the edge of the chasm, while the marshy valley would be spanned by an imposing bridge, aligned directly on the main courtyard and the entrance to the new house.[4]

After the foundation stone was laid on 18 June 1705, Vanbrugh wrote to the Duke, '*the garden wall was set agoing the same day with the house and I hope will be done against your Grace's return… the Kitchen garden Walls will likewise be so advanced that all the Plantations may be made. And in generall the whole gardens will be form'd and planted in a year from their beginning.*'[5] This statement, like so many others made by the architect, was to prove somewhat optimistic.

The initial earthworks were undertaken by Henry Wise, gardener to Queen Anne, with over 1,500 men reportedly on site, clearing the terrain, cutting hundreds of trees, moving many cubic yards of earth to level the ground and lay the foundations of Vanbrugh's vast structure, built more as a royal and a national monument than as a comfortable home.[6]

The main block of the building was designed with four square towers, flanked by two service ranges on the east and west (kitchen and stable respectively). The gardens closest to the house were seen as an extension of it and, according to the fashion of the time, reflected its architecture. Formal gardens on three aspects – south, east and west – were to be laid out on a regular pattern closely linked to the architecture of the house, while the northern aspect was reserved for the grand entrance court. The geometric lines of two main avenues to the north and the east, planted with 1,600 elms two to three trees deep on either side, were focused directly on the two principal axes of the house.[7]

John Vanbrugh, architect of Blenheim Palace. ↓
© Private Collection

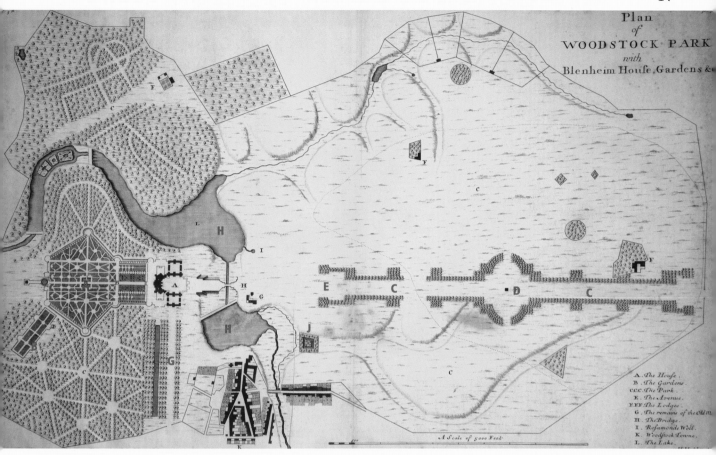

Plan of Woodstock Park, *Vitruvius Britannicus*, 1725, Vol. III, plate 71

© Private Collection

This engraving shows Vanbrugh's intended plan for the park. The extensive polygonal formal garden to the south of the house is clearly depicted (**A**), as is the eight-acre (3.2 ha) Kitchen Garden (**B**). The state approach from the north was a grand avenue planted with elms (**C**). The elliptical shape halfway down (**D**) was intended to incorporate an obelisk. Although this was not constructed, after the 1st Duke's death a column built by his widow in his memory was sited at the southern end of the avenue (**E**) (see Chapter 3). The original east avenue of elms (**F**) was aligned with the eastern bow window of the house. When Vanbrugh expanded his design to create large service courtyards flanking the main building, a second avenue of elms (**G**) was planted in line with the East Gate – the gateway to the kitchen court. The broad canal shown on this drawing (within the original east avenue) was never built.

The plan also shows Vanbrugh's intention to create lakes (**H**) on either side of the bridge, linked by a canal. This was derided by the 1st Duchess as '*a great sea round the house… in spots of dirty, stinking water*'. The scheme of waterworks in the valley was later completed to a different design by the Duchess, with the help of

Colonel John Armstrong (see Chapter 3). At the north-eastern extremity of the lake, a square-shaped feature incorporated the old Queen Pool (**J**), named after Queen Philippa (*c.*1314–69), consort of King Edward III, whose eldest son, Edward, the Black Prince, was born at Woodstock in 1330. In ancient times this was the site of two fishponds. The smaller of the two, Queen Pool, was the upper pond which was dammed when a causeway was built crossing the valley to the old medieval palace. The causeway incorporated a weir and a bridge, called Queen's Bridge. Aquatic fowl for the royal table were bred there. The larger, lower pond (called King Pool) was drained and turned into meadow in the fifteenth century.

When 'Capability' Brown created the lake for the 4th Duke of Marlborough in the mid-1760s (see Chapter 5), Queen Pool was incorporated into this larger body of water. The fisherman who had kept the 'stew' (water enclosure for keeping fish) at Queen Pool and later kept two new 'stews' at the western park boundary, lived in a house nearby. There is still a house (called Fishery Cottage) on this site, although not the original one.

The South Front of Blenheim Palace

With his strong theatrical leanings, Vanbrugh built Blenheim as a monument to the achievement of John Churchill, 1st Duke of Marlborough, '… *it cannot be doubted but if travellers many ages hence shall be shewn the Very House in which so Great a man Dwelt as they will then read the Duke of Marlborough in Story; and that they shall be told, it was not only his Favourite Habitation, but was Erected for him by the Bounty of the Queen and with the approbation of the People, as a Monument of the Greatest Services and Honours that any subject had ever done his Country…*'

The design of the house contains several elements of military symbolism. On each corner tower, four large cannonball finials (carved by Grinling Gibbons) are topped with inverted fleurs-de-lys surmounted by a ducal coronet, signifying the military defeat of the French by the Duke. In the centre of the south front (facing the Great Parterre), the entablature was originally designed to display a large equestrian statue of John Churchill, but in 1721–2 a stone bust of King Louis XIV was fixed in its place. The bust had been taken by the Duke from the Porte Royale of the Citadel at Tournai after a successful siege operation in September 1709. The Latin inscription *EUROPAE HAEC VINDEX GENIO DECORA ALTA BRITANNO* below the bust is a symbolic reference to the Duke's military genius and the nation's glory: '*The Assertor of the Liberty of Europe dedicates these lofty honours to the Genius of Britain*'.

The medieval church of St Martin at Bladon. ↑ **The church was demolished in October 1802. The 4th Duke of Marlborough had a new church built which reopened in June 1804.**
© Private Collection

The Great Parterre to the south of the new building was the most significant component of the original garden as it was overlooked from the State Apartments on the *piano nobile*. It was traditionally from these rooms (the most important in the house), that the gardens had to be seen to best advantage. The original garden was formal, strongly following French rather than Dutch influence through its scale and integration with the wider landscape, as well as its hierarchy of spaces. According to the design, in the parterres nearest the house, closely clipped plants were trained to grow in elaborate geometrical shapes, demonstrating the power and the wealth of the owner. Further away, areas of grass and topiary were punctuated with statues, sundials and basins of water, around which an ornamental wood was planted on axial lines. The focus of the view from the house down the central axis of the Great Parterre was the medieval church at Bladon (later demolished and rebuilt).[8]

Vanbrugh had incorporated military themes into the decoration of the building, embellishing its dramatic roofline with martial trophies and other ornamental sculpted emblems of victory. This iconography also extended into the gardens – eight rounded bastions (circular fortifications *'after the ancient Roman Manner'*)[9] were constructed at each angle of the polygonal Great Parterre, the bastions themselves reflecting the shape of the semi-circular bow windows on the east and west fronts of the house. This half-round shape would be repeated again in the design of the walled Kitchen Garden. However, although Vanbrugh was probably responsible for the broad brushstrokes of the garden's axial layout, the variety and manner of planting was determined by Henry Wise.[10] The Duke of Marlborough had confidence in Wise's expertise, having already conducted business with him when planting trees at Windsor Lodge.[11] This conviction was expressed in a letter to the Duchess, *'for the Gardening and Plantations I am at ease being very sure that Mr Wise will be diligent'*.[12] There is no documentary evidence to suggest that the Duke of Marlborough contributed to the design, except perhaps in inspiring Vanbrugh to produce such a martial scheme.

There are several surviving proposals for the layout of the original garden.[13] One of the earliest plans shows the Great Parterre without bastions. More importantly, it reveals an imposing scheme to the north, where a large oval plantation intersected with a star ride figures on the opposite side of the valley. The remains of the old royal manor are outlined but there is no bridge as yet over the valley.[14]

The bastioned curtain wall of the Great Parterre is the notable common feature in all the other drawings, implying that this idea was quickly developed and retained in the architect's thinking. The wall provided a walk around the perimeter of the Parterre; a viewing platform into the garden as well as into the countryside beyond.[15]

Some of the surviving designs are rough sketches which may have been drawn by Vanbrugh or his assistant at Blenheim, Nicholas Hawksmoor. However, none of the detailed drawings appear to be in either of their hands (with the exception of Hawksmoor's proposal for park gates). Although Henry Wise would have collaborated closely with Vanbrugh and incorporated his ideas, it suggests that to a large extent he had overall responsibility for producing the garden plans. Stephen Switzer's handwriting is recognisable on one of these, while another finely executed drawing dated 1709 is signed by Charles Bridgeman.[16] Both men were Wise's assistants; but while Switzer is known to have been working at Blenheim, Bridgeman, then aged nineteen, is only recorded as supplying trees from Wise's nursery at Brompton, and it is unlikely that he contributed to the design.

The geometrical outline of the south Parterre garden was divided into two areas of planting – a square-shaped terrace close to the house and a hexagonal lower section called the 'wood-work'. The terrace contained four long rectangular beds – two inner compartments of symmetrical scrollwork patterns (directly in front of the house) and two outer compartments of closely

One of the earliest designs for Blenheim's park and gardens. ↑ The shape of the Great Parterre to the south has not yet been finalised. Note the absence of bastions, the proposal of other outlying features and the imposing scheme to the north of the valley where an elaborate oval plantation is intersected with a star ride. There is no trace as yet of the Kitchen Garden.

© Bodleian Library, University of Oxford (Ms. Top Oxon. a.37*, f. 1)

clipped trees planted in straight lines, for which '*59 pyramid swedish junipers four foot high and 148 pyramidal yews five foot high*' were supplied. The hexagonal section, a formal wilderness, was planted with espaliered trees and shrubs, intersected with walks. Henry Wise supplied 9,357 hedge yews of various heights, with 831 large and 1,478 small flowering shrubs for the wood-work quarters, and '*5,900 hornbeam, privatt, and sweet bryer for the inner line…*'[17] Very few perennials were included.[18] The planting was successfully carried out by Stephen Switzer, '*out of about ten thousand Hedge-Yews, etc. that were planted under my direction at Blenheim in 1706, there were not two hundred that fail'd*'.[19] However, despite the thousands of plants supplied, they were still insufficient, which resulted in the areas of turf within the wood-work being enlarged by 1708.[20]

The principal walkway extended from the south steps of the house to the southern extremity of the Parterre, past an intended fountain pool in the wood-work. Surviving drawings reveal various designs for this body of water. On one, a rectangular basin with small projecting bastions is seen, repeating this Vanbrughian motif on a smaller scale. Two others show a pair of basins with fountains. Furthermore, in each design a round basin with a large circular fountain (280 feet/85 m in diameter) was planned for the southern extremity of the garden.[21] A colonnade, containing a grotto about five feet (1.5 m) high, was to enclose the basin around its southern aspect.[22] However, the scale

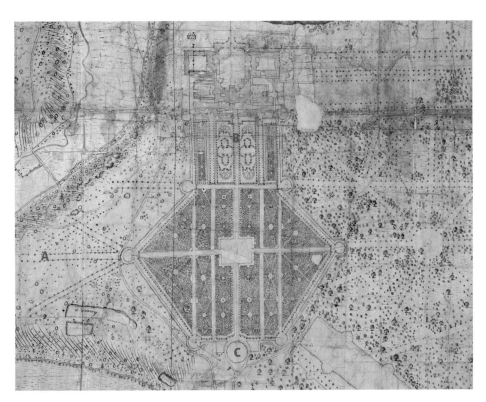

Detail from the 1719 plan (shown in full on page 38). ➜ Henry Wise's planting scheme in the wider landscape surrounding the Great Parterre includes a *patte d'oie* (three avenues branching out in the shape of a goose foot) to the west (A). The scrollwork designs of the four formally planted rectangular beds closest to the house are shown (B), as is the intended large circular basin at the southern extremity (C). The fountains within the wood-work shown on Bridgeman's 1709 plan (page 14 and overleaf) were not constructed.

of such an ambitious scheme combined with the inability to provide sufficient water pressure for the fountains at a time of limited knowledge in hydraulic engineering presented an impossible mix in providing a successful outcome.

To the west of the wood-work, a *patte d'oie* (three radiating avenues in the shape of a goose foot) made a formal feature of the irregular outline of the valley edge; while to the east a sizeable plantation of trees and shrubs was laid out in a quincunx pattern of extending lines.[23] The building accounts show the scale of Henry Wise's planting: *'52 standard lawrells, 18 cedars of Lebanon, 186 large elms and sycamores, 2,219 large espalier limes, 2,566 smaller size ditto, 2,000 small hedge hollies…'* [24]

Beyond this screen of trees, an equally impressive eight acre (3.2 ha) rectangular Kitchen Garden was built with two long bastioned walls facing due south, maximizing the absorption of heat from sunlight. The walls were fourteen feet (4.2 m) high, mostly in brick, except for a four-acre (1.6 ha) southern extension or slip garden, planted as an orchard.[25] The bricklayers Richard Stacey and Thomas Churchill constructed several sections of wall to incorporate flues heated by wood-burning furnaces (known as *hot walls*).[26] Inside this garden, two large circular basins facilitated the watering of plants.

The Kitchen Garden was a sign of conspicuous wealth, providing the house with an ample supply of fresh produce, both fruits and vegetables, including *'collyflower, lettuce, cabbage, spinage, beans, pease, carrots, onions, endives, turnips, beans'.*[27] The Duke of Marlborough, impatient to move into his new house as quickly as possible, had pressed Henry Wise to plant mature trees.[28] Hundreds of fully grown specimens were transplanted in baskets from Wise's Brompton Nursery: 202 peach and nectarines, 220 pears, 29 apricots, 134 plums, 102 cherries, 400 gooseberries and currants, 190 vines, and 262 apples.[29] The first garden to be completed and stocked, Vanbrugh proudly recorded in 1716 that *'the Kitchin garden, now the Trees are in their full Vigour and full of fruit, is really an astonishing sight. All I ever saw in England or abroad of this kind are trifles to it.'* [30]

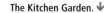

The Kitchen Garden. ↓

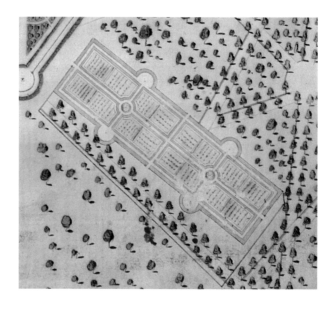

The Duke requested his wife to sample the fruit of every tree and to reject those not good enough.[31] Sarah delegated this task to friendly neighbours as well as to her housekeeper at High Lodge, a small building within the Park, previously the residence of the Ranger of the Royal Forests.[32] High Lodge had been renovated and extended to accommodate the Marlboroughs at Woodstock before their new house was ready.[33] (See box on page 54.)

A Plann of Blenheim, drawn by Charles Bridgeman, 1709. →
The principal garden at Blenheim was the Great Parterre to the south of the house, laid out in two sections: an upper square-shaped formally planted terrace and a lower hexagonal 'wood-work' or wilderness planted with trees and espaliered shrubs. A round bastion was built at each angle of the perimeter wall. Two main gravel walks cut through the Parterre. The principal one extended 2,200 feet (670 m) in a straight line from the house, a typical feature in a baroque garden, linking the Palace to the open country. It was crossed in the middle by another gravel walk 1,850 feet (564 m) long. Large areas within the Parterre, including the slopes of the terraces, were covered with grass. Turf was cut by garden labourers (using a scythe) once or twice a week depending on the season, and rolled once every two days with wooden or stone rollers. Formal gardens were expensive, both to plant and to tend.

Beyond the drawing of this plan, when he was about 19 years old and working for Henry Wise, there is no documentary evidence to substantiate Charles Bridgeman's involvement in the gardens at Blenheim. It is unlikely that he would have been responsible for any elements of its design. It was much later in his career that Bridgeman was commissioned by Sarah, Duchess of Marlborough, to lay out the gardens of another residence, Wimbledon House, a task he undertook from 1732, but which still remained to be completed at his death six years later.

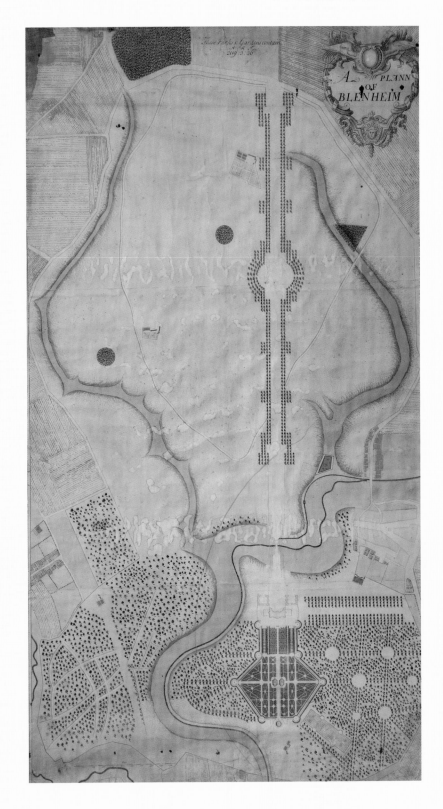

On the east front of Blenheim Palace (overlooked from the private apartments) Vanbrugh and Wise designed an elaborate sunken garden called the Duchess's flower garden, the foundations for which were dug in the summer of 1708.[34] Two early designs survive. The first reveals a narrow garden of symmetrical beds, or possible fountain basins, with a flight of steps leading out in each corner.[35] The second plan (which was executed) shows a square sunken area surrounded with terraces on three sides and a gated curtain wall.[36] A large greenhouse (now called the Orangery) bordered this garden on the north. However, when the Duchess of Marlborough protested that the greenhouse and curtain wall completely blocked her view,[37] a spiked iron *'palisade between stone peers'* was erected in place of the wall.[38] The greenhouse was finished but only after 1716 when, as we shall see, the Duchess's priority was to complete construction rather than to provide a pleasing prospect.[39] Invoices for plants supplied by Henry Wise from the Brompton Nursery inform us that this garden was stocked with violets, white Dutch corinths, wild services, carnations, polyanthus, campanulae and damask roses.[40]

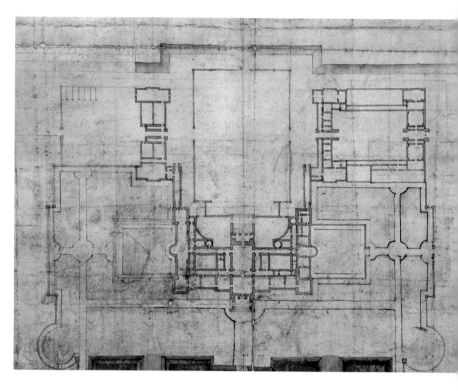

A proposal for the gardens on the east and west of the house. ↑ Sarah, Duchess of Marlborough, objected to the building of a gated curtain wall: *'I desire nothing more may be done upon that wall which is called the flower Garden under my chamber window till you give me an account how far it is designed to be carry'd up, for I apprehend it may spoil the view into the Parke, as the Orange House has done already, and I think there is nothing in a Garden or Buildings can make amends for that.'*

As the construction of Vanbrugh's building was begun from the east moving through to the west, plans for the east garden, the Great Parterre, and the Kitchen Garden were the first to be finalised. No comprehensive schemes have been found for the west garden, although one of the early drawings for the east garden shows an identical garden to the west.

Treatment of the west aspect was difficult. The ground was stony and the densely wooded hill sloped steeply into the river valley.[41] The only surviving fragment of design for the treatment of the western aspect dates from 1720, when Nicholas Hawksmoor suggested building an elaborate bridged walkway with flights of steps.[42] This proposal was not adopted. In fact, the only formal garden to be created on this side of the house was undertaken in 1924, when the 9th Duke had the present Water Terraces constructed. In the early eighteenth century, the problems concerning the completion of the building meant that this garden, along with several other schemes, was left unfinished.

As Captain General of the English and allied forces from 1702–11, the Duke of Marlborough was in Flanders fighting against King Louis XIV's armies and was therefore unable to exercise any meaningful control over the building work at Woodstock. Nor could he rightly do so as the entire project, a gift from the Queen and the nation, was under the supervision and charge of the Office of Works. However, Marlborough's overriding desire was to see the house completed and to live a retired life there.[43] He repeatedly requested his wife to visit the site and send him an account of the progress of the work. This left the Duchess of Marlborough in an unenviable position. As a woman in the early eighteenth century, she was seen to be meddling in matters that did not concern her. Moreover, her exceedingly practical nature, her quick temper and her dislike of extravagance and unreasonable expenditure soon had her protesting in splenetic terms to her husband.

Two years into the project, Vanbrugh requested additional funds from the Treasury to advance the work more speedily. When, instead, a half-built section of the south front was demolished to rebuild it in the Corinthian style, Sarah, aggravated by her perceived impracticality of the vast project, now became concerned with the wastefulness she encountered, her annoyance growing on almost every subsequent visit to Oxfordshire.

Hawksmoor's proposal for a bridged walkway and steps outside the west front. ↓
© Bodleian Library, University of Oxford (Ms. Top Oxon. a.37*, f. 14)

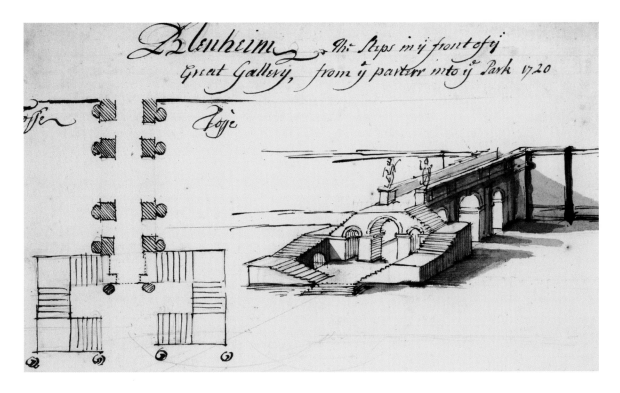

HENRY WISE (1653–1738)

Henry Wise was a horticulturist who, around 1686–7, bought a share of the Brompton Nursery founded in 1681 by George London (gardener to the Bishop of London) with three other prominent gardeners – Moses Cooke (gardener to the Earl of Essex at Cassiobury), Roger Lucre (gardener to the dowager Queen at Somerset House), and John Field (gardener to the Earl of Bedford at Bedford House in the Strand). After Lucre and Field died, Cooke sold his share, so that the vast nursery extending over more than 100 acres (40 ha) was eventually divided between the two remaining partners, London and Wise.

Drawing their inspiration from the formal gardens of France and Holland, both gardeners specialised in making topiary gardens with walks and avenues, providing their clients with geometrical planting and long vistas which were fashionable at the time. Apart from Blenheim, London and Wise were also responsible for the gardens at Cannons, Longleat, and Melbourne Hall.

In the reign of William and Mary, George London was appointed Superintendent of their Majesties Gardens, supplying plants to Hampton Court, Windsor and Kensington. At this time, Henry Wise was deputy ranger of Hyde Park. In 1695, Wise married Patience Banckes, daughter of Matthew Banckes, carpenter to the court, who was later one of the principal workmen involved in building Blenheim. In 1702, Queen Anne assigned the royal gardens to Wise's care, appointing him Superintendent. The pre-eminence of the Brompton Nursery was thus retained, until the Queen's death in 1714.

Re-appointed Superintendent on the accession of King George I, Henry Wise held his post as royal gardener until his eventual retirement around 1726. He died in December 1738, at the Priory, in Warwick, a house he had bought in 1709 (during the lucrative Blenheim contract). His thriving business had made him a wealthy man and he left his widow a considerable estate.

The Royal Collection © 2009 Her Majesty Queen Elizabeth II

Responsible for the creation of the gardens at Blenheim, and for their maintenance until 1716, Henry Wise's contract included digging, carting and the supply of trees and plants, all of which provided substantial earnings. From 1705 to 1710 he was paid £13,687 with the largest disbursement of just under £8,000 being made at the start of the works in 1705. When the building work was stopped in 1712, Wise was still owed £873 (which he later partially recovered). His total charge amounted to £14,559 of which £3,050 was for plants, including mature trees: '*Mr. Wise being pitch'd upon by the [1st] Duke to make the gardens, his Grace bad him consider, he was an old man, and could not expect to live till the Trees were grown up; and therefore he expected to have a garden as it were ready made for him. Accordingly, Mr Wise transplanted thither full-grown Trees in Baskets, which he bury'd in the Earth; which look and thrive the same, as if they had stood there thirty or forty years*'.

'I have reason to be very uneasy', she wrote in 1710, *'that there is no way can be found to put an end to perpetual expense which are to be pulled down again, at the same time as there is orders given for so many things that are necessary and of use. Surely it would be more reasonable to employ hands and money in dispatching that, than to vex me in this manner in doing things contrary to order and most certainly be pulled down'.*[44]

Although the Duchess had a passion for building, undertaking the construction of three new houses and renovating at least three others during her lifetime, she had a marked dislike of all her architects, and was happier working without them.[45] Even though she recognized that the completion of Blenheim was her husband's greatest desire, and that he had not discouraged his architect's grandiose design, Sarah's disapproval of the project's extravagance and its slow progress was laid squarely at Vanbrugh's door.[46] In the park, there were two main bones of contention between the forceful Duchess and the great architect – first the bridge and, secondly, the old ruined manor across the valley.

The bridge, according to Vanbrugh's design, was intended to perform the function of continuing the grand approach route from the Ditchley Gate, over the precipitous valley to the house. Rising to a height of 80 feet (24 m) from the valley bottom, it would carry the road directly to the main entrance courtyard of the house. Sir Christopher Wren, Surveyor-General of the Queen's Works, was consulted over the design. He conceived a

An early design, possibly by Hawksmoor illustrating Wren's proposal for a smaller bridge (A) with two circular, sweeping drives up to the house (B). ↓
© Bodleian Library, University of Oxford (Ms. Top Oxon. a.37*, f. 2)

Plan and section of a small bridge with a simple profile, possibly a part of Wren's scheme for bridging the valley. ↘

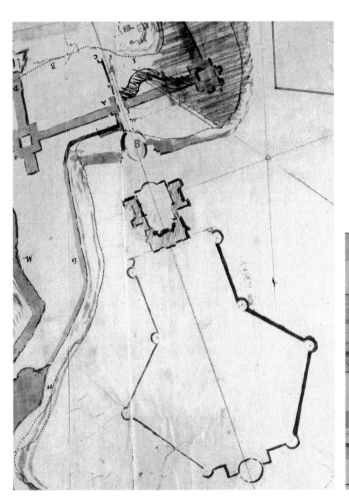

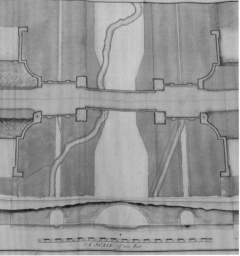

less expensive solution through a smaller bridge at a lower level, approaching the new house through two large, sweeping, circular drives up the steep bank.[47] After discussions involving Wren, Vanbrugh, Hawksmoor and even Henry Wise, Vanbrugh's scheme was eventually adopted.[48]

Designed with characteristic boldness, the bridge was a substantial building of three arches. The central arch at 100 feet (30 m) was the largest span of any bridge in the country at the time. Square projecting piers between the central and side arches were designed to break the continuous line of the bridge and were built to support four ornamental towers with an arcaded superstructure. Construction on such a scale was only possible because the foundations would be laid on land rather than under water.[49]

By 1705–6 Vanbrugh had decided to procure a 'water-engine' which would pump water from the Glyme up to a lead cistern built within the entrance tower to the kitchen court, from where the fountains of the Great Parterre and the east wing of the house would be supplied. '*A quadruple engine to raise water from the river to a height of 120 feet*' was built by Mr Robert Aldersea in March 1707/8, and installed within an arch-roofed brick 'engine-house'.[50] Henry Wise dug the watercourse to feed the engine, as well as trenches for the pipes but it apparently failed to deliver a sufficient pressure of water for the fountains.[51]

In September 1708, Wise assigned Stephen Switzer (who had been at Blenheim from the outset, initially in charge of the quarries in the park and afterwards planting in the gardens) to supervise the '*foundations of the bridge north side of the great arch adjoining to the engine house*'.[52] The mason Bartholomew Peisley keyed the 100-foot (30 m) central arch in 1710, but the east face and south arch of the structure were a long way from being finished when the Duchess put a temporary stop to all work.[53]

Sarah was concerned about the debt on the building, which by this time stood at almost £18,000.[54] Payments from the Treasury trickled through to Blenheim due to the protracted costs of continuing a continental war with no end in sight. There had

The bridge was designed by John Vanbrugh as a triple-arched edifice with four ornamental towers and an arcaded superstructure. ↑ According to the design, it was about 390 feet (119 m) long and 80 feet (24 m) high. As the Duchess chose not to complete the design, the superstructure was not built and the bridge was stopped at 50 feet (15 m). The 100-foot (30 m) wide central arch was unmatched in size at the time. The decoration included frostwork panels over the side arches (only completed on the west face) and six acroterias at each end (no longer extant).

© Private Collection

also been a radical change in the political climate with the election of a new government. The Marlboroughs' fall from royal favour, coupled with the rise of the Tories under Robert Harley, finally ended all official commitments to Blenheim. Beset by delays and the costs of Vanbrugh's modifications, and notwithstanding the substantial payment of £220,000 from the Treasury since work first began, the house was little more than a half-finished shell. Activity continued in the belief that the project would never be totally abandoned by the Queen or the Marlboroughs. However, in June 1712, when the unthinkable happened and work was indeed officially stopped, the debt was said to be around £45,000.[55]

After Queen Anne's death in 1714, King George I sanctioned additional funds but this did not go very far in settling the outstanding dues.[56] Legal action followed and bad feeling festered on every side as the Duke and Duchess refused to accept liability for a project deemed a gift, and for which they felt the Treasury was responsible. Questions were also raised regarding the inflated amounts charged by the workmen and the overgenerous rates approved by Vanbrugh.

Work at Woodstock was therefore abandoned for almost four years until the Marlboroughs decided to complete the building at their own expense. Although the gardens had been tended during this time (by as many as eleven men on a daily-wage basis under the supervision of Tilleman Bobart) and what had been planted was maturing, they were far from finished.[57] Even more substantial work remained to make the house habitable.[58]

In 1716, new contracts were signed with mason-contractors while the master craftsmen stood their ground, refusing to work until their debts were settled (although Vanbrugh, Hawksmoor and Wise did return).[59] When the Duke was incapacitated by a stroke in May, the Duchess unenthusiastically took control of the project, regarding it 'a chaos that turns ones braine but to think of it'.[60] She resolved to complete Blenheim only because of her husband's passion for the place, and his desire, greater now than ever, to leave it to posterity. However, Sarah had been at odds with Vanbrugh for too many years for a break to be long avoided.

Robert Aldersea's engine. ↓
The main technical difficulty was that the water had to be pumped a great distance but the stream that fed it was not very strong. He was paid £623 for the engine, while John Desborough was employed to look after it, earning £10 a year.
© Bodleian Library, University of Oxford (Ms. Top. Oxon. a.37, f. 118)

The Marlboroughs had anticipated the demolition of the old manor on the opposite side of the valley *'to make use of all that is there, to save money in what is done at the Bridge, for all that Building must come down and the hill must help fill up the Bottom…'*[61] In 1709, Vanbrugh made a lengthy and impassioned plea for its preservation. He had proposed growing a thicket of firs, hollies and yews through which the medieval ruins could be seen, believing *'it would make one of the Most Agreeable Objects that the best of Landskip [landscape] painters can invent. And if on the Contrary this Building is taken away, there then remains nothing but an irregular, Ragged, Ungovernable Hill, the deformities of which are not to be cured but by a vast expense; and that at last will only remove an ill Object but not produce a good one…'*[62]

His appeal was unsuccessful, because the ruins *'were not in themselves a very agreeable sight… they happened to stand very near the middle of the front of [the] very fine castle of Blenheim… in the way of the prospect down the great avenue for which a bridge of so vast an expense is made'.*[63] When it was discovered that Vanbrugh had been living in the neglected building on a regular basis since 1713, without permission and in defiance of clear instructions, diverting labour and precious resources from the new works to make parts of the crumbling old manor habitable, the Marlboroughs were *'red hot mad.'*[64] The fate of the ancient royal palace was sealed and, had the architect not been goaded into resignation, he almost certainly would have been dismissed.[65] In September 1716, Henry Wise discharged *'all the men and teams at Blenheim'* in accordance with the Duchess's instructions.[66]

Documentary evidence suggests that Vanbrugh's stance regarding the manor was not shared by the Marlboroughs or their friends, who generally considered that the ruins were better demolished.[67] The Lord Treasurer, Sidney Godolphin, reportedly declared that there could *'no more be a dispute than whether a Man that had a great Wenn upon his cheek would not have it cut out if he could.'*[68] However, it is the Duchess alone who is usually vilified for the destruction of the old manor. Setting aside the personal differences she evidently had with the architect, it is difficult to see how the vastly contrasting style of the ancient building could have fitted comfortably in full view of the new palace, conceived in an age when the rigid geometry of the setting was still fashionable and considered desirable. Even though garden styles had begun to evolve and take a new direction in the early decades of the eighteenth century, in reality, the delight of the irregular belonged to a later period. It must also be remembered that Blenheim was built on a heroic scale as a monument to the Queen's favour, an expression of the military genius of the Duke of Marlborough and his services to the nation, and that this building like no other in England sought to imitate the grandeur of Versailles.[69]

Direction of the works now passed to James Moore, a cabinet maker, who, according to Sarah, was not only honest, but had *'very good Sense… and understanding in many Trades besides his own'.*[70] To his credit, from being an uninhabitable shell, the house was sufficiently advanced within two years for the family to move into the east wing (by the summer of 1719), although construction was still ongoing on the west. Work on the bridge resumed after the fabric of the main house neared completion in September 1721. Masonry and rubble were used from the ruined manor to complete the bridge, but without its towers and arcaded superstructure.[71] Even at a reduced height, the bridge was completely out of proportion to the stream flowing below it.

After spending just two short summers at Blenheim, the Duke of Marlborough died, leaving his widow the task of completing the building. Certain western sections of the sprawling structure would eventually be finished, including the chapel containing the family tomb,[72] but Sarah abandoned work on the west service court (the stable block) and the west formal gardens on the difficult sloping hill, which were brought *'to a ruff level… for laying the turf'.*[73]

As far as the Great Parterre was concerned, only parts of the bastioned walls had been built.[74] In June 1709, the Duchess had halted any further work, sending instructions that she would *'have no expense at the lower End of the Garden where the great Bason is till further order, being a thing everybody condemns so much, I am confident my lord Marlborough will pull it down'.*[75] When the master mason, Edward Strong, protested, he received a stinging reply, *'Mr Strong… represents that it is a great prejudice to him not to go on with the Garden Wall, by reason he has prepared great quantities of stone, that he has increased his number of workmen, but chiefly that it would reflect on his reputation not to finish the work he has begun… let him know in answer to these particulars that I can't think a man's reputation can be in the least touch'd by not working upon a ruff wall, who is employed at the same time in the most considerable part of the building, both for the skill and profit… and having so many times alleg'd as a reason he wou'd not carry on the worke of the house so fast because he wanted hands, I am thoroughly perswaided he can always employ all the hands he can get in carrying on that greate worke…'*[76]

EARLY GARDENERS AT BLENHEIM
STEPHEN SWITZER, TILLEMAN BOBART AND JOHN HUGHES

Stephen Switzer (1682–1745), the son of a Hampshire farmer, trained in the formal style of gardening under London and Wise. As their young apprentice, he was involved for many years overseeing the work on the gardens at Blenheim. Switzer's first employment lasted six weeks, when for '*his care and pains in looking after the Quarries in the Park*' Vanbrugh sanctioned him a payment of 10 shillings a week. In 1706 Switzer's main accomplishment was the successful planting of about ten thousand hedge-yews of which '*there were not two hundred that fail'd*'. A year later, he supervised the stocking of the gardens and the wood-work. While witnessing the foundations of Vanbrugh's bridge being laid, he observed the removal of petrified oaks from the boggy ground. Known to have more than a passing interest in hydraulic engineering, he described the construction and operation of Mr Aldersea's water engine at Blenheim in some detail. His interest in such scientific processes led to his most important publication in 1729, *Introduction to a General System of Hydraulicks and Hydrostaticks*. Switzer was also employed in creating gardens for the Duke of Ancaster at Grimsthorpe and for Lord Bathurst at Cirencester. Although he later (1742) set up in trade, describing himself as a '*Seedsman of Westminster-Hall*', he is better remembered as a garden writer who, in the early eighteenth century, through many theoretical and practical essays on gardening, influenced both design and methods. Switzer reckoned Blenheim was amongst the greatest of Henry Wise's undertakings, a '*stupendous Work, begun and most part finish'd in three years time*'. He recorded that plants and trees were supplied not only from Wise's nursery at Brompton but also from other estates in Oxfordshire. He was responsible for purchasing many of these, principally elms. (Elms were chosen because they kept their leaves longer in the autumn and were easy to transplant and propagate.) Perhaps based partly on his experiences with Henry Wise and John Vanbrugh at

Blenheim, in 1718 he wrote, '*when you first begin to build, and make Gardens, the Gardener and Builder ought to go Hand in Hand, and to consult together*'. He advocated regularity immediately around the house but not beyond, where the view should always be new and diverting. His style of early naturalism mixed the formal and the irregular. Switzer coveted a larger role at Blenheim and wanted to be given the charge of the gardens, but Henry Wise recommended Bobart for the position.

Tilleman Bobart was the younger son of the Brunswick-born horticulturist, Jacob Bobart, the first Keeper of the Oxford Physick Gardens. The younger Bobart had worked at Hampton Court and, when he came to Blenheim, he planted some of the elms in the park. On Henry Wise's recommendation, Bobart was appointed as one of the Clerks of the Works at Blenheim on 24 September 1708, for which he received £200 a year (for four years before building work was stopped in 1712). He was re-employed thereafter as '*chief gardener upon the Spot*' at £52 a year. The Kitchen Garden was amply stocked; the hot walls had trees planted on both sides, providing vast quantities of fruit. Bobart was unceremoniously discharged in 1719 when the Marlboroughs discovered that he regularly sold produce from Blenheim to local gentlemen and to the Oxford colleges and that he had felled several trees in the park to personally profit from the timber sales. He went on to work for the Duke of Chandos at Cannons (1720–4) and in 1729 was employed at Wroxton, once again working under Henry Wise, where he directed the creation of formal terraces and a long canal.

John Hughes is a lesser-known figure of the early eighteenth century. He arrived at Blenheim in the 1720s in a supervisory capacity, assisting James Moore in his direction of the ongoing building works after Vanbrugh's departure. Hughes was in charge of the gardens from an early date even though his formal contract as Head Gardener was only signed in June 1726 and he left two years later.

After this date, the documentation becomes increasingly fragmentary, revealing only one specific gardening appointment. In 1733, Mr Thomas Tayler was appointed gardener at Blenheim at an annual wage of £20. However, it seems likely that he was a caretaker gardener. New research has revealed that Tilleman Bobart's older brother, Jacob, who had taken over charge of the Oxford Physick Gardens from his father, arranged for associates (like James Smith) or other gardeners from the locality (like Richard Payne of Ditchley), to tend the grounds at Blenheim on a part-time basis.

Vanbrugh's bridge, before 'Capability' Brown flooded the valley to make the lake. ↑

Ultimately, however, the Duchess relented and allowed work to progress on the garden walls, but only when masons were free and stone was available, *'because next the house that should be first completed'*.[77] As the wall was built to make the garden level and to keep deer out, it mainly consisted of a sunken section (ha-ha) topped with a parapet of dressed stone. By November 1714, there still remained 4,160 feet (1,268 m) of *'Great Garden Wall'* to finish. In September 1721, the masons Townsend and Peisley submitted an *'Estimate of the copeing and reparations necessary at Blenheim in ye walls beginning at ye Bastion on ye West side of ye wilderness and continued round to ye bastion on ye opposite side, except ye ashlar work of ye walls on each side of ye Grand Bason,'*[78] but the stone was only brought in for this two years later.[79] Nevertheless, the basin at the southern extremity was left unfinished and eventually covered with grass, consistent with the treatment of the other bastions.[80]

Although Blenheim was intended to be the ducal seat, handed down with the title, Sarah owned the house for her lifetime. This was in accordance with both her husband's will and the Act of Parliament through which Queen Anne had bestowed the gift.[81] After the 1st Duke's death, the dowager Duchess used Blenheim only occasionally, preferring to live at her other homes in London, St Albans and Windsor. However, during her twenty-two-year-long widowhood she did not completely abandon Blenheim, but turned her attention to particular projects in the park which were close to her heart.

3 *Finishing Flourishes*

THE DUCHESS OF MARLBOROUGH
RECALLS NICHOLAS HAWKSMOOR

The Woodstock Gate.
←

**John Churchill,
1st Duke of Marlborough,
with Colonel Armstrong.**
↓

The earliest designs for the house had included various canal schemes, some incorporating rectangular and polygonal basins.[1] Although the Marlboroughs must have known of these existing designs, they turned instead to Colonel Armstrong for assistance in devising a suitable scheme. As Chief Engineer of the English Army, John Armstrong had been one of the 1st Duke's key associates during the War of the Spanish Succession; his particular skill and knowledge had guaranteed the success of many crucial campaigns. Armstrong was now called upon to design and supervise the building of elaborate waterworks in Blenheim park, including a lake with canals and cascades. Centred around the bridge, the scheme progressed in an orderly sequence south-westwards through the valley.[2]

To create the lake, a dam was formed by constructing a stone wall against one of the raised causeways to the ancient manor. Just over three feet (1 m) deep, the lake was sited to the east of the bridge.[3] Water flowed from it over a stepped cascade (incorporated within the dam wall) into a long canal on the other side of the bridge.[4] Contemporary accounts describe the cascade as being very wide with around five steps.[5] Sarah was pleased with the design, *'Sir John [Vanbrugh] never thought of this cascade which will be the finest and the largest that ever was made.'*[6]

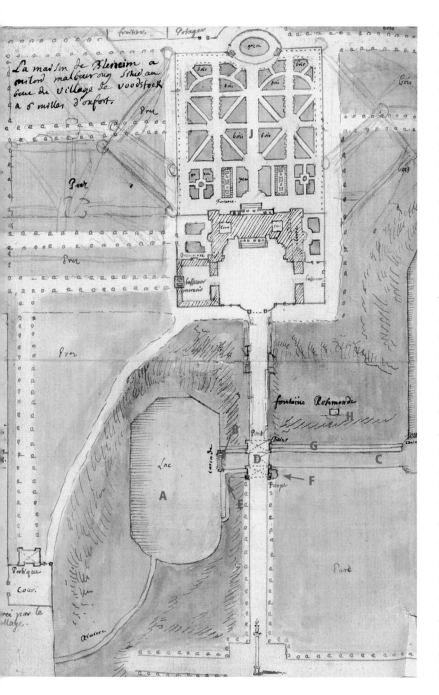

Stephen Switzer observed the *'new lake'* in 1727, *'the work of that illustrious and Right Noble Lady, the present Duchess Dowager of Marlborough'*, and it is mentioned again in a French visitor's journal a year later, accompanied by a sketch showing a large rectangular basin with cut corners.[7] Other sketches and contemporary engravings also illustrate a wide, straight canal extending under the central arch of Vanbrugh's bridge past Rosamund's Well, draining into a large circular basin to the west.[8]

Two smaller flanking canals, each ten feet (3 m) wide, were constructed under the side arches of the bridge.[9] Of these, the one through the north arch was specifically designed on a raised level to provide a current of water strong enough to operate Aldersea's engine more efficiently. On the other side, the stream was canalised through a bath house located under the southern arch of the bridge.[10] It not only carried the waste water directly to the circular basin on the other side, but could also be used to empty the lake if necessary.[11] Hawksmoor proposed a grotto under the southern arch *'finished with Rocks and Shells'* in which he intended placing a marble fountain by Bernini, gifted to the 1st Duke of Marlborough (see box on page 168–9).[12] It is not

This drawing by an unknown French visitor *c.*1728 shows Armstrong's lake pool (A) with the cascade (B) flowing into the largest of three canals (C) under the central arch of Vanbrugh's bridge (D). The short canal (E) under the northern arch fed Mr Aldersea's engine (F). The longer canal on the other side (G) carried water to and away from a bath house under the bridge's southern arch. However, the drawing is not entirely accurate – Rosamund's Well (H) is incorrectly positioned and the Great Parterre to the south of the house is shown as a rectangular garden (J). ↑

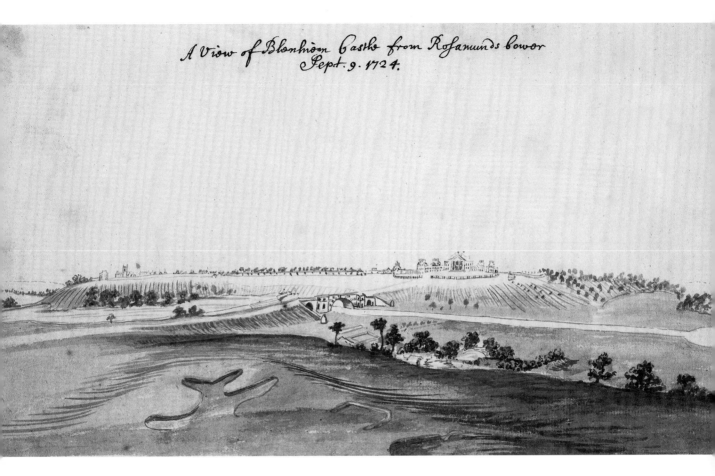

A view of Blenheim Castle from Rosamund's bower,
by William Stukely. ↑

This view was produced on his visit to Blenheim on
9 September 1724, '*In Woodstock we saw a part of
the old Palace and [Rosamund's] famous labyrinth
which is since destroyed. Her bathing place or well
(as called) is left a quadrangular receptacle of the
most pure water, immediately flowing from a little
Spring under the Hill, and shadowed with Trees, near
it some few remains of Walls and Arches… A stately
bridge from hence now leads along the grand
approach to the present castle. A cascade of water
falls from a great lake down some stone steps into
the Canal that runs under it*'. Stukely still refers to the
house by one of its early names, Blenheim Castle. His
drawing also shows two acroterias on either side of
the bridge, where the structure meets the valley,
indicating that this element of the bridge's decoration
was partially completed.

© Bodleian Library, University of Oxford (Ms. Top. Gen. d.14 f. 14v)

known if a decision on this proposal was ever taken,
as the Duke died within the month. The outer parapets
of the canals were subsequently lined with iron
balustrades, and long walks established on both sides
of the valley meadow.[13]

In 1725 Sarah wrote to a friend on the progress of the
work, '*the Lake, Cascade, Slopes above the Bridge are all
finish'd and as beautifull as can bee imagin'd, the Banks
being cover'd with a most delightful Verdure; the Canals
are allso finish'd the whole length of the Meadow under
the Wood and there are a hundred Men at Work, sloping
the Hill near Rosamund's Well; and when all the Banks
are don in the same Manner, and the whole Design
compleat'd, it will certainly bee a wonderful fine Place…
and I am glad it will bee so, because it was the dear
Duke of Marlborough's Passion to have it don*'.[14]

A PLAN of BLENHEIM
House and Gardens 1779

A Plan of Blenheim House and Gardens 1719. ←
The design of the Great Parterre (A) and the Kitchen Garden (B) have been finalised, and the bridge included (C). The old royal manor is still shown (D) labelled 'The Mansion'. Two avenues of elms have been planted to the east of the house (E). Armstrong's initial canal scheme is overdrawn in red ink (F).

The *'whole Design'* referred to describes the extension of the canal scheme, creating two more arms *'at the old rails or the lower end of Rosamund's meadow'*, which carried it further downstream into the Glyme valley.[15] Each of these extensions (undertaken by 1728) also terminated with small waterfalls running into round basins. The last arm of the canal scheme joined the River Glyme at the exact spot where 'Capability' Brown would later build his cascade dam when he flooded the valley on both sides of Vanbrugh's bridge to create a much larger lake.[16] Although Armstrong's lake and canal scheme was therefore completely submerged by Brown within forty years of its creation, two of the Duchess's other projects still remain in the park today.

Boydell's *North-east view of Blenheim House and park*, 1752, shows the canal under the bridge and densely wooded, rising ground beyond it. →

Boydell's *North-west view of Blenheim House and park*, 1752. →
The main canal was 1,840 feet long by 100 feet broad by 3 feet deep (560 x 30 x 1 m). It flowed under the central arch of the bridge, terminating in a large circular basin 300 feet (91 m) in diameter.

About five years after Vanbrugh's dismissal, Sarah recalled his tractable assistant, Nicholas Hawksmoor. On hearing of her intention to complete the house, Hawksmoor had written to the Duchess putting forward ideas and suggestions, generally expressing his concern *'for that building, like a loving Nurse that almost thinks the Child her own'*.[17] He returned to Blenheim just before the Duke's death in 1722. Responsible for finishing the interior of the Long Gallery on the west side of the house (now the Long Library), he also built a triumphal arch in the grounds.

Vanbrugh had originally intended two entrance routes to Blenheim. The most important approach, as has already been discussed, was from the north. A second carriage drive was planned from the east, in anticipation of which Henry Wise had planted the eastern avenue of elms. However, the Marlboroughs were unsuccessful in overcoming the resistance of a stubborn villager, and, failing to acquire the land necessary to establish the eastern approach, the scheme was abandoned.[18] (See page 75.) Later, when working with James Moore, the Duchess decided to develop a new route into the park which resulted in the gated entrance through the village of Woodstock. As this became the most convenient and practical road to the Palace, it quickly rendered Vanbrugh's northern ceremonial approach obsolete, and the bridge became largely ornamental once it no longer conveyed the only effective drive to the house.

Hawksmoor had put forward two proposals for the location of the gate. The first was to build the archway at the park boundary, but in a straight line leading out from the principal road through Woodstock's market place. The second option was *'to make an esplanade when you are past Chaucer's house and to place the Gate upon the left hand… this second way is most approved of by her Grace'*.[19] Although the reason behind the Duchess's angular placement of the gate is not known, it would later create one of the most surprisingly dramatic entrances to any country house, when its unconventional location was successfully combined with 'Capability' Brown's landscape alterations to provide an unexpected and breathtaking first view.

Before construction began on the new gateway, the Duchess received *'a very rediculous Petition from severall of the inhabitants of Woodstock'*. Although the nature of their submission is unknown, Sarah characteristically ordered the masons Townsend and Peisley *'to proceed without Loss of Time'*.[20]

A view of Blenheim Park, by Alexander Cozens, 1748. This angular view from the south-west includes the only known image of the bastioned wall of the Great Parterre. The small cascade (behind the three horses) was at the junction of the second and third sections of the extended canal scheme in the valley.

Modelled on a design for a Roman triumphal arch (Serlio's Arch of Titus), Hawksmoor's gate was conceived as a grand entrance, one he suggested should include *'some proper Inscription to shew the succeeding Ages to whom they were obliged for defending their liberties, and put them in mind (if possible) of their gratitude.'* [21] Using Latin on the Woodstock side, but translated on the park side, the Duchess had a personal acknowledgement inscribed: *'This gate was built the year after the death of the most illustrious John Duke of Marlborough by order of Sarah his most beloved wife, to whom he left the sole direction of the many things that remained unfinished of this fabrick. The services of this great man to his country the Pillar will tell you which the Duchess has erected for a lasting monument of his glory and her affection. MDCCXXIII [1723].'* [22]

Designed by Nicholas Hawksmoor, the Triumphal Arch (Woodstock Gate) was constructed in 1723 by the Oxford stonemason William Townsend, at a cost of £512. ↑

The mention of the Pillar (now known as the Column of Victory) within the inscription on the arch indicates that the two monuments were planned at the same time, under Hawksmoor's direction. In the early eighteenth century there had been a marked resurgence of interest in classical antiquity and a general awareness of the ancient Roman tradition of raising arches and columns to celebrate heroic victories. Although the 1st Duke of Marlborough was the greatest military commander of his time, his reputation had been tarnished during the last years of the war when his political opponents wrongly accused him of embezzlement of army funds and of deliberately prolonging the hostilities with France for personal financial gain. Despite these charges being proved false soon after his dismissal from office, the shadow cast over his distinguished military career had not been entirely effaced from contemporary recollection. Unwavering in her devotion to her husband's memory and seeking to refute these attacks on his character, Sarah built the arch and the Pillar, both visually dominating structures within the park landscape, to restore the Duke's place in history and his honour for posterity. However, in so doing she changed the meaning of Blenheim from a national monument celebrating military achievement under Queen Anne, to a more personal one, in which the 1st Duke himself was idealised. The celebration of the deed was converted into a commemoration of the doer.

Many drawings of obelisks and columns prepared by Hawksmoor survive. Some must certainly have been made when Vanbrugh was still in charge of the works, when an obelisk had indeed been intended within the ellipse of the avenue of elms created along the northern state approach. When Hawksmoor was recalled to assist in the completion of Blenheim, he resumed attempts to persuade the Duchess to place such a structure in the park, suggesting the junction of the east avenue with the new road from the triumphal arch as a possible location. An alternative submission for an obelisk on the site of the demolished manor was also rejected by Sarah, who reckoned *'if there were obelisks to bee made of what all our Kings have don of that sort the country would bee stuffed with very odd things.'*[23] However, his opportunity finally came when Sarah decided to construct 'the Pillar'.

In contrast to Hawksmoor's earlier submissions where the designs for an obelisk are relatively plain, in most of the drawings submitted for the Column of Victory the heroic symbolism is unmistakable.[24] One suggestion, for an obelisk surmounted with a large gilded star, deliberately attempted to underline Marlborough's greatness through imagery associated with the defeated Louis XIV, called the Sun King. In order that the Duchess would not fail to understand the relevance of his design, Hawksmoor attached an explanation, *'The French set up an obelisk at Arles to the late Lewis the 14th with four inscriptions in Latin full of Complements. On the top was placed the Sun the devise ye French King was fond of. But as that Parhelion or false sun was forced to leave shining [i.e. stop shining] by the influence of a British Starr, the brightest Europe has yet at any time ever seen... the emblem of a Starr may not be improperly placed on the top of this obelisk.'*[25]

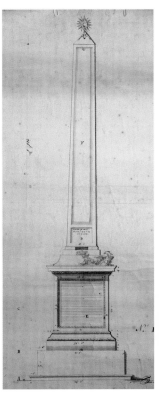 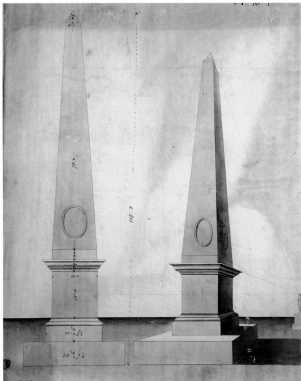

Proposals for an obelisk in Blenheim Park. ➜ ➜➜

Another drawing for the Duchess's consideration was a modified Column of Trajan, after the original built for the great Roman emperor.[26] However, the most interesting surviving design is the one incorporating a fluted Doric column with a statue of the Duke on top and eagles above the inscription on the corners of the pedestal.[27] The eagle imagery was adopted from the Imperial crest, representing Marlborough's elevation as a Prince of the Holy Roman Empire.[28] Although this design contained all the elements which were eventually adopted, Hawksmoor's proposal was not implemented at the time.

As already mentioned, the Duchess's main purpose in erecting the Pillar was to celebrate the Duke's achievements and refute the slanderous accusations which had poisoned the last years of his life. In drafting an inscription for the Pillar she turned to friends and acquaintances for help, but none could produce anything suitable.[29] The project was shelved for four years until her son-in-law, Francis Godolphin, introduced her to Henry Herbert, 9th Earl of Pembroke, rekindling her interest.[30] In the winter of 1727–8, with the help of Roger Morris, Lord Herbert reworked Hawksmoor's drawing, using the same elements but re-arranging them in the Palladian idiom.[31] Renewed attempts were then made on a fitting inscription, with a contribution even from William Townsend, the contractor employed, which Sarah found *very Poetical for a mason*.[32] Ironically, in the end it was Henry St John, Viscount Bolingbroke, a political enemy who nevertheless hero-worshipped the Duke, who provided the wording to satisfy the Duchess. That she was *much moved* every time she read it, was, she admitted, a *sign that it is good*.[33]

The Column of Victory was sited directly on Vanbrugh's original north-south axis, at the southern end of the main approach avenue. Constructed from 1727–31, the fluted Doric column was, at 100 feet (30 m) high, on the same scale as the original Column of Trajan.[34] At the top stood a 34-foot (10.3 m) lead statue of the Duke of Marlborough dressed as a Roman general, holding a commander's baton in his left hand and a Winged Victory elevated in his right hand. The Winged Victory was not only a symbol of military success but also a representation of triumph over death. Four eagles carved in stone were set in each corner around the statue.

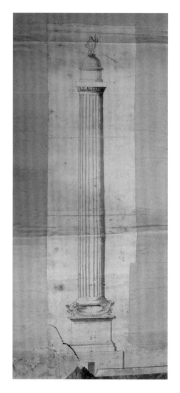

Hawksmoor's design for '*the pillar*'. ↑

The 1st Duke of Marlborough's armorial bearing. ↙ The Princedom of Mindelheim, a small territory in Bavaria, was bestowed on John Churchill, Duke of Marlborough, on his elevation as a Prince of the Holy Roman Empire – his reward from the Austrian Habsburg emperors after the Blenheim campaign, for saving Vienna from a possible French invasion during the War of the Spanish Succession. This entitled the Duke to incorporate the Imperial double-headed eagle in his coat of arms and to style himself 'Marlborough Mindelheim'.

The Column of Victory was begun in 1727 and completed in roughly three years. The column was Sarah, Duchess of Marlborough's lasting memorial to her husband. It continued to impress visitors even after the military achievement of the Duke had faded from public consciousness. At the turn of the 20th century Nathaniel Hawthorne remarked: *'I never had so positive and material an idea of what Fame really is – of what the admiration of his country can do for a successful warrior.'*

Although William Townsend (the stonemason undertaking the work) operated quarries at Headington in Oxford, the output from his own enterprise was insufficient for his needs during the building boom of the early eighteenth century. Most of the stone for the column was therefore procured from the quarries of another Headington mason, John Green.[35] The pedestal was cased with white statuary marble slabs, three inches (7.6 cm) thick, supplied by Henry Flitcroft.[36] Three faces were inscribed with the Acts of Parliament through which Blenheim had been bestowed on the 1st Duke for posterity.[37] Bolingbroke's inscription, describing Marlborough's campaigns and public services, was placed on the fourth side (facing Blenheim Palace). The inscriptions on all the faces were drawn on wooden boards to test the spacing. The words were then marked out on the marble slabs but before the marble was cut Sarah sent her secretary, James Stephens,

THE MARLBOROUGH LINE OF SUCCESSION

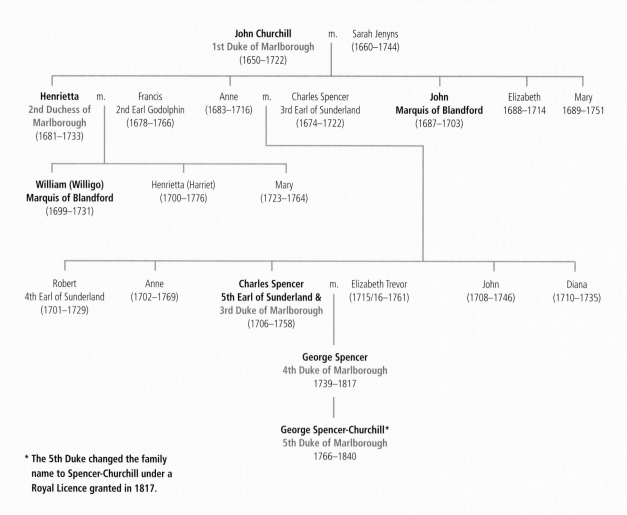

* The 5th Duke changed the family name to Spencer-Churchill under a Royal Licence granted in 1817.

Sarah Churchill, 1st Duchess of Marlborough (1660–1744). ↑
The Duchess was often at odds with Vanbrugh; her love of all
things plain and simple conflicting with his exuberance. In a
letter written in 1716, just after her husband had suffered a
stroke, she explains, '*I have no mind to fall out with Sir John
and much less to vex the Duke of Marlborough at a time
when his health is so bad. At the same time I think I owe it
to him and to my family to preserve if I can having a great
estate thrown away in levelling of hills, filling up precipices
and making bridges in the air, for no reason that I or
anybody else can see but to have it said hereafter that
Sir John Vanbrugh did that thing which never was done
before*'. However, despite their differences, the Duchess
and Vanbrugh had one thing in common – a desire to see
Blenheim Palace completed.

to check the accuracy of the lettering. In a project that had taken almost ten years to complete, and one so close to her heart, the Duchess made certain the column was perfect in '*every Particular to make it as durable as possible*'.[38]

A woman of unparalleled ability, Sarah, Duchess of Marlborough, continued building well into her old age. In the early 1730s she was further preoccupied with constructing a new house at Wimbledon, with gardens laid out by Charles Bridgeman.[39] Bridgeman's accounts and his widow's correspondence with the Duchess relate entirely to these gardens rather than to Blenheim, although this discrepancy has persisted for many years.[40]

At the age of 78 Sarah briefly contemplated finishing a gateway near Bladon to the south of the Great Parterre.[41] But, despite all her activity, she regarded the ducal seat as a '*wild, unmerciful house*' and scarcely used it in old age.[42] With no surviving sons, after the 1st Duke's death in 1722, their eldest daughter, Henrietta, became Duchess of Marlborough in her own right. However, Henrietta did not inherit Blenheim, as Sarah (who retained a life interest) outlived her. When Henrietta died in 1733 with her only son (William 'Willigo' Godolphin) having predeceased her, the title passed to her nephew, Charles Spencer of Althorp. As the 3rd Duke of Marlborough, Charles finally claimed possession of Blenheim after his grandmother, Sarah's death. Sweeping change was not long in coming.

Lombardy poplars were first planted at Blenheim by the 3rd Duke in the 1750s, their earliest known introduction into the English landscape.

4 *An Important Transition*
THE 3RD DUKE'S ALTERATIONS

For many years Charles Spencer, 3rd Duke of Marlborough, had had a difficult relationship with his grandmother, continually encountering her disapproval of his financial management, or rather his lack of it. As Marquis of Blandford, the titular heir to the dukedom, Charles had squandered his generous annual income and run up huge debts on the expectation of his inheritance. On his accession to the title in 1733 he owed over £150,000.[1]

His fondness for commissioning costly alterations at his properties had prompted Sarah to discover her grandson's intentions regarding Blenheim, which he would ultimately inherit. *'As for the question… about my building at Blenheim, that depends upon her'*, Charles commented caustically, *'if she will be so good as to di[e] soon that I may be able to clear my debts, I believe I shall build, but if she is spiteful enough to live much longer I fear I shall not…'*[2]

Apprehensive that he might squander the family fortune in refashioning Blenheim, on which vast sums of money had only recently been spent, Sarah (in her capacity as Ranger of Windsor Park) decided to allow her grandson the use of the Lodge in Little Park.[3] During the five years he spent there, the 3rd Duke laid out extensive gardens with gravel walks, an island, a mount, a greenhouse, and a wilderness extending down to the river Thames. In 1738, when this latest lavish expenditure came to her notice, Sarah evicted her grandson and his garden reverted to parkland.

The 3rd Duke of Marlborough's Lodge ↑↑ **at Windsor Little Park, where he laid out the grounds at great expense.** ↑

© Private Collection

For the next ten years the 3rd Duke lived at Langley, a newly acquired estate in Buckinghamshire, where once again he spent unreservedly on the gardens, planting avenues of firs and building a 27-acre (11 ha) lake.[4] The accounts show large sums owed to Roger Morris (£6,000–£8,000) and Thomas Greening (£2,000). Gardener to King George II, Greening was most likely responsible for the new planting scheme[5] while Morris, the architect employed by Charles Spencer at two other properties, Althorp and Monkey Island near Bray, designed a domed temple in the grounds at Langley, which offered views to Windsor Castle four miles (6.4 km) away.[6]

It has previously been thought that when the 3rd Duke finally moved to Blenheim in 1748, he lacked immediate funds with which to make any alterations. In fact, Vanbrugh and Wise's original design appears unchanged in a description published by Mr Salmon: *'The gardens consist of 77 acres encompassed by a stone wall and laid out in the form of a hexagon, having a round bastion at each angle of 200 ft. diameter. There is in this garden a Wilderness of a vast extent with vistas cut through it. The Grand Gravel Walk which runs from the house southward is 2,200 ft. long and there is another which crosses it in the middle 1,850 ft. in length. Noble Terraces (from whence we have an extensive view of the country) run from Bastion to Bastion....'* [7]

Langley Park in Buckinghamshire was purchased by Charles, 3rd Duke, in 1738 and sold by his son, George, 4th Duke, in 1788. ↑
© Private Collection

However, Salmon also describes the Palace with a completed stable court, and a greenhouse to the west, neither of which were ever built.[8] This puts into doubt the accuracy of his report and it is reasonable to think that he was describing the intended plan of the site rather than providing an eye-witness account. A very similar description in Macky's *Journey through England*, but where the author clearly states *'as these Designs are not yet brought to perfection, I can only give you an Idea of them'* makes it likely that this was indeed the case.[9]

Although in 1716, when the 1st Duke and Duchess of Marlborough took over the finishing of Blenheim themselves, the Duchess had noted *'all the walls of the gardens to do, except those that inclose the Kitchin ground'*, based on an examination of surviving documents and drawings, it is believed that the bastioned perimeter walls of the Great Parterre were built, as there was *'no dispute whether it is to be done or not'.* However, as already mentioned, the basin and grotto scheme at its southern extremity was not completed, and by 1728 the basin pool had been filled in and grassed over.[10]

Whatever the state of completion of the Great Parterre, it would have been entirely unfashionable by the time the 3rd Duke moved to Blenheim, when the taste for a more naturalistic style had developed in preference to *'gardening with levels and lines'*, even though these older formal gardens were still admired. However, in view of the 3rd Duke's known interest in arboriculture and in creating new garden layouts, it is highly likely that he would be inclined to remodel the landscape around the house as soon as he was able.

A fresh examination of family records has revealed that the Duke's financial position was not quite as difficult as previously believed. A new Trust, established roughly two

THE HA-HA

The division between ornamental grounds and the outlying parkland was defined by a sunken barrier called the ha-ha. Developed from French military engineering, it had been used in gardens from the late-seventeenth century onwards. In his translation of D'Argenville's *Theory and Practise of Gardening* (1709), John James describes the feature: *'At present, we frequently make Through Views call'd Ah-ah, which are openings in the walls, without grills, to the very level of the Walks, with a large and deep ditch at the foot of them, lined on both sides to sustain the earth, and prevent the getting over, which surprises the eye upon coming near it, and makes one cry, Ah! Ah! from whence it takes its name'.*

months after the death of Sarah, Duchess of Marlborough, in 1744, administered the estate and the 3rd Duke's debts.[11] For the next decade the interest payments continued to be properly managed and the debts were gradually written down. During this time regular cash payments were made to the Duke on account, the largest of which was £12,000.[12]

The 3rd Duke took legal advice on the future management of the estate and, through an Act passed in 1756, conveyed the interest on the lease of Langley to his eldest son and heir, George, Marquis of Blandford, just before he turned eighteen.[13] The Act further established that £10,000 could be spent on rebuilding Langley for the Marquis.[14] Significantly, it also allowed the Duke to receive a payment of £30,000 and other smaller amounts against the surrender and discharge of several leases. This enabled substantial cash disbursements, totalling around £65,000 in just two years.[15] Such sums would certainly have enabled the Duke to undertake major changes at Blenheim where, by 1759, the gardens were already being described in contemporary guidebooks as *'now a very large plot of ground, well contrived by sinking the outer wall into a Foss, to give a view quite round, and take off the disagreeable appearance of Confinement and limitation to the Eye. It is within well adorned with Walks, Greens, Espaliers and Vistas to divers remarkable objects that offer themselves in the circumjacent country. The descent to the Water on the south and west exceeds most gardens in this kingdom'.*[16]

Elizabeth, Duchess of Marlborough (1715/6–1761). ↑

Charles Spencer, 3rd Duke of Marlborough (1706–1758). ↑
Charles Spencer was Sarah Marlborough's oldest surviving grandson. When he became 3rd Duke of Marlborough in 1733, his younger brother John Spencer gained control of the Spencer's ancestral home, Althorp. Both brothers resented their grandmother's autocratic management of the family finances even though John, as the Duchess's favourite, stood to inherit her vast personal fortune. When, at a family get-together, Sarah compared herself to a great tree with '*all her branches flourishing*', he remarked unkindly that the branches would thrive better when the root was underground!

A previously unknown survey plan drawn a few years later in 1763 also indicates that the most significant change to the gardens – the removal of the western bastioned walls of the Great Parterre – was likely to have been initiated by the 3rd Duke. The sloping ground of the western aspect meant that the garden wall on this side would have been built higher than on the east. Its removal enabled the garden to be merged with the park.[17] (See Chapter 5.) Additionally, a number of Lombardy poplars were planted in the grounds, their first known introduction in England.[18] A new farm covered with furze (gorse) was created for the dairy herd in the north-west of the park, becoming known as Furze Plat Farm.[19] Although no records have been discovered naming those responsible for the changes, the work was well under way before the Duke's sudden death in 1758, during the Seven Years War. A contemporary account published shortly afterwards describing the gardens as '*spacious and agreeable; they originally consisted of about 100 acres, but the late Duke made large additions and elegant improvements. The noble descent to the water on the south and west, covered with flowering shrubs, and embellished with other natural beauties, will hardly be paralleled by any Garden in this Kingdom*', leaves us in no doubt that the 3rd Duke had already begun an ambitious scheme of alterations.[20]

The family at Blenheim found their lives dramatically changed by the Duke's sudden death. While the young Marquis of Blandford acceded to the title, becoming the 4th Duke of Marlborough and inheriting the ducal estate, it was decided that his mother would return to Langley as dowager Duchess, when the rebuilding work there was completed.[21]

HIGH LODGE

High Lodge, previously known as Ranger's Lodge, was in earlier times the residence of the Ranger of the Royal Forests. When occupied by Sir Henry Lee (Ranger from 1570–1610, in Queen Elizabeth I's reign) in 1577 it was described as a building with two gardens and a wood yard. The house is better remembered for its connections with John Wilmot, the rakish Earl of Rochester, Comptroller of the Park in the reign of King Charles II, and Keeper of the King's Hawks. Rochester was a famously ribald and popular Restoration poet, who died at the Lodge in July 1680.

In 1706, the building was renovated (**A**) for the 1st Duke and Duchess of Marlborough who used it on their visits to Woodstock while Blenheim was being constructed. The Lodge was enlarged with the addition of a new wing, windows were replaced throughout, new paving laid and new fittings provided in the kitchen. The building lay empty from 1719 when the family moved into the newly completed private apartments in the east wing of Blenheim Palace. Sarah, Duchess of Marlborough, then allowed John Ashworth (a young man of means who had fallen on bad times) to use the Lodge, appointing him as a deer-keeper in the park.[26]

In the 1750s the 3rd Duke of Marlborough undertook renovations at Blenheim, which included some work at High Lodge. These renovations were concluded in spring 1764, a few years after the 3rd Duke's sudden death, when the upholsterer Charles Arbuckle supplied the Lodge with '*132 fine Chints paper pencilled in oyl, 144 of border, 118 of Lumberhand paper and fourteen chairs*'.[27] The parapet of the building was crenellated and a canted bay added (**B**). This remodelling in the Gothic style has in modern times been attributed to Lancelot 'Capability' Brown on stylistic grounds. Well before Brown's arrival at Blenheim, Stephen Switzer had advocated the use of this style for

estate buildings. The transformation of High Lodge made it an eye-catching sculptural object, which completed the vista to the south-west of the Palace.

The Lodge played its part in the late-eighteenth-century pleasure grounds formed by the 4th Duke, at a time when visiting the menagerie and the Kitchen Garden, as well as boating and fishing on the lake, all became popular. A highlight on the park circuit, distant views could be glimpsed from its tall central tower.

In the late nineteenth and twentieth centuries it was used by the family as a spot for luncheon during elaborate shooting parties, one of which, in 1896 (**C**), was attended by the Prince of Wales (later King Edward VII). Food was sent out from the Palace kitchens in padded baskets and reheated on a stove in a tent. High Lodge was then divided into two residences, occupied by Palace staff until the 1970s.

Ancient Woodland

The landscape around High Lodge has long been a forest consisting mainly of oak trees. This naturally regenerating ancient woodland was preserved and maintained as a deliberate contrast to the formal avenues, sweeping lawns, man-made lake and managed landscape surrounding the Palace. Several ancient oaks still survive, the largest and oldest of which show signs of early pollarding. The girth of some trees measures between 24 to 30 feet (7–9 m) which suggests that they date back 300–500 years. Some of these are now well past their prime, with hollowed trunks and 'stag heads'. They are not removed as their timber is worthless but the part they play in the woodland eco-system, providing a natural habitat for beetles and other insect life, is valuable.

High Lodge

At first, modest expenditure was undertaken in refurnishing Langley, some rooms at Blenheim and at Marlborough House in London. The upholsterer Charles Arbuckle was engaged for five years from January 1759 at all three properties. In 1764 Arbuckle provided wallpaper and chairs for High Lodge in Blenheim Park, which had undergone a recent remodelling in the Gothic style.[22] The old casements on both storeys were converted into pointed windows. A canted bay and tower were incorporated into the front façade, and a crenellated parapet ran along the entire roofline. Although records relating to this period confirm Stiff Leadbetter and Roger Morris as the only documented architects to be commissioned by the family, the reconstruction of High Lodge has traditionally been accredited (on stylistic grounds) to Lancelot 'Capability' Brown.[23] Admittedly the records for Brown's work are fragmentary, but they do nevertheless show that the 4th Duke had consulted him by 1763 for improvements to the grounds at Langley.[24]

Having inherited a vast estate and a great fortune at the age of just nineteen, the 4th Duke had both the time and the money to gratify his tastes and interests. However, it was only after his marriage to Lady Caroline Russell (daughter of the Duke of Bedford) in August 1762, that he set about transforming Blenheim into the most fashionably splendid family home.[25] Vanbrugh's monumental Palace was finally to be given its uniquely majestic setting.

North view of Blenheim, by C.W. Radclyffe, detail.

5 'Nothing Equal to This'
'CAPABILITY' BROWN &
THE 4TH DUKE'S LANDSCAPE GARDEN

By the middle decades of the eighteenth century, the conception of a fashionable garden had changed dramatically from the old formal style to a new enthusiasm for natural scenery. Aristocratic landowners completing their classical education on the Grand Tour were inspired by Italian landscapes and the pastoral paintings of Claude, Poussin and Salvator Rosa. Change was initiated not only through the gardens of Switzer, Bridgeman and Kent, but also as a result of the publications of Addison, Steele and the celebrated Alexander Pope, who famously remarked *'All gardening is landscape painting'*.[1] However, the new art of composing natural landscapes reached its highest point in the work of Lancelot 'Capability' Brown.

So much has already been written on Brown's life and career that it would be mere repetition to detail it again instead of concentrating on what he achieved at Blenheim and discussing his practice and working methods on this site. It is sufficient therefore to mention that he was a Northumbrian who worked at Stowe before setting up independently and moving to Hammersmith in 1751. Through contacts made while at Stowe, Brown's business grew rapidly. His curious nickname originated from his habit of surveying a new location for its capabilities; his talent amply revealed in the inspired implementation of each task. He won many notable commissions, building his reputation as a landscape gardener, architect and engineer, and making him a highly successful businessman.[2]

At the height of his career, Brown was invited by the 4th Duke of Marlborough to improve the grounds at Langley. But the Duke also wanted to make essential changes at Blenheim, and wrote to him in June 1763, *'I have received your letter; and will send to town for your plan for Langley, which I like very well, but as I cannot begin to make alterations (at least expensive ones) at this place and at Langley at the same time; I have a notion I shall begin here immediately; so that the sooner you come the better'.*[3]

For the prestigious Blenheim commission Brown embarked on a detailed survey of the park, engaging John Spyers to carry out the task. Charles Richardson, a resident of the neighbouring village of Combe, who witnessed the survey, recorded: *'Mr Spiers of Twickenham, his assistant and a lad named James Stuckly of Combe carried the chain'.*[4] Brown paid Spyers £25 on 3 January 1764; it is likely that a part of this disbursement (if not all) related to the survey and the drawing subsequently produced.[5]

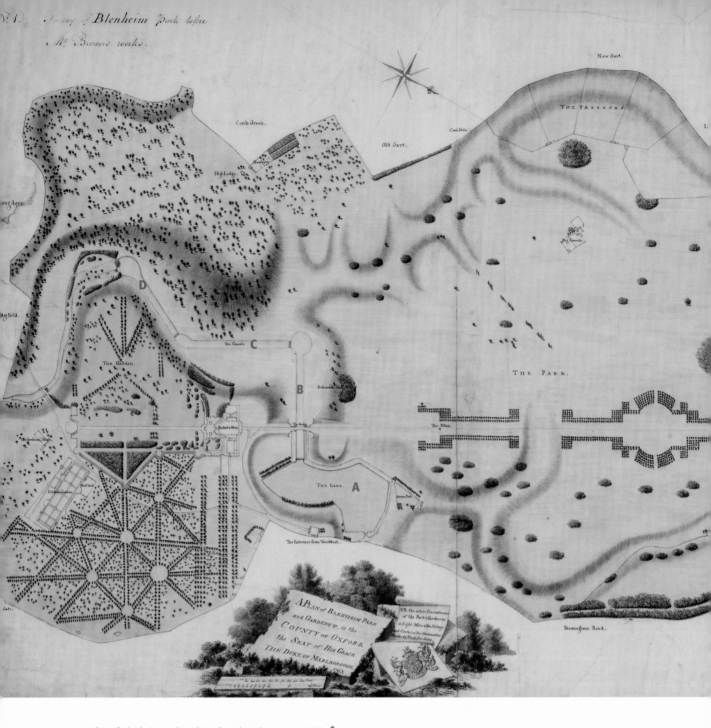

A Plan of Blenheim Park and Gardens, by John Spyers, 1763. ↑

Spyers came from a family of Twickenham nurserymen and was trained by his uncle, Joshua.
In November 1748, the family supplied trees for Horace Walpole's garden at Strawberry Hill and
prepared a survey of the grounds a couple of years later. The survey of Blenheim Park was carried
out in 1763 and should be counted as Spyers' first commission for 'Capability' Brown. He remained
Brown's draughtsman for almost twenty years, until Brown's death in 1783.

The drawing details Colonel Armstrong's surviving scheme – the lake (**A**) and three arms of the
canal (**B**, **C**, **D**) extending into the Glyme valley. The last section of canal drained into two parallel
watercourses before rejoining the river. 'Capability' Brown built his cascade dam at this point and
converted the two watercourses into a widened stretch of river which continued downstream.

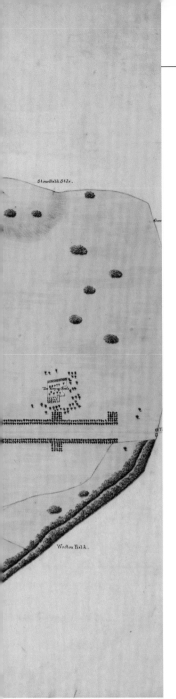

The drawing reveals the 3rd Duke's half-finished alterations and additions to the grounds. Although it is not certain how much further his son carried the scheme before Brown's assistance was sought at Blenheim, from what is known of the 4th Duke's early life, it seems highly unlikely that he took anything forward. After his father's death, the exceedingly shy young man was sent on the Grand Tour to complete his education. His travels in Italy in 1760–1 stimulated a life-long interest in classical antiquity, but the Tour was hurriedly aborted in order to discharge a ceremonial role at the coronation of King George III. On his return, an unusually brief political career followed before the Duke retired from active public life, turning his attention fully to estate business and his personal interests.

The 1763 survey plan provides a most valuable indication of the layout of the grounds at Blenheim in the transitional period after Henry Wise, but before 'Capability' Brown's intervention. It clearly shows that only the east bastioned wall of Vanbrugh and Wise's Great Parterre remained, there were a few residual traces of the wood-work, and the compartmented plantings had all but disappeared. In the park, the grand avenue to the north and the east avenue appear fully planted. Other notable features like Wise's *patte d'oie* to the west and the quincunx plantations to the east also survived. However, Wise's flower garden for the 1st Duchess had already been replaced with a lawn framed with planting.

Several belts of trees are also shown, most likely planted by the 3rd Duke who had a keen interest in arboriculture. Those worth mentioning are a long shelter belt at the north-eastern boundary of the park; wedge-shaped clusters on the slope to the west of the house; a kidney-shaped clump around Rosamund's Well; two large circular clumps in the north-west of the park; and finally, a densely planted enclosure where the last arm of Armstrong's canal scheme drained into the river. Interestingly, at this spot (where Brown later sited his cascade) the canal drained into two parallel watercourses which extended some distance before joining up again to flow as a river near the then boundary of the park.

The survey also confirms that the park comprised roughly 2,000 acres (809 ha) at the time and its circumference measured over eight miles (12.9 km). Additional land purchases had yet to be made by the 4th Duke to bring the estate to its present boundaries. However, the most significant findings relate to Brown's contract at Blenheim, his conduct and reputation, for although he would remove the remaining parterre walls and submerge Armstrong's canal and cascade scheme, Brown did not make any damaging alterations to the landscape, nor were his designs as destructive of earlier compositions as has traditionally been thought. Brown had already gained experience in grand-scale landscaping through his work at Alnwick, Luton Hoo and Bowood.[6] Although Blenheim dwarfed most other estates, the elements of Brown's style of gardening worked best on a larger scale, and the Blenheim commission, if not his masterpiece, would certainly become one of his most celebrated sites.

Lancelot Brown's work typically included the careful management of four elements – water, trees, buildings and ground. Around the house, he would create sweeping lawns which came right up to the building, framed by groups of trees or dotted with single majestic specimens. In the middle distance, a body of water with curving shores would be formed, precise planting always screening out any termination points. In the far distance, the rising ground would have a dense canopy of trees joining the skyline. Around the perimeter of the estate, an irregular belt of trees would be planted (often called a

South East View of Blenheim Palace, by C.W. Radclyffe. ↑ Brown created an extensive lawn to the south of the Palace, framed with carefully planted clumps of trees.

shelter belt), to conceal the boundary walls and give the appearance of the owner's possessions being infinite. Straight lines vanished altogether, but Brown did not merely replace them with curves. Realising the importance of contours, he adjusted landscapes vertically as well as horizontally by removing earth or mounding it, exploiting the lie of the land to create sweeping vistas up hills and down valleys. Groups of trees were deliberately scattered to control views. His parks were created to imitate the English countryside but they were in fact highly contrived tableaux, meticulously calculated and manufactured. Walks and drives were planned exactly to provide varying vistas and sudden changes of scene, contriving visual delay and creating anticipation. The density of trees was also entirely managed. Brown was praised for his painterly compositions, but he worked more like a sculptor, his landscapes designed to be viewed from all angles. He produced gloriously contoured scenery that appeared as if formed by Nature.

At Blenheim, several existing architectural and landscape elements were disposed to Brown's advantage. There was already a river, a prominent natural valley, a monumental bridge and an impressive house built on a wide plateau. Additionally, the unusual placement of Hawksmoor's Woodstock Gate with its capacity for surprise provided a device for a dramatic initial panorama.

Brown enlarged the existing arrangement of water features (the small lake, the stepped cascade and canals with connecting cascade pools) by flooding the valley to create one large sheet of water with curving shores. In submerging the earlier scheme, Brown not only unified it but completed it in the latest fashion. His plan for this remodelling still exists at Blenheim Palace.[7] Although undated, it was probably made in 1763–4. The lake at Blenheim was Brown's largest, and the proposal for its creation was almost certainly one of the earliest designs he submitted for the 4th Duke's approval.[8]

LANCELOT 'CAPABILITY' BROWN (1716–1783)

'Capability' Brown, a renowned landscape gardener of the eighteenth century, earned his curious nickname through his assessment of an estate for its capabilities. Working flexibly, Brown sometimes offered a design but did not carry out the work himself. Whenever he secured a contract, Brown appointed a foreman or associate to direct all manual operations on site, only paying periodic visits to check progress. Employing up to twenty foremen at different stages of his career, he was never directly responsible for hiring labourers. This part of his business was undertaken by the foreman, or by using the estate's labour force. Only on rare occasions would he oversee the work himself.

At Blenheim, Brown employed Benjamin Read as his associate. Read was in charge of the implementation of the project, as well as the supervision of contract labourers. The average labourer would earn about eight shillings for a six-day week. Brown's commission at Blenheim (from 1763 to 1774) was a demanding but highly remunerative project for which he was paid just over £21,500.

In a letter written a few years before his death, Brown explained his working methods, '*to produce these effects there wants a good plan, good execution, a perfect knowledge of the country and the objects in it, whether natural or artificial, and infinite delicacy in the planting… so much beauty depending on the size of the trees and the colour of their leaves to produce the effect of light and shade so very essential to the perfecting* [of] *a good Plan, as also hiding what is disagreeable and shewing what is beautifull*'.

By the time of his death, Brown had such an immense reputation that the generally critical Horace Walpole lamented, '*Lady Nature's second Husband is dead*'. His tomb was inscribed with the words '*more than genius slumbers here*'.

Early Surveying and Measuring

In order to produce accurate estate plans, surveyors in the eighteenth century used geometry and the principles of triangulation to measure distances across the landscape. The process was begun by establishing a baseline between two points which was measured with a steel chain; the accuracy of the baseline was vital as it formed the first side of the triangle from which all the other lengths would be worked out. A fixed distant point (a tree, a building, or a marker flag) was then selected and its angle to the baseline measured by using an instrument called a theodolite. The distance between the other end of the baseline and the tree or building was then determined by calculating the hypotenuse of the triangle created.

The theodolite was a surveying instrument comprising a scale with two fixed and two moveable sights. Even a very basic model could produce fairly accurate results.

A number of different instruments existed for specific surveying and measuring work. Establishing levels for ornamental lakes would have required staking out by trial and error, to estimate the amount of earth-removal and clay-lining work required. Mathematical skills (especially geometry) and a good knowledge of engineering were required for calculations in reconfiguring the terrain.

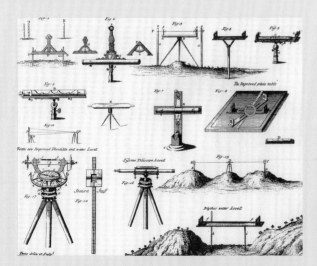

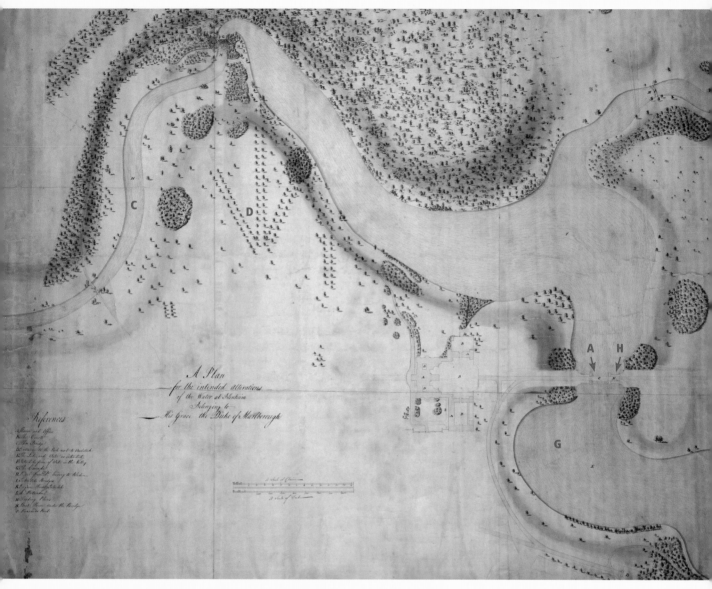

A Plan for the intended Alterations of the Water at Blenheim, by Lancelot Brown

The plan, undated, but probably *c.*1763–4 shows Brown's scheme for a new artificial lake extending on either side of Vanbrugh's Great Bridge (**A**), with clumps of beech trees planted at the corners of the bridge. The cascade dam (**B**) is tucked away around a bend, the termination point hidden behind a screen of planting. Downstream from the cascade, the Glyme is shown as a widened serpentine river (**C**). The trees dotted on the landscape are typical of Brown's draughtsmanship and include a mix of conifers and deciduous specimens. He retained the *patte d'oie* of trees (**D**) to the south-west of the house while adding a few new clumps, but planned dense new planting on the rising ground above the cascade (**E**). A similar screen of planting is shown near the Hawksmoor's Triumphal Arch (**F**), hiding the entry of the Glyme into the park. Notably, the island in the middle of the upper lake, which was created out of the remnants of the old causeway, is not shown at all (**G**) and was probably decided on later, as work progressed.

Brown created a boathouse within the bridge (under the north arch) (**H**) and positioned a pumphouse near the cascade (not the present one) to operate the sluices for the dam. The water engine installed under the north arch by Robert Aldersea half a century earlier was moved several times as work progressed. It was temporarily placed where the Glyme enters the park. Soon afterwards it was moved to the head of the water at the cascade before it was finally relocated at a new 'engine house' built to accommodate it, near the old Woodstock Gate (located further to the north).

Every man-made lake needs a dam to contain the water; the profile and surface area of the lake depends on the height of the dam. In making the lake and dam at Blenheim, Brown took the architectural detail of Vanbrugh's Grand Bridge as his point of reference – the level of water in the lake was precisely aligned with the horizontal moulding between the ground and first-floor windows of the bridge. The moulding was broadened to accommodate seasonal fluctuations and extreme weather.[9] The floor of the central room at the bridge's north end was filled with stone and rubble, raising it above water level to make a convenient boathouse.[10] But by far the main concern for Brown at the time was the flooding of the bridge under water.

Vanbrugh had built the bridge on meadowland, with foundations that were never intended to be submerged. The task of strengthening the bridge was undertaken in 1764 before the lake was created. According to the contemporary observations of Charles Richardson, the 4th Duke ordered the complete levelling of all the walls of the old manor which were still standing so that they *were supplied to repair the bridge and in particular to secure its foundation … They sunk all round below the foundation at a great expense, cased and terraced it above high water mark and rose the floors of the rooms within…'*[11]

If any written contracts were made with the Duke of Marlborough, they have not come to light. Apart from the lake plan mentioned earlier, Lancelot Brown's 1764 drawing of the cascade is all that remains.[12] In the decade he worked at Blenheim, Brown actually built two dams; first, the cascade dam for the lake, and later the Lince or Bladon dam which contained the reservoir formed in widening the river Glyme downstream.[13]

Aerial photo of Blenheim Park, 1961. Taken in the morning on a dry summer's day, this photograph shows the outline of Armstrong's old canal scheme submerged beneath Brown's lake.
↑
© Oxfordshire County Council Photographic Archive

The cascade dam had not only to contain and maintain water at an optimum level but also had to be watertight and strong enough to withstand significant water pressure, to resist ripple erosion and to prevent moles and other creatures from burrowing through. Although technical knowledge was still limited at the time, Brown drew on the skills pioneered by John Grundy, a Spalding-based engineer in the 1740s (for the Fenland drainage projects).[14] Having habitually used rammed clay as a watertight method of building dams for ornamental lakes since the 1750s, Brown was experienced in these early engineering techniques before coming to Blenheim.

A drawing for the cascade, by Lancelot Brown, 1764. ←
The cascade is, in fact, the overflow section of Brown's dam across the valley, built to create the lake. In his 1770 publication, *Observations on Modern Gardening*, Thomas Whately described water as *'the most interesting object in a landscape'*. Cascades provided the viewer with a different type of water, i.e. rapidly moving white water, which pleased not only the eye, but the sense of hearing too. By placing the cascade around a bend and concealing it with planting, Brown made the most of the technique of visual delay. Visitors were (and still are) able to hear the cascade before they see it, which heightens their anticipation and appreciation of the scene.

The cascade dam consists of two sections with foundations on solid limestone bedrock: a long earthfill embankment constructed with a clay core at least five feet (1.5 m) wide to the height of the dam, and a masonry overflow section (the cascade) which forms the western end of the structure. For the core of the dam, Brown used local clay mixed with a small amount of limestone gravel. It has a sloping upstream face (i.e. the side inside the lake) but a more vertical downstream one. The clay in the core had to be well tempered – not too soft, nor too stiff. It was typically layered in 6 inch (15 cm) courses, before being extensively and firmly rammed, each course being sprinkled with sand which prevented the hammers from sticking. The core was supported on both sides by sloping earth embankments. The crest of the embankment and the downstream slope were covered with grass. The cascade section was covered with layers of clay, random-fill limestone and a few well-placed rocks over which the run-off flowed, maintaining the level of the lake.[15]

A system of pumps and sluices installed to the side of the dam allowed water levels to be controlled. The water was pumped to reservoirs in the park from where the Palace and Kitchen Garden were supplied, also providing for areas under cultivation and livestock. Excess water was discharged through the sluices directly into the river downstream of the cascade, and served to safely lower the level of the lake in the winter months when the cascade froze over, and in extreme wet weather.

The Cascade, by
C.W. Radclyffe. →
The light iron
bridge in front
of it was a
later addition.

However, while adding to the aesthetic enjoyment of the grounds, the cascade compromised the strength of the dam in more than one way. The eroding force of the waterfall is obvious, but the problem caused by the ornamental planting surrounding it, a device frequently used by Brown to conceal the termination points of water, was more destructive. Tree roots create fissures which can endanger the structure and cause leaks in the embankment and this has required successive Dukes to carry out expensive repairs ever since.[16]

In accordance with general practice, the lake was probably formed by clearing out the vegetation in the meadows, removing the larger stones and rocks and filling any holes in order to level out the valley bottom. Armstrong's earlier canal and cascade scheme was left as constructed. The ground around it was lined with layers of clay (later termed 'puddled' clay) worked systematically from the bottom of the valley upwards.[17] The first layers were mixed with lime to stop animal life from worming through and also to absorb excess water. Every layer was rammed down by gangs of men working in teams, each team working with a different type of hammer. The first layer was the thickest (around 4 feet/ 1.2 m), gradually becoming thinner nearer the top, each layer being worked at right angles to the preceding one. The lining was smoothed and covered with 2 inches (5 cm) of chalk before a final layer of clay was rammed down. The sloping walls of the valley were similarly lined while the lake was allowed to fill, so that the clay would not dry out or crack during the process. An extra layer of clay was usually applied to the sides to prevent cracks going through the bottom of the lining during very dry summers.[18]

*A Plan for the alterations from Pritchard's gate
to the new gate*, by Lancelot Brown.
© Woodstock Town Hall

Both sections of the lake on either side of Vanbrugh's bridge follow the serpentine shores of a natural valley, which led William Gilpin to remark '*ye ground falls easily on every side: not ye least mark of a spade (if any hath been used) is left*'.[19] The neat turf edges usually curved out of sight which made the exact size of the lake indiscernible. The sweeping banks of lawn extended up the slopes of the valley, reaching as far as the front steps of the house where grass now completely covered Vanbrugh's paved north entrance court.

As work progressed, a small island (then called Coach Road Island, later known as Queen Elisabeth's Island) materialized to the east of the bridge. This was a remnant section of the lower causeway leading to the old royal manor, which had also been used by Armstrong in his earlier lake and cascade scheme.[20] The island appears to have been included in the scheme as work progressed, as it does not feature in Brown's *Intended Alterations* plan.[21]

However, it is clearly visible (planted with trees) in Brown's later drawing, *A Plan for the alterations from Pritchard's gate to the new gate*.[22] This design proposed a series of

gothicised buildings with a long castellated wall adjoining the village, extending from Woodstock Gate to a new gate at Hensington, created by the 4th Duke of Marlborough. (See box on page 75.) However, the Duke did not proceed with Brown's complex scheme. He also rejected another plan submitted for a Gothic bathing house at Rosamund's Well.[23] It seems rather odd that Brown offered so many proposals in the Gothic style even though the Duke was known to favour neo-classical architecture. None of these Gothic designs was in fact implemented within the Palace precincts, although, as we shall see later, a farm edifice was built further afield.

The cascade and lake took about four years to complete and there is no doubt it was a great accomplishment, universally praised not merely by Brown's contemporaries, but ever since. Tourists flocked to Blenheim to see the latest improvements and almost a dozen coaching inns flourished in the neighbourhood at this time.[24] In August 1767, Brown received a congratulatory letter from Baron Cadogan of Caversham Park, '… *we saw it to the greatest perfection, and indeed it <u>beggars</u> all description, as it would the owner of it had he not forty or fifty thousand pounds a year to be doing with. The water is by much the finest artificial thing I ever saw; when I say that I include the banks,*

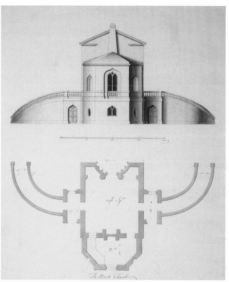

Two design proposals by Lancelot Brown for the front and rear of a Bathing House at Rosamund's Well.

and the advantageous manner in which you have set it off… The Park is much underplanted notwithstanding the verge round it, but I take for granted these are faults that will mend…'[25] Vanbrugh's Grand Bridge had finally been provided with such a worthy setting, that even the habitually acerbic Horace Walpole admitted the lake *'is now amazingly beautiful and puts the bridge's nose out of joint'.*[26]

'Capability' Brown's improvements changed the views both to and from the house. Extensive lawns now swept right up to the steps on all four principal fronts. Brown used grass as a connecting medium which allowed a visual integration of the park, bringing it much closer to the building.[27] He had created a lake unparalleled in size[28] and beauty, but this alteration in the landscape resulted in the best prospect no longer being commanded from the house, where none of the principal rooms faced the water. Instead the finest view was now obtained on entering into the grounds from

Woodstock Gate; Sarah's practicality in establishing the gate and Brown's genius in conceiving the landscape beyond it provided a most dramatic entrance into the park. It was this majestic sequence of views – the bridge, the lake, the column, the woods, and the palatial house – which prompted King George III to remark, when visiting Blenheim in 1786, *'We have nothing equal to this'.*[29]

Around the time of the King's visit, the 4th Duke launched a magnificent pleasure

An 18th-century engraving of pleasure boats on the lake. ↓
© Private Collection

A View of the Lake with Bridge and Obelisk, by John Warwick Smith. The lake is one of the largest areas of open water in Oxfordshire and is important for breeding and wintering wildfowl, including the great crested grebe, herons, Canada geese and the gadwall.

boat on the lake, appropriately named *The Sovereign*.[30] As angling became increasingly popular, the water was also used for fishing. Richard Beckley, the Duke's long-serving fisherman, operated large weighted nets for his catch, but his duties also included attending gentlemen anglers who had been granted permission to indulge their sport.[31] Lord Macclesfield recorded a visit in 1786: *'the Duke of Marlborough after having so obligingly given leave to me to take a few days fishing in Blenheim water, informed me that it was necessary for me to give 2 or 3 days notice to the fisherman… We found everything ready and had a pretty good days sport, as we caught 7 tolerable Jack and a brace of good perch, one full 2 lb weight. As we fished with snap tackle, we threw in the small fish which we took…'*[32]

The new landscape owed much to Lancelot Brown's creative genius, but the contribution of the team of workmen and their impeccable execution of Brown's design should not be overlooked. Although Brown paid regular visits, the construction of the cascade dam, the creation of the lake and his later work to the south of the Palace was overseen by his associate on site, the project foreman, Benjamin Read.

Read was a pavior (a man working on conduits) when Brown is thought to have met him at Stowe.[33] He was subsequently employed by Brown at Croome in the 1750s, one of their larger commissions involving the extensive drainage of the Earl of Coventry's land in Warwickshire, where Read successfully supervised the creation of a new river.[34] His skill in the management of water and his understanding of the problems encountered in such work was possibly sufficient reason for Brown to employ him again at Blenheim.

Brown's account with Drummonds Bank records the amounts paid to Benjamin Read over eleven years from 1763 when the Blenheim contract began. The steady flow of money makes it apparent that work proceeded actively throughout the decade; but the commission was generally divided into two parts over two periods. First, when the lake, the cascade and several tree-planting schemes were completed to the north of the Palace between 1763 and 1770. Secondly, from 1771 to 1773, when the River Glyme was widened into its sweeping serpentine form, and another cascade constructed near Bladon.[35]

The view from Woodstock Gate, called 'The Finest View in England'. ↓ For many years, the scale of the bridge had been out of proportion to the stream of the River Glyme beneath it, before Brown's new lake and cascade became the focus of any visit to the grounds at Blenheim Palace.

An analysis of these payment records reveals interesting details. Brown did not always make payments to Read on the basis of the sums he received from the Duke, as on several occasions payments made were greater than the sums received. However, the Duke issued drafts whenever requested and if Brown was overdrawn on the Blenheim contract, it was more likely because of his relaxed accounting rather than any withholding on the Duke's part.[36] However, Brown prepared an account of the work undertaken until October 1770 and received a full settlement of all claims in the spring of 1771.[37] This was probably the mid point at which the work to the north of the house had ended and the stage to the south just begun.

By the close of his contract, Brown had received a substantial £21,537 from the Duke of Marlborough. His business with the 4th Duke was lucrative; the difference between his receipts and his disbursements totalled £3,930. However, although work ended in September 1773, two payments were made to Benjamin Read in 1774 which did not fit the usual pattern. The smaller sum (£89:4s) was probably the final settlement of Read's tally, but the larger amount, a substantial £400 paid on 1 March, is of much greater interest.[38]

ACCOUNTS RELATING TO BROWN'S BLENHEIM CONTRACT
(1763–1774)

Extract from 'Capability' Brown's account book:

Received of His Grace the Duke of Marlborough at Blenheim

		£ : s	
1764	February	1,100	
	October 20	800	1,900:00
1765	January 16	500	
	April 3	400	
	August 12	500	1,400:00
1766	January 24	1,000	
	June 11	800	1,800:00
1767	February	1,000	1,000:00
1768	February 12	1,500	
	April	600	
	November 25	1,500	3,600:00
1769	June 25	1,200	1,200:00
1770	March 30	*1,500	*4,050:00
1771	Balance of all accounts		
	to 27 October 1770	*2,550	
	July 29	**1,500**	
	December 10	**1,200**	2,700:00
1772	March	500	
	August	**1,200**	1,700:00
1773	May 13	**1,000**	1,000:00
1774	February 17	**1,000**	
	in March received a Balance		
	& all Demands	187:14	1,187:14
	TOTAL		21,537:14

**Amounts paid by Brown
to Benjamin Read:** [39]

YEAR	£
1763	670
1764	1,730
1765	1,620
1766	1,405
1767	1,670
1768	1,885
1769	1,485
1770	1,645
1771	2,135
1772	2,198
1773	675
1774	489
TOTAL	17,607

*Figures in bold type show the sums deposited
by Brown directly into his Drummonds account.*

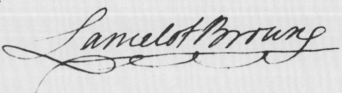

As Brown's agent, Read would have kept a nominal roll of workmen with a record of their pay to reclaim this from Brown. For his trouble in keeping these accounts, in managing the labour and in organising the work, he would expect to be paid. This was a common form of contractual arrangement during the eighteenth century. It would appear therefore, that the money received by Read at the conclusion of the work was either in remuneration of his supervisory role, or more likely the payment of an agreed fee or gratuity, especially if one considers that £400 is roughly 10% of Brown's profit, as calculated earlier.[40]

However, Read's involvement with Blenheim did not end when Brown's business there ceased. New research has revealed that he was retained by the 4th Duke. The estate accounts for 1775 (the year after Brown's contract ended) describe Benjamin Read as the *Foreman of the Works*, with an annual salary of £105.[41] In fact he remained at Blenheim for the rest of his working life, '*forming ornamental plantations and enriching the Park and Pleasure grounds*' until the age of 60, when his death at Woodstock in 1794 was recorded.[42] Employed at Blenheim for three decades, but not always under Brown's direction, it seems certain that some landscape modifications were in fact carried out by Read in collaboration with the Duke, after Brown's departure.

A late-18th-century watercolour of the view from the Palace towards the Column of Victory. Despite the scale and grandeur of Blenheim's landscape, its vocabulary is deceptively simple – the principal components are trees, grass and water. Brown's planting of beech stands at the four corners of the bridge, and other clumps around the lake, are unmistakable.

Read was most likely responsible for enclosing the cascade gardens in the 1780s, when John Byng observed a '*Frenchly-adorn'd fountain*' and a Chinese bridge '*of mean effect*'.[43] Accounts for 1784–5 show that roughly £2,800 was spent by Read in that year alone.[44] Estate records also describe a new walk laid out by him in the grounds, which was inadequately made with a mixture of loamy sand and pebbles proving difficult to negotiate in wet weather.[45] By 1788, he was occupied with every aspect of Park maintenance. A memorandum issued by the Duke in February clearly records the division of staff responsibilities: the farmer was accountable for '*all business with respect to the Stock… Cattle, Sheep, Horses… and all the Common Farming business… with 2 Men, 2 Boys, 2 Shepherds and 2 Dairy Maids*', and that '*everything that respects the Ornament or keeping the Park clean and neat, beyond the Ordinary business of a Farmer, Mr Read is to be applied to, and to find proper persons to do it*'.[46]

The 4th Duke took an active interest in laying out new gardens and in constructing garden buildings. As we shall see in the next chapter, several imposing garden temples were commissioned, but other structures were simpler, such as the small rustic pavilion built with a '*grotesque front*' set with pebbles and sand.[47] Walking around the grounds with the Duchess was a favourite and regular pastime, and it was reported that she only drank water from the spring at Rosamund's Well.[48] Brown had planted an avenue of Scots firs along the line of the fence to conceal the dead walk leading from Woodstock Gate towards the Palace, but in the mid-1780s, in a public-spirited gesture, the Duke had it cut it down because it spoilt the view from the vicarage on the other side of the boundary wall.[49]

George, 4th Duke (1739–1817) ⬅⬅ and Caroline, Duchess of Marlborough (1743–1811). ⬅

THE HENSINGTON GATE

The Hensington Gate comprises two substantial piers, probably designed by Nicholas Hawksmoor. The gate was originally conceived as part of an outer boundary wall scheme at the far end of Henry Wise's original East Avenue, directly aligned with the bow window of the private apartments. The intended gateway was to be constructed in Burford ashlar, with '*shafts and columns, wav'd shafts of Rustic Peers, and circular arch heads*'. The frosted sections of the columns on each pier and the enriched scrolls were carved by Grinling Gibbons in April 1709. However, the scheme was not realised: despite the 1st Duchess's generous offer, the Marlboroughs were unable to purchase the plot of land adjacent to the Oxford Road from a stubborn villager, William Hands. Some elements already carved, such as the columns and the scrolls, were then used for an entrance known as 'Bladen Gate', erected after 1738 beyond the formal parterre garden to the south of Blenheim Palace.

In the early eighteenth century, the park did not extend as far as the village of Bladon. The 4th Duke enlarged the estate in 1767 by incorporating the fields between the southern perimeter of the original park wall and the village, emparking an area called the Lince.

Soon afterwards, financial difficulty forced William Hands' family to sell their land, which allowed the 4th Duke of Marlborough to acquire it. In the mid-1770s, the Duke moved the old Bladen Gate (already dismantled) to its present position at a newly created entrance to the park, called Hensington Gate. It would appear that William Chambers directed its reconstruction (see Chapter 6).

A plan of
Blenheim Park,
by Thomas Pride,
1772. ←

As regards planting, 'Capability' Brown did not merely have a highly developed sense of scale and proportion but, more importantly, he had a real appreciation of how the landscape would evolve. Trees were the most important element of his gardens and he used them to enhance, to conceal and to reveal. Their disposition and grouping on the sides and summit of the valley forming the lake was finely conceived and cleverly executed, each clump addressing the contour of the land. Openings within groups of trees were intentional, to lead the eye out to the lake or the house. He mixed foliage in various shades of green and graduated planting according to tree heights, predominantly planting hardwoods such as oak, beech, elm, sweet chestnut, ash and lime. Brown also introduced conifers into the wider landscape, dotting around individual Scots fir and pine specimens in the mix of hardwoods. Plane trees were often planted near the water's edge and pines to conceal, but beech was the most ubiquitous.[50] Cedar of Lebanon was the only exotic species used for distinctive planting in visually critical places.[51] To create irregular vistas, many mature trees were retained in the new landscape and sometimes fully grown specimens were moved to new locations by teams of men and horses employing Brown's novel 'transplanting machine'.[52] If he was not assisted in this by James Shipley, the Head Gardener at Blenheim, this work was certainly witnessed and carried on by Shipley after Brown's departure.

Not much is known of Shipley's background, but it is probably no coincidence that he arrived at Blenheim in the same year as Brown. In 1764, he is described as '*Kitchen Gardener at Blenheim*' (with an annual wage of £30) with the Gardener, Robert Purvis, earning £50. There is a gap in subsequent records but Purvis had departed by 1771 and Richard Franklin had been appointed, on a lower wage of £20.[53]

For almost twenty years from 1775 (after Brown's departure, when his salary was raised to £40), James Shipley had complete charge over the management of the gardens.[54] Lord Torrington, the Hon. John Byng, recorded a visit in 1787: '*I really felt myself when in the flower-garden, in the midst of perfume, to have a conception of paradise… My guide was a little boy of twelve years of age… and we were so lucky as to meet Mr Shipley, the head gardener, at the gate of the kitchen garden, who carried us in*'.[55] Returning again in July 1792, Torrington was received once more by Shipley, '*who made me eat fruit and walk about with him*'.[56] However, he was disappointed with the size of the hothouses, '*all small and low and kept principally for grapes*' and even more dismayed to find that birds venturing over the garden walls were shot, '*… to hear the firing of guns… Oh fye! What, for a few cherries, destroy all the songsters? And here will they come to perish. Stretch forth Marlborough, thy hand of mercy, and of pity; and let not this infamous slaughter prevail*'.[57]

James Shipley must have gained enough experience in arboriculture after working with Brown and Read at Blenheim to be considered something of an expert in the locality. John Wills, the Warden of Wadham College in Oxford, consulted him in 1796, when '*it was agreed to adopt the plan of alterations in the Fellows Garden recommended by*

Mr Shipley, the Duke of Marlborough's gardener; and it was ordered that all the trees marked by Mr Shipley should be immediately cut down…'[58] It is also likely that he had set up independently in business by this time, as after 1795 he disappears from the Palace staff records.[59]

Brown planted many hundreds of beech trees around the lake, including four small stands close to the water's edge around Vanbrugh's bridge, screening the corners where the walls adjoined the valley.[60] He extended the shelter belt of woodland planted by the 3rd Duke on the north-east perimeter, to conceal the real boundary of the entire park. The perimeter belt was broken and varied with blocks of trees of differing maturity on the horizon, and its inner edge was formed with irregular groups of trees so as to avoid uniformity.[61] Several large clumps of hardwoods were also planted, the largest covering fourteen acres (5.6 ha).[62] The organization of these wooded areas led to the development of nurseries on the estate, producing valuable timber.

While retaining the frozen geometry of the eastern avenue and quincunx plantations of elms and limes established by Henry Wise, the grand avenue to the north was broken up into groups and clumps of different forms and magnitudes, probably seeking to create variety in the sequence of views and to include tantalising glimpses of the house from various points on the 'circuit ride'.[63] The removal of this formal element was substantially carried out by Read even though Brown had started to break up the avenue around 1771–2.[64] A perimeter ride was in place before 1772, but by 1806 a new ride had been created diverting the course of Vanbrugh's main approach road from its rigid north-south orientation, re-routing it past important elements of the newly constructed landscape. This meant that it did not merely take in the house, the lake and the bridge, but also, at a suitable distance, the farm at Furze Plat, the paddocks, the kennels, *'ploughed pieces'* of arable land, and tree plantations.[65]

One of the considerations in landscape gardening was that the estate should not merely provide pleasure, but profit. This idea had been advocated by John Evelyn in his treatise on trees, *Sylva*, published in 1664 and developed in the early eighteenth century by Stephen Switzer in his *Ichnographia Rustica*.[66] Although Sarah, Duchess of Marlborough, had remarked in 1713, that *'there will never be any Advantage made of the Parke at Woodstock'*, within the space of sixty years the situation was changed.[67] The 4th Duke had spent vast sums on landscaping his grounds, but once the expense had been made, the gardens generated revenue. Sheep and cattle grazed the parkland, producing wool and milk before being slaughtered and eaten. Deer still provided sport in the park as well as food.[68] Trees were regularly harvested and restocked. The plantations in north park yielded winter fodder for all the animals, including the heavy horses and asses employed in both farming and gardening operations. The lake and river were exploited for fishing. Aquatic fowl were bred near Coach Road Island (Queen Elizabeth's Island) and at the fishery near the old Queen Pool, while game birds were reared at the Lince, in the new *'pheasant grounds, planted, defended and gated for the Duke's private sport'.*[69]

GARDENERS' WAGES

In the eighteenth century, the Head Gardener at Blenheim was also called the Kitchen Gardener. He ranked among the most important members of staff, working closely with the Head Cook or Chef every day in deciding what fruit and vegetables would be delivered for the Duke's table.

In 1764, Thomas Carter, the Cook, earned £45 a year, while Robert Purvis, the Gardener's salary was £50. Only three others – the Confectioner (John Fitzwater, £52:10s), the Fisherman (Richard Beckley, £60) and the Clerk of the Kitchen or House Steward (Charles Turner, £60) earned more than him. However, by the end of the year, changes were made in the staffing of the gardens and day-workers were taken on. This coincided with 'Capability' Brown's arrival and his re-landscaping of the grounds.

Before the end of that year, James Shipley had been appointed as Kitchen Gardener earning £30 per annum. In 1771 and 1772, Shipley was assisted by Richard Franklin who was paid £20 annually. Franklin then disappears from the records. From 1775–90 Shipley was earning £40 a year.

From 1812 onwards, the Head Gardener was on £50 annually, but the records do not provide his name. In 1816 (the last year of the 4th Duke's life), the post was unoccupied. Mr Whitman, the new gardener arrived on 15 February 1817, one of the first appointments made by the horticulturally fanatical 5th Duke (see Chapter 7).

In the early nineteenth century, vegetables were grown in long rows within the rectangular beds of the Kitchen Garden (called 'quarters') and the hothouses continued to be heated with wood-burning stoves.

The Kitchen Garden at Blenheim with a view of one of the large, circular basins used by the gardeners for watering plants.
© Private Collection

More important in terms of its impact on the landscape was the alteration of the scene to the south of the house. This was achieved in stages, by removing what was left of the bastioned parterre to create a vast open lawn instead, framed on both sides with the deep green foliage of ornamental cedars.[70] Two to three thousand sheep grazed on a piece of rough land to the south of the

The Fishery at Queen Pool. ↑

Aerial photograph showing the widened stretch of the River Glyme near Bladon. ↓

lawn.[71] The lawn, the sheep and the freely roaming deer in the park were kept entirely separated by the clever placement of new ha-has.[72] At a suitable distance, in the gardens or 'pleasure-grounds' to the south-west of the house, flowering shrubs were planted amongst the trees. Brown created walks, built garden seats, and generally dealt with every request made by the Duke or Duchess, as a letter reveals, *'I hope Mr Read has altered the level of the ground at the Oak Tree which Her Grace wished to have altered. I have lost the dimensions I took of the space under the New Stairs which Her Grace wished to have a Seat in; which prevents me from sending a sketch for that purpose'.*[73] But his most remarkable work to the south was on the River Glyme, altering its course and substantially widening it by building a second cascade dam.

It may be remembered that Colonel Armstrong's old canal scheme split into two channels before joining the river. The land between the watercourses was dug out and the river *'deepened about 10 feet and widened about 40 feet'.* Some stretches of water were contained with curved embankment walls built in stone; the river was effectively managed by employing canal technology.[74] Just as he had done with the lake earlier, Brown included a small island in the enlarged river and constructed a second dam at the Lince, where the River Glyme joined the Evenlode (a tributary of the Thames). The Lince was a parcel of land in the south of the park purchased by the 4th Duke in 1767, which addition brought the boundary

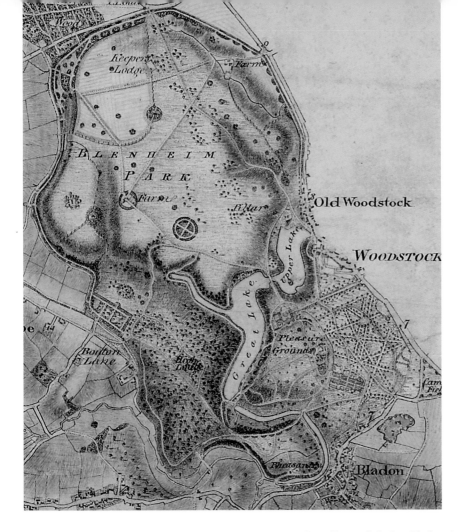

Detail of Ordnance Survey drawing, 1817. ←
The straight line of Vanbrugh's old approach road was altered to an irregular winding route by the time of the 4th Duke's death, in 1817, and the north avenue was also broken up.

to its present limits, bordering the village of Bladon.[75] The Lince dam is remarkable because instead of being built across the river, it runs for roughly half a mile (800 m) parallel to it. Here again, a cascade courses over one end of the embankment. Built of rubble limestone to a height of roughly 13 feet (4 m), it was protected by covering its sloping, inner or upstream face with clay and stone pitching.[76] By building this dam and widening the river, Brown created a substantial water feature, particularly admired by early visitors, which led to his alleged remark that the Thames would never forgive him.[77] The remodelling required substantial manpower and materials, and was consequently the most expensive element of Brown's undertaking. During building works, Read was paid several sizeable amounts from 1770 to 1772.[78]

As mentioned earlier, none of Brown's designs for decorative Gothic schemes was executed, except perhaps his proposal for a utilitarian building in the park for which he submitted plans in August 1765: *'I have enclosed to your Grace the Sketch for the Front of the cart House, Granery, etc. I mean the granery to have two Floors besides Stages for Corn between them for the easy turning of the Grain, and letting it fall*

The lower cascade built by 'Capability' Brown at the Lince near Bladon, where the River Glyme meets the Evenlode, a tributary of the Thames. ↓

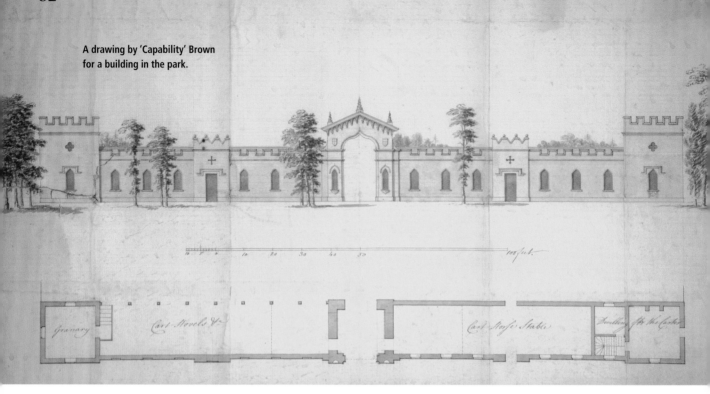

A drawing by 'Capability' Brown for a building in the park.

from one floor to the other which is the best way of keeping it sweet… If a Barn is wanted, the middle part may be very easy made by taking a piece of the Cart House on one side and a piece of the supposed Stable on the other, and the arch will make a good Entrance or barn door… and I flatter myself that the Effect of the Building would be very proper for the situation'.[79]

The farm building constructed near the kennels included a menagerie of animals where blue cow-deer, a Spanish ass, moose from America and a tiger gifted by Lord Clive of India were housed.[80] Only part of this building survives today, in an altered form. The farm was rebuilt by the 6th Duke (see Chapter 8) and, although it no longer serves its original purpose, estate business is still undertaken here. From the late 1980s it has become the operational base of the Blenheim Water bottling plant. This is rather fitting because at Blenheim most of Brown's 'improvements' were associated with water. He incorporated all of his favourite and famous devices here – the lake formed a large *'sheet of water'*, the stream of the Glyme was widened into a *'noble river'*, and in building two dams he created very different but equally impressive *'cascades'*.

The Blenheim Water bottling plant is currently based at Park Farm. ↑ Natural mineral water is drawn from an aquifer within the park. The spring eventually flows out at Rosamund's Well. The commercial bottling of water began shortly before the 10th Duke's death in 1972.

South and North views of Blenheim, by C.W. Radclyffe. ←↙

Brown brought a seamless quality to the park with the grass sweeping right up to the steps of the house. However, in so doing, he broke the formal link between the house and its gardens. Although a beautiful lake had been created to the north, on the south front the view from every window of the socially important State Apartments overlooked a vast but insignificant open expanse of grass, framed by a few groups of trees. However, at the time, such naturalistic views were not only admired, but desired.

The deer in the park are worth noting. The 4th Duke was Ranger of Wychwood forest – responsible for the deer, the open forest and coppicing. Roughly 100 animals were killed every year, six of which were sent to the King.

Brown's final work at the Lince was undertaken roughly when William Gilpin visited and remarked on the splendour of the alterations, *'The cascade, where ye head is made, is ye most beautiful and easy artificial cascade I ever saw. Below ye cascade ye water is still continued and forms a beautiful curve. A new bridge is just erected, beyond which lies ye town of Bladon…'*[81] The new bridge, built in 1772–3 on the site of an older structure, was designed by Sir William Chambers, the foremost architect of his age, who worked at Blenheim concurrently with Brown. Chambers was chiefly employed by the 4th Duke of Marlborough in renovating the interiors of the palace, but his work soon extended outside, and by the time Brown had quit the scene in 1774, Chambers' influence was predominant.[82]

6 Introducing Classicism

SIR WILLIAM CHAMBERS'
GARDEN BUILDINGS

The Temple of Diana.
←

Before 'Capability' Brown's departure, the 4th Duke had introduced several neo-classical elements into the landscape. These were implemented by Sir William Chambers, architect to King George III. Although the exact date of Chambers' involvement at Blenheim is uncertain, he was known to be working there from 1769 onwards. When Stiff Leadbetter (the architect engaged to renovate Marlborough House in London) died in 1766, Chambers took over the contract. Apart from this, he was also approached in connection with a Town Hall to be built at the Duke's expense in Woodstock.[1] Soon afterwards plans were prepared for a new residence for Thomas Walker, the Duke's Steward and Town Clerk, but Chambers could only proceed with this building when a suitable plot of land at Hensington was leased from Merton College some years later.[2]

The first surviving record of Chambers' involvement in Blenheim Park appears in a letter recommending old stone which *'will save His Grace a considerable expense'* to be used for a gate.[3] Although the letter does not specify which gate, Chambers was probably referring to the Hensington Gate. (See box on page 75.) It is likely that this was when 'Capability' Brown submitted his own design for a new gate along with his scheme for the crenellated park wall and gothicised buildings, in an attempt to win the contract.[4]

'Capability' Brown's design for a new gate. ↓

Chambers was not on good terms with Brown. Tradition has it that his ill feeling dated from the commission for Claremont in 1768, when his design was rejected in favour of Brown's. He subsequently made a veiled attack on Brown for his lack of classical education and modest background, unjustly condemning his natural style of gardening as differing *'very little from common fields, so closely*

is common nature copied in most of them… a stranger is often at a loss to know whether he be walking in a meadow or in a pleasure ground, made and kept at a very considerable expense…'[5] However, there is no evidence of the two men working inharmoniously at Blenheim in the early 1770s when Brown widened the River Glyme and built the Lince dam while Chambers was engaged in constructing a new bridge. Their joint enterprise substantially changed the prospect to the south of the Palace.

The New Bridge was designed as a triple-arched stone structure with a balustraded parapet. The piers at both ends carried four sphinxes, each on a stone plinth. Chambers explored the possibility of acquiring *'any sphinxes ready cast'* but when this proved unfeasible, John Cheere, the foremost contemporary supplier of sculptural work and garden statuary, was contracted to make them.[6] However, when the sphinxes were sent to Blenheim in August 1773, the bridge was not ready. Soon afterwards an attempt to lift them into place failed, *'owing to some little warpage in the metal'* which, as Chambers explained to the Duke, *'may easily be filed down so as to fit to the plinths exactly, which will be better than to sink down the plinths, as the wet would lodge there and burst the stone when the frosts come to it. I think it will be best to fasten the sphynxs to the stone which may be done by making holes through the hanging drapery and… running these holes afterwards full of lead'.*[7]

The land around the New Bridge was known as Long Orchard and belonged to a Mr Nixon before the 4th Duke purchased it, demolished the field boundaries and added it to the park.[8] Mr Wakeman, the Duke's poulterer, was lodged in a small thatched Shepherd's Cot, built *'of the trunks of trees fancifully arranged'* set up between the New Bridge and the cascade.[9] But fifteen years after creating the new setting, the Duke further redeveloped the Lince. A Georgian Lodge was constructed near the lower cascade and Benjamin Read was subsequently occupied with planting a dense cover of trees, significantly altering Lancelot Brown's original landscaping of the area.[10]

Similarly, to the north of the Palace, despite Brown's work in securing the foundations of Vanbrugh's bridge, the structure was strengthened further. Chambers was appointed to supervise this task over two years in the 1770s.[11] The Duke also ordered the level of the ground all along the valley line north of the bridge to be lowered by six feet (1.8 m), and along the brow curving around to Woodstock Gate by fifteen feet (4.6 m), so that a better view of the lake could be had all round.[12] These changes (most likely supervised by Read) altered the view of the lake.[13]

The New Bridge was designed by William Chambers and built in 1772–3. It was called New Bridge to distinguish it from Vanbrugh's earlier structure, and is still known by this name today. →

Sir William Chambers (1723–96). ↑
© Private Collection

View of Bladon from the Gardens, by C.W. Radclyffe. ↑

On his tour around the grounds in April 1786, Thomas Jefferson noted '*2,500 acres of which 200 is garden, 150 water, 12 Kitchen Garden, and the rest park. 200 people employed to keep it in order, and to make alterations and additions; about 50 of these employed in pleasure grounds. The turf is mowed once in 10 days in summer*.'[14] The maintenance of the new landscape was by this account even more labour-intensive than the upkeep of the old formal garden, although Jefferson (and other visitors) may have been provided with slightly inflated workforce figures.[15]

In the pleasure grounds, Jefferson recorded a thin scattering of trees and '*small thickets of shrubs, in oval raised beds, cultivated, and flowers among the shrubs. The gravelled walks are broad. Art appears too much*.'[16] William Gilpin had made a similar observation earlier, in 1772, when he recorded '*several little patches of flowers, and flowering shrubs, artificially disposed, and introduced; which shewed the hand of art to have been straying… But when we saw these scenes the work was new*'.[17]

The creation of this new flower garden by the 4th Duke in 1771–2 may well have been another instance of collaboration between Chambers and Brown at Blenheim. Strikingly similar to the garden created by Brown's friend, William Mason, at nearby Nuneham, the 4th Duke's garden (based on the plan of Madame de Pompadour's *flower basket* at Versailles) was an oval grove of complex planting with fan-shaped flower beds in a radial design.[18] It was located to the south-east of the Palace, slightly off the principal circuit walk. William Mavor, the author of early guidebooks to Blenheim, was struck by '*the sudden burst of so much beauty*', effusively describing it as a '*wilderness of sweets… The outline is elegant; the execution*

The Flower Garden at Nuneham.
© Private Collection

charming…in the centre of variously arranged bouquets… is an obelisk of porphyry, surrounded with four white marble vases filled with annual flowers. On the north is a neat temple, properly dedicated to Flora; and during the summer months every interstice left by the trunks of the surrounding grove is replenished with oranges, lemons, and other exotic trees, shrubs and plants of the greatest delicacy and the richest odour…' [19]

While it is a possibility that the garden was laid out by Brown, it was dotted with architectural elements by Chambers. Most likely responsible for the vases mentioned by Mavor, Chambers certainly designed the large ornamental tripod marking the entrance to the garden (for which a drawing survives),[20] as well as a small temple dedicated to Flora, the goddess of spring, flowers and blossoming. This open-fronted garden pavilion was built within the flower garden after modifications were made to its size, as discussed in a letter to the Duke, *'I have marked upon the plan the depth which I think the little building in the flower Garden may be reduced to without hurting the look.'*[21]

The orange and lemon trees described in the garden were moved into the greenhouse (Orangery) every winter until 1787, when it was converted into a theatre for family entertainment.[22] Chambers prepared designs for an imposing new greenhouse in stone, one hundred feet (30 m) long with large windows on three sides.[23] Possibly proving too expensive, it was not built but a more economical structure was located in the Kitchen Garden, along with a pine and a grape house.[24] The Head Gardener was re-lodged in a new residence built into the south-west wall. However, the most radical change to the walled garden was made by 1772 with the introduction of a stately Palladian Gateway.[25] Once Chambers had provided this classical pedimented

The Temple of Flora. ↑ Dedicated to Flora, the goddess of spring, flowers and blossoming, the temple has an open-fronted alcove framed in an elliptical arch, with a sculpted wreath within the pediment. It was originally located in the 4th Duke's flower garden but was moved in the mid-1830s to its present location.

Design for the Palladian Gateway by William Chambers, drawing by John Yenn. →
This new gateway built within the west wall of the Kitchen Garden in 1772 allowed the family and their visitors a distinguished entrance into the walled garden. Gardeners and other workmen continued to use the old entrance, undisturbed in their duties. The family were thus spared from the noise and bustle of the working areas of the Kitchen Garden or the whiff of manure which would have been carted there from the stables.

© Royal Academy of Arts, London

entrance, the Kitchen Garden could be viewed by the family and visitors through the west wall, and was included from then on in the circuit walk of the grounds.

Chambers' second garden temple dedicated to Diana, the goddess of hunting, was built in 1773 in the ionic style and located in the pleasure grounds. The surviving design shows it was flanked on both sides by two large ornamental tripod vases, but these are sadly no longer extant. The rear wall of the temple was decorated with an oval bas-relief of Hippolytus offering a wreath of flowers to Diana. On either side are two smaller oval medallions with verses from Euripides, one in Greek, the other an English translation.[26] The dedication on the medallions and the decoration of this temple were probably decided by Jacob Bryant, a classical scholar. Bryant had a long association with the 4th Duke, tutoring him at Eton College, accompanying him on his Grand Tour and remaining a trusted friend and advisor thereafter.

Chambers' classicising embellishments were rapturously described in early guidebooks: *'The gardens have been considerably enlarged and thrown into the form they now wear by the present Duke, who has further beautified them by the addition of some well placed ornaments; particularly the Temple of Diana and*

**Design for the Temple of Diana
by William Chambers,
drawing by John Yenn.** ↑

© Royal Academy of Arts, London

The decoration on the back wall of the temple (three medallions,
one with a bas-relief of Hippolytus offering a wreath to Diana and
two with verses from Euripides) was probably chosen by the
Duke's tutor and classical scholar, Jacob Bryant. ↓

an elegant little Temple in what is called the flower garden; to which we may add two noble bronzes and some copies of Antique Vases, in stone.[27]

The two bronzes mentioned were moved by 1787 from the Palace to the gardens.[28] Originally commissioned in 1711 by the 1st Duke of Marlborough from the renowned Florentine sculptor, Massimiliano Soldani Benzi, the four bronzes produced were based on marble statues in the Tribuna of the Uffizi.[29] Of these, two standing figures (the Venus de Medici and the Clapping Faun) were left indoors, while two crouching figures (the Wrestlers and the Arrotino or Knife Grinder) were repositioned on large stone pedestals in the grounds. One was placed not far from the Temple of Diana, while the other was located in the vicinity of the cascade, in an area which was only incorporated into the pleasure grounds in the mid-1770s.[30]

This mid-1770s addition, the only restricted part of the pleasure grounds accessed through a locked gate, was just another in a long list of never-ending changes the 4th Duke made by *'throwing a neat Chinese bridge… near the cascade and enclosing and laying down in the most elegant style a pretty large tract of the opposite hill. But the most capital object is a magnificent fountain… which has recently been erected in the vale.'*[31] The marble fountain, sculpted by Gian Lorenzo Bernini as a one-third scale copy of the Fountain of the Four Rivers at the Piazza Navona in Rome, was allegedly a gift

Sketch of the Arrotino in the Pleasure Grounds at Blenheim, by S.H. Grimm. ⬇

to the 1st Duke of Marlborough from the Spanish Ambassador.[32] Although
Hawksmoor had earlier offered suggestions for its placement, the fountain was not
erected until the 4th Duke decided to install it in a large oval basin near the cascade.
(See box on pages 168–9.) Years of neglect necessitated repairs, which Chambers
and the sculptor Richard Hayward undertook in 1774 *'on the spot where it is to be
erected and built up as fast as it is repaired else it will be very liable to accidents
in its removal from one place to another. This may be begun in the Spring and as
no very great nicety will be necessary in the repair it will soon
be done.'*[33]

A short distance from the fountain, an underground mineral
spring[34] called New Found Well was channelled to flow into
an ancient roman sarcophagus from where the water spilled
through the mouths of two stone lions, before disappearing
again into the ground.[35] Several grottos were also introduced
into this area where the 5th Duke would later develop an
extensive Rock Garden.[36] New Found Well was later refashioned
with a lion's mask on top (pictured here) and was subsequently
dismantled in the twentieth century. The roman sarcophagus

The Cascade,
by F. Bauer. ↑

The lion's head in the
Secret Garden. ↓

The sarcophagus in the
Water Terrace Garden. ↘

(adorned with figures of Hercules, Ariadne and Dionysus in bas-relief) is now located outside the chapel on the Water Terraces, while the single lion's head above it was set up by the 10th Duke in his Private Garden and has been recently re-established in the Secret Garden.

In 1775, all the statues were removed from the top of the north elevation of the house (except for three above the pediment) and many were placed in the shrubbery around the cascade, not far from the bronzes.[37] Although statues had always served as ornamentation within garden schemes, by the mid-eighteenth century the circuit walk had developed to such an extent that they were conventionally viewed standing alone in the landscape, quite detached from the house. Although this fashion was short-lived, apart from the Soldani bronzes, almost all the other statuary is now lost.

The East Gate, by C.W. Radclyffe. ←
The entrance gate to the kitchen court was designed by John Vanbrugh and later embellished by William Chambers with lions' heads, statues in niches, swags and a garlanded tablet. The inscription on the tablet (with details of the grant bestowed by Queen Anne on the 1st Duke of Marlborough) was added afterwards by the 9th Duke.

Only two stone figures removed from the roof of the Palace survive today as Chambers placed them in niches in Vanbrugh's East Gate in his attempt to alleviate the gate's fundamentally martial appearance. He also added lions' heads, swags, intertwined laurels and a garlanded tablet.[38] (The inscription on the tablet was carved much later, during the 9th Duke's tenure.) Four pyramidal vases carved with mask heads, flames and roses were placed on top of the gate.[39]

Other proposals for garden buildings and park pavilions were offered by William Chambers and his assistant John Yenn, notably for a lodge at Ditchley Gate, and a bath at Rosamund's Well, but none of these was executed.[40] By 1784, after Chambers became increasingly preoccupied with the Somerset House project in London, Yenn more or less took over all his business for the 4th Duke – at Blenheim, Sion Hill House (Isleworth) and Marlborough House (London).[41] Over the years Yenn had produced a number of drawings for the Duke's approval, some executed under the direction of his great mentor, and others made later when he worked independently but in Chambers' style.[42]

Detail of an engraving by J.P. Neale, 1823. ↓
Note the sphinxes on either side of the front steps.
© Private Collection

One of the designs Yenn produced was *'for an Addition, to the top of the Pedestals on which the Sphinx's were fixt to the Bridge over the Lake at Blenheim'.*[43] Such a title necessitates clarification. The bridge in question was, in fact, Chambers' New Bridge, spanning the River Glyme (which had been widened by 'Capability' Brown).

An unexecuted design for a bath at Rosamund's Well, by John Yenn. →
© Royal Academy of Arts, London

In the late eighteenth century this sinuous body of water was sometimes called a lake because it spread far beyond its original channel. Rather confusingly, several statements about the splendour of the lake at Blenheim, *'certainly the most superb piece of water in this Kingdom'* were, in fact, making reference to this section of the transformed river rather than the lake in the valley to the north of the Palace.[44] As far as the sphinxes on the bridge were concerned, it is not quite clear why they were moved to the front steps of the house and placed on either side of the trophies there, but this may be linked to the difficulties in fixing them on the bridge.[45] Elegantly fluted stone caps (designed by Yenn) were placed on the bridge in place of the sphinxes, and still remain in situ today.

Rosamund's Well. ↓

In 1789 Yenn was commissioned by the Duke to produce a design for a third classical garden temple, called the Temple of Health. Built at a time when such garden structures were falling out of fashion, the Temple of Health specifically celebrated King George III's return to good health after his first bout of illness. It was located off the visitor route at the eastern edge of the pleasure gardens adjoining the park, but not too far away from the ornamental tripod and the flower garden.[46] A small open-fronted structure with a pair of Corinthian columns supporting each side of the pediment, the building's symbolism is conveyed in the decoration on its rear wall – a bas-relief medallion portrait of the King set alongside a marble plaque inscribed in Latin which, translated, reads:

> 'To God, the greatest preserver
> and to Divine Providence
> for the recovered well-being
> of George the Third, the best,
> most pious King.
> George, Duke of Marlborough,
> his wish satisfied, his vow fulfilled,
> joyfully and willingly dedicated
> this marble as some witness
> to a grateful spirit.
> In the year of man's good fortune
> 1789'.

The building was typical of a certain type of eighteenth-century garden structure, not built to punctuate the scenery but more emblematical, making a definite statement of the Duke's political fidelity while still reminding the visitor of the sophistication of the owner's taste.

After several decades of continual alterations and improvements, 'sticking up twelve trees here and thirteen there', very little change was undertaken in the grounds after Benjamin Read's death in 1794.[47] This loss was compounded by a greater tragedy of a more personal nature a year later, when the Marlboroughs' favourite son, Lord Henry, died in Berlin at the start of a promising diplomatic career, aged just 24. The already reclusive 56-year-old Duke ceased mixing socially and retreated so far into the shell of his

Design for the Temple of Health by John Yenn. ↑
© Royal Academy of Arts, London

The Temple of Health. ↓

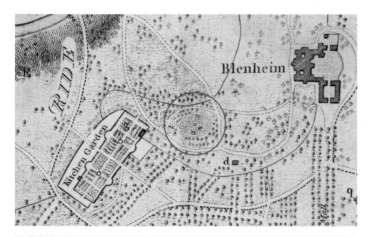

Details from two engravings by Neele. The 4th Duke's flower garden shown in the 1797 edition ↑↑ has been replaced with the aviary in the 1814 edition. ↑

baroque palace that the Earl of Pembroke referred to him as his *'oyster brother-in-law'*.[48] Charitable works followed, the most notable being the almshouses built outside the Hensington Gate two years later, endowed by the Duchess.[49] At about the same time, a purpose-built China Gallery was constructed in the grounds, to display a large collection of valuable oriental porcelain which had been offered to the Marlboroughs by Samuel Spalding.[50]

It was only in the twilight of his life that the Duke was tempted to modify his gardens once more. He redesigned the flower garden after successfully negotiating the purchase of a magnificent wire aviary from the executors of Harriet, Lady Reade, in 1812.[51] The aviary was removed from her country house at Shipton-under-Wychwood, and put up in a semi-circular arrangement near the Temple of Flora.[52] Its twelve compartments were stocked with *'curious birds, both foreign and native'*, including *'Mandarine Ducks of China, American Drakes and water fowl'* as well as *'Curassoa birds'* and numerous gold and silver pheasants reared at the Lince.[53] The aviary was a highly fashionable acquisition which, along with the menagerie in the park, highlighted the Georgian ideal of creating a comprehensive landscape paradise.

Over more than half a century, until his death in 1817, George, 4th Duke of Marlborough, had constructed a virtually new landscape at Blenheim which convinced many contemporary onlookers, like Mrs Delany, of the vast superiority of taste *'in the days of George III from those of Anne'*.[54] However, the formal gardens of the Queen Anne period, like the naturalistic landscapes of the later eighteenth century, were in the style of their own age: the 1st Duke's gardens saw Nature mastered, while the 4th Duke's made Nature mistress. Nevertheless, the serenity of the Brownian landscape had such an enduring appeal that it was not only left largely untouched by later Dukes but great efforts were made then, and continue to be made now, to preserve it.

Fagus sylvatica, watercolour by Susan Blandford, later Duchess of Marlborough.

7 Collecting Plants, Growing Debts

THE 5TH DUKE'S HORTICULTURAL PURSUITS

George, 5th Duke of Marlborough (1766–1840). ↑

The 4th Duke's passion in laying out his grounds and his unrestrained expenditure in its execution had not gone unnoticed by his eldest son and heir, George, Marquis of Blandford, later 5th Duke. Born in 1766 when 'Capability' Brown was creating the lake, and watching his father undertake the complete transformation of Blenheim, the Marquis's keen interest in gardening was probably stimulated at an early age. Blandford became a botanist and plant collector with such a propensity for eccentric overspending that he eventually discredited his noble ancestry. His insolvency took the Marlboroughs through one of the darker chapters in their history and saw the splendour of Blenheim Palace fade temporarily into an embarrassing dilapidation.

From his early years, Blandford was hard to discipline.[1] The 4th Duke had been a withdrawn and distant father tending to cocoon his children, but the rigidly controlling Duchess Caroline proved unforgiving and remorseless when they strayed. Blandford was initially tutored at home by the Rev. William Coxe and William Mavor (the author of Blenheim's early guidebooks), until old enough to go to Eton. He was not sent on the Grand Tour, but to Paris for three months instead. By the time he came of age, he had acquired an interest in rare books, a passion for plant collecting and a reputation for wild extravagance.

After his marriage in 1791 to Susan Stewart (daughter of the 7th Earl of Galloway), the Blandfords rented Culham Court near Henley, moving to Bill Hill near Wokingham three years later.[2] In the first years of their life together, from 1794 to 1804, Susan executed an exquisite series of flower paintings.[3] It is not known when or how she developed her skill, although by now drawing had become established as a desirable female talent, with flowers considered a suitable subject matter. Susan Blandford's

Susan, Duchess
of Marlborough
(1767–1841). ←

Florilegium, or book of botanical illustrations, containing roughly
one hundred watercolour plant portraits, is her lasting legacy.

This was an age when voyages to far-flung corners of the world saw
numerous new species of trees and shrubs imported into England.
By the early nineteenth century, the trickle of new plants had grown into a
flood. Humphry Repton had succeeded Lancelot Brown as the pre-eminent
garden designer of his time, introducing clumped 'shrubberies' and coining
the term 'arboretum' for a special collection of trees. The Marquis of Blandford
was strongly influenced by Repton's style and adopted many of his ideas, not
only at Bill Hill and at Whiteknights, but later at Blenheim Palace too.

Surviving documents reveal Blandford's acquisitive nature and his single-minded
pursuit of newly imported horticultural exotics to augment his collection.
After the eminent naturalist Sir Joseph Banks had undertaken a great
expedition with Captain Cook on board the *Endeavour* to Tahiti, New
Zealand and Australia, he was placed in charge of the Royal Botanic Gardens
at Kew, transforming it into an important centre for new plant arrivals and
their propagation. Blandford visited Kew and was offered some *'remnants of
His Majesty's gardens… to carry home'.* From then on, he would write to the
superintendent, William Aiton, requesting new plants *'when they had a stock of
anything which was not from some cause or another prevented from leaving the gardens.'*[4]

Houstonia coccinea.

In August 1796, Aiton supplied half a dozen specimens, including a *Camellia japonica* and a gardenia, but they were sent reluctantly; a note at the bottom of Aiton's list emphasised that '*Lord Blandford never added any plant to the Royal Collection!*'[5] Repeated demands from the Marquis led Aiton to reply that '*the King was not very fond of parting with his Plants*' but when the Marquis complained determinedly to Sir Joseph Banks about his superintendent, who '*absolutely refuses me everything*', Aiton was forced to supply a *Houstonia coccinea* and other specimens.[6]

From this record we also discover that in 1797 Blandford shipped two hundred English plants to the Botanical Gardens in Jamaica.[7] They were exchanged through Thomas Dancer (a Jamaican physician passionately interested in horticulture) for 200–300 native plants including '*a great many new genera*', received a year later.[8] The delivery of Dancer's plants was anticipated at Whiteknights, a property near Reading, bought for Blandford in 1798.[9] Almost immediately the Marquis undertook an intensive redevelopment of the grounds, with little regard to cost. This process would continue over the next nineteen years of his occupation.

The Marquis bought plants from various sources, notably the Vineyard Nursery in Hammersmith, run by Lee and Kennedy, where by 1804, according to Mr Lee, his bill exceeded £15,000.[10] Another major supplier was John Fraser, an importer of American plants and a botanical traveller, whose discoveries in Newfoundland, Georgia and the

Phlox subulata.

Gardenia pubescens.

Whiteknights,
a property near
Reading, bought
in 1798.
© Private Collection

Carolinas led to the introduction of the Fraser magnolia and the
Fraser fir into England.[11] In Mrs Hofland's *Descriptive Account
of the Mansion and Gardens of Whiteknights*, there are several
references to American plants, including the Fraser magnolia,
which was said to be *'the first ever imported'*.[12] Possibly the phlox
so delicately painted by Susan Blandford had also been supplied
by Fraser.[13]

John Fraser recognised in the Marquis of Blandford not only an
important patron but also a serious collector when he named
a new discovery *Blandfordia cordata* in his honour. The story
is interesting. The plant was observed by Fraser in 1786 on his
journey through the mountains in Georgia near the source of
the Savannah river. It was brought back to England in 1800.
Andrews's *Botanist's Repository* described the tender greenhouse
plant with an illustration of a specimen from the collection at
Whiteknights. The entry concludes, *'Little need be urged for the
propriety of our naming a plant from the Marquis of Blandford;
and thus dedicating this small part of our labours to his lordship;
as few, at present, patronize the science through all its branches,
with so much vigour and liberality, or who have equal knowledge*

The *Blandfordia nobilis* (pictured below),
and the *Blandfordia cordata*, were named
in honour of George, Marquis of Blandford,
later 5th Duke of Marlborough. ↓
© Private Collection

in its theory and practice.[14] However, Fraser's name for this flowering plant was not accepted since it had already been labelled as *Galax aphylla* under the Linnaean binomial system.

The ornamental garden at Whiteknights had few rivals. Rare and exotic plants, trees and shrubs were introduced on a lavish scale. The Marquis was never satisfied with just a single new specimen, usually purchasing several at a time, even when they cost from five to twenty guineas each. Once the same plants became commonly available they could be bought for as little as two to three shillings.[15] He constantly extended the limits of his garden, expanding his botanical collection to cram in every novelty, thereby creating a busy succession of gardens, rather than a harmoniously planned arrangement.

Without an income to match it, the expenditure lavished on such fanatical collecting would inevitably end in a crash. Money was not merely squandered on the gardens; the Marquis's library of rare books was estimated to have cost £25,000. This, along with his collections of watches, rings, snuff boxes, pictures and jewels, was all financed by heavy borrowing. In the year following his mother's death, his father (the 4th Duke) attempted to ease his indebtedness by instructing Blenheim's trustees to mortgage Whiteknights. Sir Charles Cockerell, with Archibald and Henry Traill, advanced £45,000 for the

Berberis vulgaris.

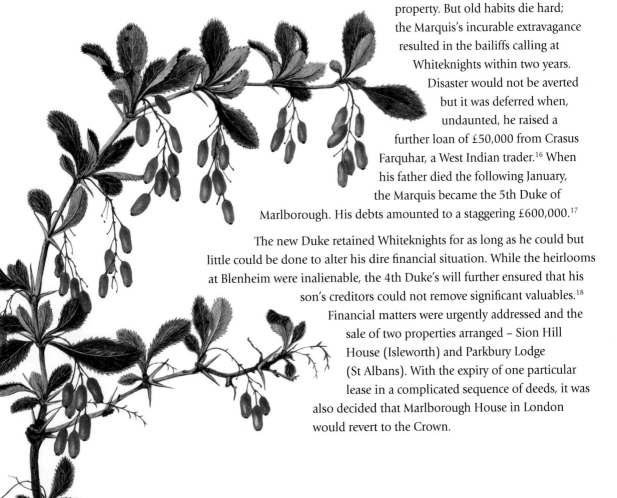

property. But old habits die hard; the Marquis's incurable extravagance resulted in the bailiffs calling at Whiteknights within two years. Disaster would not be averted but it was deferred when, undaunted, he raised a further loan of £50,000 from Crasus Farquhar, a West Indian trader.[16] When his father died the following January, the Marquis became the 5th Duke of Marlborough. His debts amounted to a staggering £600,000.[17]

The new Duke retained Whiteknights for as long as he could but little could be done to alter his dire financial situation. While the heirlooms at Blenheim were inalienable, the 4th Duke's will further ensured that his son's creditors could not remove significant valuables.[18] Financial matters were urgently addressed and the sale of two properties arranged – Sion Hill House (Isleworth) and Parkbury Lodge (St Albans). With the expiry of one particular lease in a complicated sequence of deeds, it was also decided that Marlborough House in London would revert to the Crown.

WHITEKNIGHTS

In 1819 the Marquis of Blandford published a *Descriptive Account* of his property at Whiteknights. It took three years for Barbara Hofland to write the text and for her husband Thomas to illustrate it. Mrs Hofland leads the reader through every section of the 280 acres (113 ha) of ground, divided into three distinct areas – the Botanic Gardens (close to the house), the New Gardens, and the Woods.

The **Botanic Gardens** contained '*an unrivalled storehouse of Flora*'. The entrance was through a latticed, arched gate covered with clematis and *Corchorus japonica* and a door '*adorned by three Oriental arches, surmounted with crescents, on which Jessmine and Corchorus grow luxuriantly.*' A border surrounding the garden was entirely planted with North American specimens, while the lawn, edged on one aspect with roses, was dotted with baskets (circular cast-iron structures simulating basketwork) planted with begonia and scarlet sage. There was also a Linnaean Garden arranged by botanical type, described as a '*science museum*', and in an impressive greenhouse called the Temple of Pomona, a central bed was reserved for some of the rarest plants. Six further greenhouses were located nearby, each containing different collections of plants, including two aquatic houses.

Despite Mrs Hofland's sugared prose, an astonishing variety of planting is observed with specimens from every corner of the globe – North America, Japan, China, Egypt, the Cape of Good Hope and Botany Bay. By far the most captivating spectacle of the Botanic Garden was an extraordinary 20-foot (6 m) high Magnolia Wall, entirely covered with *Magnolia grandiflora* along its length. The flowers were '*spotless, pearly white, and when fully expanded, from ten to twelve inches in diameter.*' Established in 1800 with *Magnolia macrophylla*, *Magnolia conspicua*, *Magnolia aucminata*, *Magnolia glauca* and *Magnolia purpurea*, the most remarkable effect of this feature was its fragrance.

The Conservatory was filled with more exotic plants '*placed in jars, vases and bowls, of scarce, costly and elegant china*'. Near this building, a fountain designed by the Marquis's aunt, Lady Diana Beauclerk, was enclosed within a Hexagon Treillage.[19] The fountain, consisting of '*three dolphins supporting a large escalop from which flows a… Jet d'eau in four distinct forms, falling into the basin below*' was elaborately decorated with shells, blue john, seaweed, fungi and mosses.

The **New Gardens** lay further afield from the house and were approached by crossing the lake over an iron bridge. Verdant lawns, another American border '*thickly planted with the most valuable shrubs and flowers*', an oak grove and a red cedar grove (*Juniperus virginiana*) featured in this garden. Like the Botanic Gardens, it too was peppered with rustic seats – small but elaborate structures constructed in a variety of timbers, with thatched roofs and covered with climbing plants.

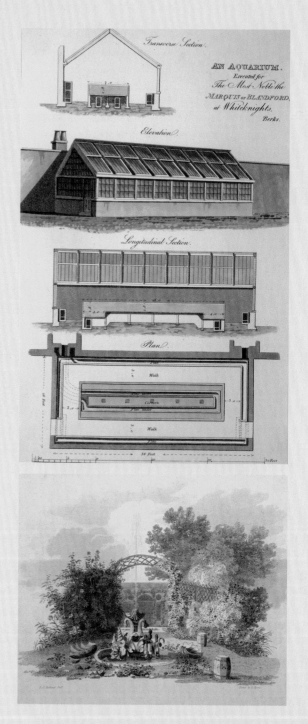

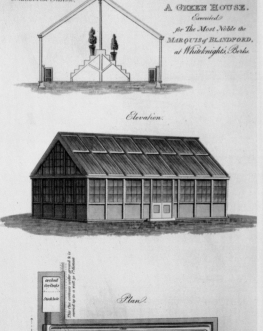

The third section of the pleasure grounds, called **the Woods**, was '*approached through a fence formed of large stones, which have obtained the name of Grey Wethers from their resemblance to sheep*'. This section was embellished with a Catalpa walk, a 1,200-foot (364 m) Laburnum bower, a 600-foot (182 m) Acacia walk and a French Chantilly Garden. Another Flower Garden was filled with begonias, scarlet geraniums, purple rhododendrons and, in the Rose Garden nearby, '*every possible variety of the Rose, the Queen of flowers*'. Two fountains, a rustic bridge, wooden pavilions (including a Swiss Cottage) formed part of the picturesque effect. Passing the Vineyard and yet another American border, the visitor arrived at an impressive grotto. Here, branches of coral hung from the roof of the rockwork, seaweed and green ferns were intermingled with pink, white and black shells, and masses of violet spar, shining ores and large shells decorated the walls.

There is nothing to suggest that the Marquis had any professional help in establishing these gardens, apart from the dealers through whom he acquired his stock of rare new plant specimens (some of which failed to survive when they were planted in unsuitable soils or sites through the lack of established practical experience). However, the rustic temples and seats within the gardens were designed by J.B. Papworth and, in 1810, Francis Bernasconi submitted a bill '*for stucco work under the direction of S.P. Cockeral, architect at the ruin in the Park*' and '*at the Bridge*'. The architect in question was the notable Samuel Pepys Cockerell, of Sezincote fame, who had built the entrance gates and the bridge at Whiteknights for its previous owner, William Byam Martin, in 1785.

At a time when the general interest in gardening was growing rapidly, an undertaking on such a scale naturally attracted visitors; some were fulsome in their praise, others brandished sharper pens. Mary Russell Mitford was one of the latter: '*I am very happy to have seen Lord Blandford's… as I should if I had not, always have fancied it something superior. In good truth I was greatly disappointed. The park as they call it (if about eighty acres, without deer, can be called a park), is level, flat and uninteresting; the trees are ill clumped; the walk around it is entirely unvaried, and the piece of water looks like a large duck pond, from the termination not being concealed. If the hothouses were placed together instead of being dispersed they might make a respectable appearance… their contents might be interesting to a botanist, but gave me no pleasure. The thing I liked best was the garden in which the conservatory is situated; the shrubs there are really very fine, particularly the azaleas, and the American honeysuckles both pink and yellow; the rhododendrons are superb*'. In all fairness, at the time of her visit in 1807, the planting was far from mature, when it would have made a much greater impression. In fact the gardens were so renowned that King George III visited in 1810. In 1817, Queen Charlotte returned, accompanied by the Princesses Augusta and Elizabeth. However, there is no doubt that the main focus of Blandford's elaborate creation was horticultural.

At Whiteknights, in October 1819 everything moveable was stripped and everything saleable was sold (furniture, pictures, fine wines, the iron bridge, the Chinese temple, farming stock and equipment). But enough survived in the garden for it to remain interesting to horticulturalists for years afterwards.[20] Over twelve days from 7 June 1819, Mr Evans of Pall Mall conducted the sale of the contents of the library.[21] Luckily, lot 3592, *'a volume containing 89 drawings of plants by the Duchess of Marlborough painted in a most beautiful and delicate manner'* was withdrawn from auction. As Susan had long been estranged from her husband it is not exactly clear why her *Florilegium* was saved. One possible reason may have been her agreement to move to Blenheim to make a fresh start, after the grant of an annual income of £30,000 was made to her under the 4th Duke's will.

Her 'plant-mad' husband now embarked on moving many specimens from Whiteknights to Blenheim before they were sold in a plant auction.[22] The new gardener at Blenheim, Mr Whitman, supervised this work employing 35 casual labourers, before Mr Jones, the old gardener at Whiteknights (since 1802), was reassigned to Blenheim in 1830.[23]

The 5th Duke made random alterations to the grounds which led Prince Pücker-Muskau to note that Brown's *'rich draperies'* had been transformed *'into a harlequin jacket of*

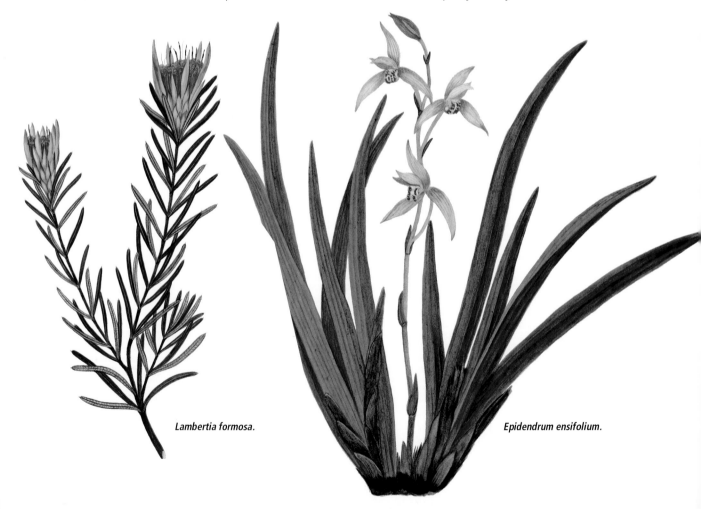

Lambertia formosa.

Epidendrum ensifolium.

little clumps and beds'.[24] The lawn to the east of the Palace reverted to a flower garden with twenty oval beds of flowering shrubs, including at least two hundred different kinds of roses.[25] A number of American plants were introduced near the aviary. Geraniums were planted in several small clumps, each clump containing a different type of flower, providing constant colour from May to October.[26] However, the most significant initial changes were made in the pleasure grounds to the west of the house.

In the 1820s, the 5th Duke, *'who is known to possess more botanical taste and skill than any other nobleman in the kingdom…[was] laying out a very large piece of ground, which, when finished, will be the finest botanical and flower garden in England'.*[27] These modifications were executed *'not only under the inspection of His Grace, but by his constant direction'.*[28] While the work was being carried out, the gardens were closed to the public and, when reopened, not only was entry severely restricted, but the area was fenced off by planting furze bushes *'so as to render it impervious to the sight: a very great deformity, and one which shows, on the part of those who put it there, an utter disregard of the general beauty of the place'.*[29] This resulted in a change to the former circuit walk around the gardens, as most visitors had to turn back and retrace their steps from the cascade until a new walk was formed parallel to the fence.

Crocus vernus var.   *Arum fatidum.*

The brothers Joseph and Pierre Dufour, manufacturers of panoramic wallpapers in Mâcon, produced '*Views of India*', an idealised and highly decorative series made available from 1815. This wallpaper was used by the 5th Duke in 1824 to decorate the 'Indian Room' which is now one of the oldest surviving historical interiors at Blenheim Palace. ←↑

For the privileged few, the gardens' circuit now began at the west front of the Palace. The western undercroft (beneath the Long Library) was converted into a series of Arcade Rooms.[30] The walls and ceiling of the first room were draped in Waterloo blue muslin, ornamented at intervals with black rosettes.[31] In 1824 an adjacent room was decorated with painted panoramic wallpaper representing *Views of India*.[32] Ten years later the oriental theme spilt into a third room – the Bamboo Room.[33] Plants were arranged inside each room and along every corridor in pots, tubs and on stands.[34] Glazed doors and large windows down to the ground connected the rooms with the landscape and invited the visitor out into the new Arcade Gardens.

Outside, *Magnolia grandiflora* were trained up the walls.[35] An octagonal timber pavilion erected nearby was '*entirely composed of various coloured woods with their natural bark… supported by columns of yew*'.[36] Obviously the Duke's taste in garden buildings had not changed since Whiteknights, but a certain piece of green circular trelliswork with gilt balls was generally considered to be the '*ne plus ultra of bad taste and absurdity*'.[37]

Planting was established either '*in dug patches… seldom contain[ing] more than a single tree or shrub, or a standard rose, with a few flowers round its base*' or in large masses, especially azaleas and rhododendrons which were bordered '*by young oaks, twisted so as to form a wreath*'. The surface of each flower bed was sunk below the level of the surrounding lawn, the drop ranging from seven inches to 1½ feet (18–45 cm).[38] On the whole, however, the effect was not harmonious, and the grounds acquired a '*spotty, frittered appearance*'.[39]

The Arcade Garden led to the New Holland or Botany Bay Garden, planted with mimosa, metrosidero, pittosporum, and other curious Australian specimens. The next area was an eight-acre (3.2 ha) Chinese Garden, where every species of camellia and other valuable oriental plants could be found. In the winter this entire garden was protected and covered by a moss-house. The descriptions of these gardens as Chinese or New Holland denoted the origin of the plants rather than a gardening style.

Created in the 1830s, the 5th Duke's Rock Garden extended over an acre (0.4 ha) of ground. The garden was planted with a large number of rare and highly valuable alpine species. Each plant was provided a separate nidus. Rock stairs passed from one level of the garden to another. ←
© Private Collection

The Rock Garden was a part of the private pleasure grounds and could only be entered when pressure was applied on a particularly ingenious pivoting boulder. ↗

The walk then led down to the lakeside from where the view across the water could be admired all along the Terrace Garden, consisting entirely of American varieties (for which nine thousand loads of bog earth were carted to provide suitable soil for planting).[40] The great novelty of this seemingly unending succession of gardens was an Aquatic Garden filled with rare plants and surrounded by rock-work. Nearby, in a further half-acre (0.2 ha) area occupied by the Dahlia Garden, two hundred plants of every known variety were displayed.[41] The Temple of Flora was moved to a new location in this garden.[42] The visitor then entered an elaborate Rose Garden (not to be confused with the present one) within sight of the cascade which contained 'island beds' of many thousands of roses, both standard and dwarf.

While the flower gardens at Blenheim Palace were still kept separate from the park, in accordance with Reptonian principles – 'a flower garden should be an object detached and distinct from the general scenery of the place' – the plants themselves were now treated more as curiosities to be possessed, examined closely and admired. Each specific ornamental area was filled with the rarest and most expensive specimens, displaying the Duke's love of new plants rather than his skill in garden design. The art of gardening had essentially been transformed into a science.

Amongst the quantities of magnolias, peonies, azaleas, kalmias, rhododendrons and wisterias, a long line of tulip trees was established. Oaks flourished side by side with Judas trees, catalpas, deciduous cypresses, Lombardy poplars and a Portugal laurel, 'the branches of which are 100 yards round at the base'.[43]

The Swiss Cottage was a rustic building built to house the watchman of the Private Garden. ↗

The 4th Duke had already created a Private Garden near the cascade (where the Bernini fountain and New Found Well were located) and 'rock seats' had been placed as a backdrop to Brown's cascade by the late eighteenth century.[44] The 5th Duke further developed this area into an elaborate Rock Garden, which by 1835 extended over an acre (0.4 ha) of ground. Reminiscent of the *Grey Wethers* at Whiteknights (see box on pages 104–5) he set up a rock barrier which could only be penetrated by pressing on a pivoting boulder to enter a *'spot in the highest style of picturesque beauty'*.[45] The garden was created with limestone rocks natural to the locality, planted with rare alpine shrubs and mosses. Access from one part of the garden to another was gained by a series of well-contrived stairs, which ran in oblique lines across the steep bank. At the pinnacle of the Rock Garden, an altar of large stone pillars called a 'Druid's Temple' was allowed to overgrow with mosses.[46]

The Rock Garden led over a rustic bridge to the Garden of Springs. Here, the Duke constructed a most curious sequence of fountains. A granite obelisk was placed on a pyramidal base formed with corals and shells from Mauritius.'… *From the centre of the top of the obelisk issues a jet… from the four corners of the foundation issue single jets and around the edge of the basin are eight jets playing towards the centre and they are surrounded with hardy aquatic plants. The effect is most pleasing. On either side of this fountain are two miniature ones standing on pedestals.'*[47] By 1836, the Chinese Bridge over the cascade pool was replaced with a light iron structure called the Swiss Bridge and a watchman was housed in a Swiss Cottage nearby, to keep guard over the valuable planted areas.[48]

Progressively emptying the greenhouses at Whiteknights of their most precious plants, Mr Jones, the 5th Duke's gardener, conveyed them to Blenheim, where they were displayed in the Arcade rooms, the greenhouse, a small hothouse, an aquatic house, a stove and vineries. An *Inventory of hardy, half hardy, greenhouse and exotic plants… of His Grace the Duke of Marlborough at Blenheim*, prepared in March 1824, enables us in some small measure to better understand the plant-collecting mania which so gripped the 5th Duke, predictably and pitifully resulting in his ruin.[49] The full inventory runs into many pages and has therefore been summarised:

Location	*Number of plants*	
In the Arcade	*516*	*(amaryllis, myrtle, oleander, camellia, ixia, orange, dahlia, hyacinth, gladiolus)*
Front of Arcade	*163*	*plus 22 painted garden seats*
Two Graperies	*584*	*(chrysanthemum, camellia, geranium, carnation, magnolia, lobelia, orange)*
Small Hot House	*80*	*(yucca, heliotrope, orange)*
Aquatic House	*77*	*pots on shelves and plants in a 'water pit'*
Conservatory	*1,751*	*(chrysanthemum, aloe, olea, exica, jasmine, honeysuckle)*
Stove	*464*	*plus 208 pots of seeds (amaryllis, geranium)*

The list also accounts for the birds in the aviary and menagerie: twenty eight silver cocks, twelve silver hens, fifteen gold cocks, seven gold hens, three hen pheasants, ten Poland pheasants, two storks and a peacock.

Further changes were made to the east of the Palace where an area beyond the aviary was turned into a new garden. A large pool of water, fed by an underground spring, was filled with hardy aquatics.[50] The water was encircled by a lawn dotted with *'ailanthirs, arbora Judae, magnolias'* and other fragrant shrubs. Some years later, a twelve-acre (4.8 ha) plot in front of the aviary was transformed into an arboretum planted *'with the choicest and most beautiful Forest Trees'*, and in the summer of 1834, an archery ground was formed on the lawn between the east flower garden and the aviary.[51]

In addition to the hothouses already located around the Kitchen Garden, the 5th Duke built a tent-shaped greenhouse in the angle of the building outside the Arcade Rooms.[52] He also erected a new melon house, locating it near the chapel in the

View of the west front from the Private Gardens, by C.W. Radclyffe. ↓ *Magnolia grandiflora* were trained up the walls and the tent-shaped greenhouse is shown in the corner of the building.

THE BLENHEIM ORANGE APPLE

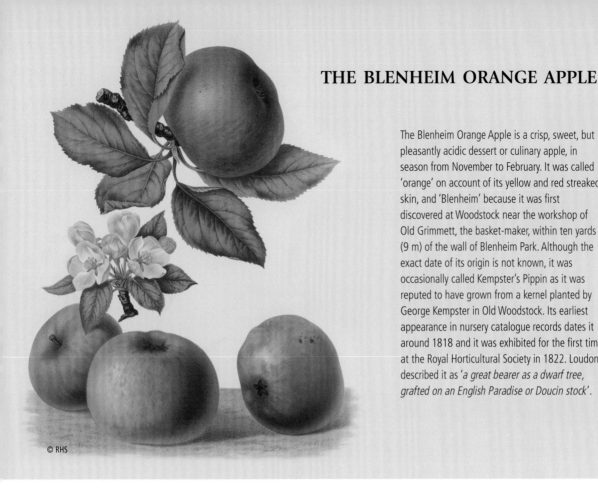

© RHS

The Blenheim Orange Apple is a crisp, sweet, but pleasantly acidic dessert or culinary apple, in season from November to February. It was called 'orange' on account of its yellow and red streaked skin, and 'Blenheim' because it was first discovered at Woodstock near the workshop of Old Grimmett, the basket-maker, within ten yards (9 m) of the wall of Blenheim Park. Although the exact date of its origin is not known, it was occasionally called Kempster's Pippin as it was reputed to have grown from a kernel planted by George Kempster in Old Woodstock. Its earliest appearance in nursery catalogue records dates it around 1818 and it was exhibited for the first time at the Royal Horticultural Society in 1822. Loudon described it as *'a great bearer as a dwarf tree, grafted on an English Paradise or Doucin stock'*.

unfinished stable court, where it extended so far out that it impaired the long architectural vista through Vanbrugh's succession of courtyards.[53]

These incessant modifications were expensive. Despite an annual income nearing £60,000, the Duke was so significantly in debt that his estates were administered for the benefit of his creditors while he subsisted on a pension of £5,000 a year.[54] His entangled finances left nothing for the Palace or the grounds to be properly maintained. Decay became apparent everywhere: the grass was overgrown, windows broken, wallflowers appeared through masonry joints, and a confusion of weeds spread throughout the lake.[55]

Overloaded with liabilities, charges were levied for shooting and fishing by the hour, which led to great public outcry.[56] As early as 1818 (the year following the 5th Duke's accession to the title), trees were felled in the park and the timber sold to raise funds.[57] To stop any further felling, his eldest son (then Marquis of Blandford, later 6th Duke), brought a case in the Chancery Court. Although this failed, a subsequent application granted an injunction. However, the 5th Duke continued to cut down trees regardless of the ruling and many old oaks were lost.[58] When his son finally took over in 1840 as 6th Duke, his first action was to petition Parliament to raise funds for immediate repairs to the house and the surrounding grounds. In an ironic volte-face, he raised some of the money through timber sales, initiating the largest tree-felling operation in Blenheim Park.

8 *Melons, Roses, Orchids*

GLASSHOUSES & GARDENING
FOR THE VICTORIAN DUKES

Prize fruit grown at Blenheim, by George Lance, 1848 (detail). ← Pineapples were difficult to grow in England, requiring constant heat for two years before producing any fruit. They were cultivated in pine houses and closely monitored by the Head Gardener.

Almost immediately on his succession, George, 6th Duke of Marlborough, arranged a loan of £25,000 for *'repairs and reinstatements'* at Blenheim. The money was raised with a mortgage on Blenheim Park, through an Act of Parliament passed in 1841.[1] As a precautionary measure, the Act capped additional borrowing at £10,000 since the 6th Duke had a misspent youth, frittering away as much as £15,000 on one occasion alone at the Doncaster Races in 1827.[2] The first disbursement of £27,224 was made in November 1842, with a further £6,500 in July 1843.[3] In order to meet the mortgage repayments, timber sales up to £10,000 were allowed, provided the trees marked out were *'at their full growth and height… or in a state of decay or proper to be cut down for the improvement of other timber… without injury to the appearance of Blenheim Park'.*[4]

Initial repairs begun in May 1840 were more showy than substantial – repainting the iron fencing around the courtyards and re-gilding the balls on the top of the Palace.[5] However, by 1841 major restoration got under way, supervised by the architect Thomas Allason.[6] For the next few years *'almost every part* [was] *in disorder'*, the bridge was repaired (James Payne), the masonry restored (Robert Johnson), new lead supplied for the roof (Walker Parker & Co.) and all the locks, including those to the garden gates, were replaced by Charles Smith & Son of Birmingham.[7] Although the expenditure was made in incremental amounts, it was by no means insubstantial: £19,067 had been disbursed by January 1842 and £34,997 by February 1844. Later, through land sales and other disposals of property, the Duke was freely able to continue the alterations with the total outflow allegedly amounting to £80,000 by the end of his tenure.[8]

By commissioning a comprehensive survey of the estate called the *Magnificent Improvements Plan*, the 6th Duke left a useful record which provides us with details of the garden layout and planting, as well as more general usage of the grounds in the mid to late 1840s when the drawing is likely to have been made.[9] Most of the arable land was in the open part of the park to the north of the Palace. A new ice house, probably constructed by the 4th Duke rather than his cash-strapped successor, had been added to the one originally built by Vanbrugh and Wise for the 1st Duke at the eastern boundary of the park.

A fisherman's cottage with an extensive Fishery and an adjoining Duckery had been established in the north-east corner of the lake (Queen Pool).[10] The China Gallery built by the 4th Duke is marked but it was demolished by 1846, when the 6th Duke moved the porcelain into the Palace where it would not be exposed to any further damage or theft.[11] An area of parkland near High Lodge was called 'Queens Garden', although the reason for this designation is unknown. Paddocks for grazing horses were retained in the west of the park. Large stretches of land adjoining the River Glyme at the Lince are marked as ozier beds, with birch and ash plantations recorded nearby. The 5th Duke's arboretum is clearly visible to the south-east of the house, but a second arboretum planted by the 6th Duke to the south-west was not yet established.

Long after the 'repairs' were concluded, like his father and grandfather before him, the 6th Duke continually effected 'improvements'. A new keeper's lodge was built in the late 1840s (called Spring-Lock Gate Cottage because of its proximity to the pivoting boulder entrance to the Rock Garden).[12] A cowhouse in the west quarter of the park was relocated by 1881 to Home Farm where new pasturage was created when the tree-felling operations ceased.[13] The bronze statues of the Wrestlers and the Arrotino (which the 4th Duke had positioned in the gardens) were returned to the Great Hall of the Palace by 1846.[14] A number of coach-houses and an open-sided riding school were constructed in the stable court after the 5th Duke's melon house was demolished.[15]

The hothouses of the Kitchen Garden were repaired and rebuilt to enable delicate and exotic fruits such as melons, peaches, apricots, nectarines, figs and pineapples (then greatly sought after as status symbols) to be grown.[16] The hothouses were dotted all around the garden, with some clustered near the old timber yard, for practical reasons (at Blenheim, wood-fired stoves continued long after the general conversion to coal).[17] The exotic produce from the 6th Duke's greenhouses was recorded in a

painting by the Victorian artist George Lance, displayed at the Royal Academy exhibition in 1848.[18] Listed in the catalogue as *'Prize fruit grown at Blenheim'*, the still life includes pineapples, peaches, grapes, pears, cherries, raspberries and gooseberries. Even without knowing the title of the painting, the view of Blenheim Palace in the background, with the ducal coat of arms above the pineapples, eliminates any ambiguity regarding the source of the fruit. The picture was purchased by the 6th Duke for 200 guineas.[19]

However, if the 6th Duke sought to make a statement about the renewed magnificence of Blenheim, he could not have chosen better than to install a splendid pair of massive black iron gates within Vanbrugh's east entrance. The gates were decorated with gilded roundels displaying the Churchill and Spencer crests, the Marlborough family arms, and the letters 'M M' representing *Marlborough Mindelheim*. Each folding section of the gates at 22½ feet high (6.85 m) weighed four tons (4.06 tonnes), turning on ball-and-socket pivot hinges. They were made in 1852 by Bramah, Prestage and Ball of Piccadilly for £1,000.[20]

Prize fruit grown at Blenheim, by George Lance. ↓ Details show a view of Blenheim Palace and the ducal coat of arms. ↗ ↗↗

In the kitchen court, other changes were initiated. Towards the end of the eighteenth century, the 4th Duke had converted Vanbrugh's greenhouse into a private theatre for family entertainment (alongside a picture gallery where a series of nine large paintings on leather by Titian were displayed).[21]

Since the theatre had become totally neglected, the 6th Duke filled the room with plants (but retained the picture gallery). On the other side of the court, the old laundry was converted into a new dairy, with tiled walls and a stone fountain.[22]

However, the 6th Duke's most ambitious repair project was to 'Capability' Brown's dam. Sixty-five years after its construction, the embankment had sprung several leaks and *'the head or dam of the lake [was] so much out of repair that it does not retain the water so high as it ought to do by several feet; and the water of the stream, instead of falling over the cascade as it used to do, finds its way underground, and rises up like springs… in the flat ground below'.*[23] In 1840 the water in the lake was entirely drawn off, the lake dredged, and all the aquatic weeds removed.[24] Subsequently, major repairs were carried out involving the reconstruction of certain sections of the original dam and the widening of its clay core under the direction of Mr Anderson, an engineer of the Grand Junction Water Works Company.[25] The total cost of the repairs amounted to more than £1,000. It was also at this time that the cascade's rockwork was remodelled to produce a more rugged-looking, fashionably picturesque waterfall, *'the effect of which when in full force is not to be surpassed perhaps by any artificial fall of waters whatever; and equals in beauty and interest most of those natural Cascades, of greater dimensions, which are met with in mountainous districts'.*[26] The work took over two years, with the last recorded payment being made in November 1843.[27] (Further repairs to the dam are currently being undertaken, see page 121.)

Since most of the costly repairs and renovations had been undertaken with borrowed money, especially in the early years of the 6th Duke's tenure, a programme of repayments had to be established. In balancing the books, an important source of income was derived from the annual sale of timber. The timber sales, managed by Thomas Glover and Thomas Waters, involved the felling of hundreds of trees, comprehensively denuding thickly foliated areas, especially in Little Park (to the south-east of the Palace, now called Low Park).[28]

The axe fell first on the centre of three rows of elms forming the right-hand side of the east avenue approach which had been planted in 1707–8 by Henry Wise. Glover reasoned that

Iron gates installed by the 6th Duke in 1852. ↑

George, 6th Duke of Marlborough (1793–1857). ↓

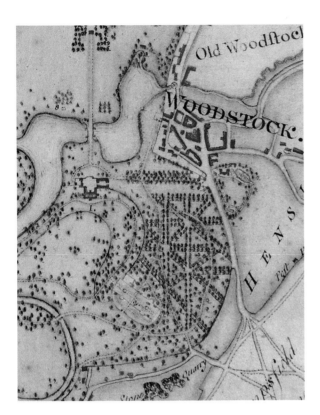

Detail from Pride's survey, 1772. ↑
Many trees planted by Henry Wise in a
quincunx pattern to the south-east of
the house survived 'Capability' Brown's
landscaping but were felled not long
afterwards by the 6th Duke.

Timber Sale poster. ↓
© Private Collection

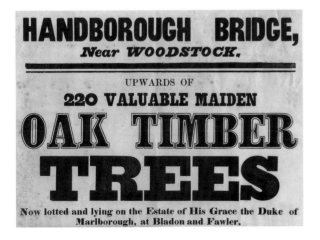

'the whole of this row should be taken down for the improvement and growth and foliage of the other two rows. As there are only two rows of trees on the left hand side of the avenue, the removal of this centre row will make the avenue uniform in its appearance'. A further 89 elms were removed between the Kitchen Garden and Eagle Gate as the *'trees are so thick in this part of the Park as to prevent the growth of the Pasture.'*

Around £1,000 was raised from the first sale of 122 elms and similar operations were undertaken over eight years from 1845. By carrying out the felling in a finely orchestrated process of gradual thinning out, the scheme was deceptive, allowing Glover and Waters to claim not to have caused any *'injury to the appearance of Blenheim Park'*. Having survived 'Capability' Brown's earlier remodelling, Henry Wise's quincunx plantations were almost completely removed to *'render the Pasturage more useful'*.[29] The greatest continuous deliberate reduction in the numbers of mature elms, limes and oaks in the park occurred during this period.[30]

The 6th Duke also raised money through the reopening and renting of old stone pits near Combe and on other outlying parts of the estate.[31] Sarah, Duchess of Marlborough, had put a stop to the extraction of gravel from the park quarries, fearing it would leave too many disfiguring holes in the ground, but the 6th Duke resumed its production and sale.[32] Pressure was further taken off strained finances through a number of lucrative land sales (for the most part to newly formed railway companies) which provided a windfall of around £50,000.[33] Although some smaller estates and houses near Blenheim Park were purchased with the proceeds, the pace of these land sales marked a turning point which would eventually lead to an even greater sell-off of the Marlboroughs' assets by the next two generations.

REPAIRS IN 2009 TO BROWN'S CASCADE DAM

Compliance with Environment Agency legislation under the Reservoirs Act, 1975, requires the Blenheim Estates to undertake extensive renovation works on 'Capability' Brown's dam through the course of 2009. The Reservoirs Act further requires the dam to withstand a one in 10,000 year flood event without major failure. To achieve this, the downstream face of the embankment and the sides of the cascade spill-over have to be strengthened to allow over-topping while preventing failure of the structure.

Blenheim Palace is a designated World Heritage Site and a Grade I listed landscape. This necessitates these important and considerable engineering works to be carried out with minimum impact on the setting. All the planting will be removed, except for those trees believed to be crucial to the landscape. The first stage of the proposed work will involve replacing the clay core of the dam which has developed small leaks. A 23-foot-deep by 3-foot-wide (7 m x 1 m) trench will be dug in small stages to the underlying bedrock, and backfilled with bentonite slurry, setting hard to form a new core along the whole length of the dam.

A 262-foot (80 m) slipway will be created along the crest of the existing dam. The top layer of soil will be removed to lay a grid of cellular, interlocking concrete blocks. The soil layer will then be put back and seeded with grass.

When these works are completed, they will allow the lake to flow over the embankment in a controlled manner in extreme or severe weather conditions, while minimising the aesthetic impact on the landscape.

The circuit through the pleasure grounds to the south of the house was modified yet again. The established entry into the gardens was through a small arched doorway in the angle of the east front garden (now called Snake Gate). Visitors were guided through a flowering shrubbery, then along the south front of the Palace, to arrive at a flight of steps at the western extremity of the building from where the view down the grassy slope to

West view of Blenheim Palace. ↑ The grassy slope down to the lake was planted with a scattering of trees and shrubs.
© Private Collection

the lake had to be admired. Descending into the private gardens, past magnolias and beds of roses, the route led to a circular Rustic Temple (covered with Irish ivy) which offered views both to High Lodge and to new farm buildings in the park.[34]

By 1852, the 6th Duke had planted a significant number of new trees – golden yew, catalpa, table thorn, yellow chestnut, scarlet oak and copper beech – introducing coloured foliage into Brown's landscape for the first time. Pines encircled a Chinese Temple and, on advancing towards an Eskimo Hut near the cascade, visitors could admire a tooth-ache tree (*Zanthoxylum*), a gum Benjamin, a *Virgilia lutea* and a beautiful *Cedrus deodar*. These new plantations formed the foundation of the present arboretum in this part of the grounds. The circuit looped around the Rock Garden to the American Garden, past the Temple of Diana, before cutting across the south lawn to the old arboretum established by the 5th Duke (south-east of the Palace). After admiring the hothouses of the Kitchen Garden the visitor returned to the gate via the aviary and past the Temple of Health.[35]

The 5th Duke had previously upset visitors by charging for shooting and fishing by the hour. However, a real hullabaloo erupted when the 6th Duke imposed a fee of 10 shillings for every six visitors. The injustice of this system of charging was openly condemned: '*If only one person enters the gate, he must pay for six; and if there are seven in company, two tickets are required to admit them.*'[36] The clamour grew in the national press as some tourists noted their displeasure at having to tip repeatedly for each of the different tours – the Palace, the gardens and the park.[37] Others demanded free access simply because Blenheim had been partly built from Treasury funds.[38] However flawed the logic behind this reasoning was, the perception that Blenheim was inhabited by a grasping owner with avaricious staff had to be dispelled. The Duke's solicitor weighed in, stating that the grant of Woodstock Manor by Queen Anne gave no automatic right of entry and a notice was published: *'The Duke gives tickets as a favour and these are only an admission to his private gardens. There is admission without any ticket three days in the week – a privilege which is rarely granted in other places… The public gardens and arboretum may be visited every day without tickets and the park as well – on foot. But if a man accompanies the party on horseback, he should be given something for his trouble'.*[39] It was further explained that the charge covered the damage caused by the visiting public.

However, as a result of the continued protests, the fee was dropped to 5 shillings for a party of six, but the clamour did not end until entry was standardised at a shilling per head[40] and the Duke himself wrote in *The Times*, *'…each person desirous of visiting the interior of Blenheim, its treasures of art and science, would be free from all charges on payment of the sum of 1 shilling and no more… in respect of the gardens, they are open all day and every day (except Sundays) to the public. The gardener has permission for his own and his men's attendance upon the visitors, to require the sum of 2 pence per head and no more… No anonymous scribbler, whether 'a commissioner of taxes' or 'one fleeced at Blenheim' shall tempt me into a renewed discussion'.*[41] Although access to the park and public gardens was free every day of the week, the private gardens could only be viewed *'with a Ticket of Admission from His Grace'.*[42]

There was no doubt that the rapid increase of visitors resulted in a number of problems for the family, not least of which was the constant invasion of their privacy. The 6th Duke's second son, Lord Alfred Spencer-Churchill, openly protested when he came across more than fifty groups of visitors one day.[43] Blenheim Palace had long been a popular attraction even in the earliest days of its construction, although its appeal greatly increased after 'Capability' Brown's modifications to its landscape. However, its proximity to London, Oxford and Birmingham, recently connected by a network of new railways, had led to such a sudden explosion of numbers that the crush of tourists was commonly observed and equally condemned by the public, many of whom were appalled when forced to fall in *'with a corps of thirty observers – what a plague and fatigue!'*[44] When the 7th Duke took over in 1857, tickets of admission were still sold at a shilling a head, but the proceeds were donated to charitable institutions, and visiting times to the Palace and private gardens were strictly limited.[45]

A late 19th-century admission ticket. ↓

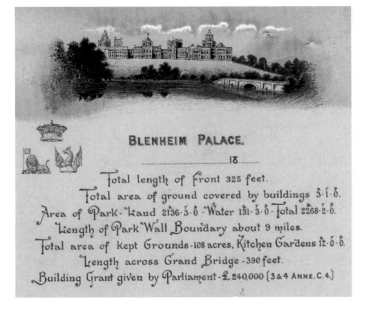

BLENHEIM PALACE.

…………………18………

Total length of front 325 feet.
Total area of ground covered by buildings 3·1·0.
Area of Park-Land 2136·3·0 Water 131·3·0 Total 2268·2·0.
Length of Park Wall Boundary about 9 miles.
Total area of kept Grounds-108 acres. Kitchen Gardens 12·0·0.
Length across Grand Bridge -390 feet.
Building Grant given by Parliament-£ 240,000 (3 & 4 ANNE.C.4.)

Described as *'a complete, full-blown, Victorian prig'*, John Winston, 7th Duke of Marlborough, made a number of alterations to the gardens just as each of his predecessors had done, but of all the Victorian Dukes, the changes he made were the most long lasting.[46] First, a new circular rose garden (called the Rosary) was created in the western pleasure grounds in place of the 5th Duke's Chinese Garden. Rose gardens had long been a standard element of pleasure grounds, usually hidden behind a screen of trees and shrubs away from the house.

To the east of the Rose Garden, in a seven-acre (2.8 ha) complex of enclosed paddocks and wooden sheds, a dozen emus with their chicks and over fifteen kangaroos roamed freely. They were cared for by Mr Long, the Duke's 72-year-old gamekeeper, also an expert in rearing pheasants.[47] According to a contemporary report, the emus and kangaroos *'seem quite at home, and live on the most friendly terms, both being natives of the same country.'*[48]

On the morning of 5 February 1861, disaster struck Blenheim when a large fire broke out in the bakehouse roof and spread to a part of the adjacent greenhouse, in the south-east corner of the kitchen court (where the Titians were displayed). The bakehouse and the gallery, including all the paintings, were destroyed. The damage, though substantial, had been contained although the roof required complete rebuilding. As the development of

John Winston, 7th Duke of Marlborough (1822–83). ↑

Initially, climbing rose bushes were trained up the circular ironwork trellis along the perimeter of the Rose Garden, until its remodelling (see page 129). →
© Private Collection

The Garden is currently planted with climbing Iceberg and rambling Albertine on the trellises. Modern varieties of hybrid tea and floribunda rose bushes (Troika, Peace, Silver Jubilee, Blessings, City of Belfast and Royal William) are planted in the beds. ←

Victorian ornamental iron rib-and-girder construction based on Paxton's Crystal Palace structure had become fashionable, the new panelled roof was made with rough plate glass supported on iron beams. This resulted in the greenhouse (then called the Conservatory, now the Orangery) being top lit for the first time. At least two drawings for the ironwork were put forward, around 1862, before the work was carried out.[49] Within a few years a choice collection of flowering plants filled the room once again.[50]

The cost of keeping the grounds continued to rise. With over 140 acres (56 ha) of grass to be kept manicured around the Palace, the invention of the lawn-mowing machine must have been particularly welcome at Blenheim, where initially a number of steam-powered mowers were purchased to produce *'the most velvety and beautifully shaven turf'*.[51] The growth of mechanisation allowed other efficiencies to be achieved – a milking machine was used on the estate's sizeable dairy herd.[52]

The fire in 1861. ↑

Other tiresome tasks, such as the cutting of weeds in the lake, were by now usually sub-contracted. The weeds were cleared on a weekly basis every July, and fortnightly throughout the rest of the summer. In October 1876, further repairs to the cascade embankment were carried out by Smith & Co. when a Mr Bridgeman was paid £146 for 18 weeks' labour.[53] Three years later Briggs & Sons were called in to examine the embankment again.[54] On this occasion, the level of water in the lake was lowered, which resulted in Queen Elizabeth's Island becoming larger.[55]

In the Victorian period, a new burden was placed on gardeners when the fashion for carpet bedding took off. Thousands of plants were arranged closely together in different patterns creating a colourful floral carpet, but each plant needed regular clipping. In order to provide a sufficient quantity of new plants for the beds and borders in every season, there was a corresponding growth in

WILLIAM CRUMP – HEAD GARDENER

© Private Collection

William W. Crump had a genuine talent for horticulture. Born at Pontesbury, he began his career in charge of glasshouse production at Powis Castle, where importance was given to the cultivation of pineapples, peaches and herbaceous flowers for the terraces. Moving on to Heckfield Place (Hampshire) as general foreman, Crump accepted a step down in order to gain valuable experience under Mr Wildsmith (a specialist Head Gardener in the cultivation of fruit and flowering plants). After a short stint at Lamberhurst, Crump arrived at Blenheim Palace, at the age of 23, where he would become particularly successful as a fruit grower.

Crump regularly exhibited at the annual shows of the Botanic Gardens in Oxford and Manchester, often winning gold medals and silver cups. He was awarded a blue riband at the International Potato Show (Crystal Palace) and was twice winner of the lucrative Ten Guinea Packing Prize awarded by Mr J. Webber of Covent Garden for the best-packed boxes of first-class fruit. Crump often displayed fruits and vegetables from Blenheim's Kitchen Garden at the Great Summer Show, the principal event of the Royal Horticultural Society, frequently earning a creditable mention.

On the death of the 7th Duke of Marlborough in 1883, Crump left Blenheim for Madresfield Court, where he remained for 36 years until retirement. By the end of his career, he had earned the title of 'The Grand Old Man of Horticulture'. Improving the growth of many newly introduced species and advancing horticultural techniques through successful experimentation in pruning, training and grafting plants, he was the recipient of the Veitchian Gold Medal, and one of the first sixty selected to receive the prestigious RHS Victoria Medal of Honour in 1897, Queen Victoria's Golden Jubilee Year.

Cutting the Grass

The first mowers employed at Blenheim were horse-drawn, steam-driven machines. They removed the need for large numbers of labourers with scythes. Staff numbers remained high until the advent of machinery, which led to the Victorian obsession with well-kept, manicured lawns and smoothly cut verges. Even today one member of staff is fully employed in maintaining the grassed areas around the Palace. Mowing is generally undertaken in rotation so that the grass is cut once every eight days. However, the south lawn is always kept immaculate which requires mowing twice a week during the summer months.

the number of greenhouses and gardeners. Large-scale carpet bedding arrived at Blenheim in the 1860s when the 7th Duke created a new Italian Garden.

The Italian Garden was located along the east front of the Palace. Previously the site of the flower garden created by Henry Wise for the 1st Duchess of Marlborough, it was later laid to lawn by the 3rd Duke and altered again by the 5th Duke who planted roses and other flowering shrubs in circular beds. The 7th Duke now created a formal garden setting once again, providing an appropriate transitional space from the symmetrical architecture of the house to the informality of the landscape.[56]

In the Italian Garden, four large beds (with carpet bedding in a complex arrangement of colours) were laid out symmetrically on either side of a broad central walk covered with white gravel. A central bed with two smaller circular beds at either end were inserted into the walk, which was aligned directly with the eastern bow window.[57] Within the overall design, the planting in the beds varied from year to year. The beds were intermingled with Irish and golden yews and clipped Portugal laurels.[58] Long continuous borders, seven-feet wide (2 m), ran on both sides of the garden. Planted in an intricately interwoven design, each floral mass was edged with dwarf box and surrounded with white gravel. Flights of steps led out of the garden on three sides; the fourth side adjoined the Palace's east front.[59]

The Italian Garden created by the 7th Duke. ↑
© Private Collection

Research also reveals that a second geometrical flower garden was established to the west of the Palace, beyond the chapel, which was best viewed from the bow window of the Long Library. However, the sloping ground down to the lake made this formal garden more difficult to establish and it was therefore considered *'of poorish design'*, even though it provided *'a pleasing variety to the surrounding irregularity'*.[60] The 'irregularity'

The Rose Garden after replanting and the installation of the fountain. ↑↓

© Private Collection

© Private Collection

referred to a new plantation of young conifers which strongly contrasted in their form and foliage with 'Capability' Brown's cedars, already grown to an imposing height.

In the 1870s, the 7th Duke employed a string of Head Gardeners. After William Lee left, John Austin (the Under Gardener) took his place in December 1871.[61] Their annual wage was £100. However, Austin was gone before the year was out and was immediately replaced by Mr Temple at a higher salary of £120.[62]

Temple remained Head Gardener at Blenheim for four years, during which time he entirely replanted the Italian Garden, introducing a number of specimen variegated hollies and offering vivid contrasts in the floral beds. In 1874 these were planted with thousands of roses, cinerarias, azaleas, camellias and primulas. He lowered his labour costs by reducing the size of the beds and increasing the breadth of the turf surrounds. A new terrace was constructed outside the Conservatory, bordering the garden to the north, which Temple edged with artificial stone.[63]

Views around the lake were opened up by cutting the laurels much lower and by removing a dense screen of shrubs. Temple also planted a selection of young specimen conifers among the cedars near the aviary. When the Rose Garden was damaged by deer he fenced it in and redesigned the garden with four beds fanning out in a petal-shaped pattern. It was replanted with new dwarf rose bushes at intervals with the standards. The central focal point was a fountain with three marble figures (a Numan, a conch-blowing Triton and a putto) placed within a circular pool.[64]

By the mid-nineteenth century, many tender plants were grown in glasshouses and hothouses, or through forcing in dark-houses. Temple increased culinary production in the Kitchen Garden, building on the success of one of his predecessors, Robert Turnbull, who was famous for his grape-growing achievements.[65] Turnbull had established eight vine houses by the mid-1860s, where several different varieties were grown – Black Hamburg, Foster's White seedling, West's St Peter's, Muscat of Alexandria and Golden Champion. As the most important glasshouse crop, requiring meticulous attention – training, pruning, watering, the right level of heating and correct ventilation – these grapes would only be consumed at the Duke's table. After grapes, peaches were the second most important fruit cultivated under glass, in three peach houses. As far as pineapples were concerned, two varieties of this exotic fruit – Queen and Smooth-leaved Cayenne – were grown in two separate pineries. Figs were grown abundantly on the back walls of the glasshouses, along with cherries, plums, nectarines and greengages.[66]

The Kitchen Garden at Blenheim Palace is an eighteenth-century walled garden, designed by Sir John Vanbrugh and originally stocked by Henry Wise from the Brompton Nursery. Built at the same time as the house, it is the only part of the original garden scheme to survive.

The garden, covering eight acres (3.2 ha), was constructed on an east-west axis with the two longest walls facing due south, to maximize the absorption of heat from sunlight. The walls, incorporating semi-circular bastions, are roughly fourteen feet (4.3 m) high, mostly in brick, except for a four-acre (1.6 ha) southern extension or slip garden (planted as an orchard). The garden walls were built as 'hot walls' (double brick walls with inner flues) by the master bricklayers, Richard Stacey and Thomas Churchill. While being expensive to build, hot walls were the most heat-retentive. The flues built between the outer and inner walls were heated through stoke holes located at base level on the outside of the outer wall. The flues ran in long horizontal lengths, up each section of the wall, opening into a chimney on the top. They were wood fired, due to ample stocks of freely available timber from the park. A large wood store was located adjacent to the outer wall of the north-western corner. Wood was burnt in the fire stacks until the nineteenth century, when it became more economical to use coal.

Originally, the garden was internally divided into two, each half further sub-divided into four plots of approximately an acre (0.4 ha) each. This multi-sectional layout is commonly seen in kitchen gardens. A pond was located in each half of the garden to facilitate watering (see page 79). Manure was plentiful as well, carted from both the farm and stables.

In the early eighteenth century the garden was planted with rows of cauliflower, lettuce, cabbage, spinach, beans, peas, carrots, leeks, onions, endives, turnips, parsnip and beans. The fruits included peaches, nectarines, dwarf pears, apricots, plums, vines, figs, quinces, fillbeards, barberries, gooseberries, currants, dwarf and standard cherries, apples and codlings. The 1st Duke requested his wife to sample the fruit of every tree and to reject those not good enough. During this early period in the garden's history, melons were grown under glass cloches and over forty flowering shrubs were dotted around in coloured pots.

In 1772, William Chambers built a Palladian Gate into the west wall. This allowed the Kitchen Garden to be viewed on the 'garden circuit tour'. The Kitchen Garden was an estate's prized possession, and favoured guests would be able to leave with a basket of produce selected by the Head Gardener. Seasonal plantings were carefully managed by using appropriate methods of cultivation, i.e. either by planting in the warmest beds and through forcing, or by planting in the coolest spots and through early picking and storing. The quality and range of the produce was always important as it needed to arrive at the Duke's table at the peak of perfection in every season.

The Kitchen Gardener was well paid and from the late-eighteenth century lived in the Gardener's House built into the south-west section of the garden wall. He appointed the foremen of the gardens – usually two – one for the Kitchen Garden and another for the pleasure grounds. He also hired casual labourers on a daily-wage basis. The staff had to deal promptly with garden pests (rabbits, hares, moles and birds) which were sometimes unsympathetically destroyed; gunpowder featured regularly in lists of supplementary supplies.

By the mid-twentieth century, planting usually included potatoes, peas, runner beans, tomatoes, asparagus, sprouts, lettuce, leeks, spinach, onion and cabbage in the beds, and fuchsias, pelargoniums, gardenias, chrysanthemums and orchids in the greenhouses. Apple trees were grown in the orchard, soft fruits (cherries and plums) trained along the walls, and strawberries were forced.

In 1991, a large hedge maze was established at the eastern extremity of the Kitchen Garden (see pages 182–3). A few hothouses now remain where grapes, peaches, figs and melons continue to be grown. Some vegetables (asparagus, sea kale, peas, carrots, celery, artichokes, broad and runner beans) and soft fruits (strawberries, raspberries, gooseberries, redcurrants and blackcurrants) are still planted in the beds, and espaliered trees continue to yield cherries, pears and plums.

The number of hothouses had already increased by the late-eighteenth century for the cultivation of melons, peaches, grapes, apricots, nectarines, figs and pineapples. The hothouses were dotted all around the garden, with the largest cluster near the timber yard, for practical reasons. Figs were grown abundantly on the back walls of the glasshouses along with peaches and plums. Apricot trees were trained around the garden walls. The quarters within the Kitchen Garden were neatly edged with box hedges along the intersecting walks.

In addition to the Victorian fashion for carpet bedding, the requirements for floral displays inside the house made huge demands on Blenheim's nineteenth-century gardeners to provide a sufficient quantity of flowering plants. These included begonias, cyclamens, primulas, ferns, crotons and palms. In the 1870s, the 7th Duke of Marlborough possessed one of the largest orchid collections in the country.

18th-century Head Gardeners' house

The 8th Duke constructed an impressive range of new hothouses replacing most of the earlier scattered structures, the centrepiece of which was a magnificent orchid house. Three Gardeners' Bothies were also built facing the north wall of the Kitchen Garden, with a new residence for the Head Gardener nearby.

In 1899, the planting lists included 'pelargoniums, Begonia semperflorens, alternantheras, lobelias, ageratums, iresine, tuberous begonias, centaurea ragusina candidissima and yellow calceolarias'. All these, as well as quantities of chrysanthemums, clematis, hydrangeas, hyacinths, rhododendrons, lilac, gladioli, tulips, azaleas, roses, palms and exotic orchids, were grown in the glasshouses.

19th-century Head Gardeners' house

Even though there were twenty hothouses within the Kitchen Garden at this time, providing a remarkable 485 running feet (148 m) of planting under glass, they did not form an impressive sight as they were scattered around the garden,[67] but a boiler system supplied by Edward Weekes (installed by the 6th Duke) still worked efficiently enough to heat three vineries and a mushroom house.[68] Temple gradually renewed the entire stock of apricot trees trained along the garden walls. Over three hundred brick pits were used for growing strawberries and for vegetable forcing. There is no doubt that the Kitchen Garden flourished under Mr Temple, but its heyday was undoubtedly from 1876 onwards, when William Crump was appointed Head Gardener.[69]

The early years of Crump's service at Blenheim coincided with a period of prolonged family absence. The 7th Duke had been appointed Lord Lieutenant of Ireland for four years from 1876 when '*Blenheim was handed over to housekeepers and agents and its household was bodily transported to the Viceregal Lodge*'.[70] As Head Gardener, Crump managed the pleasure grounds and the Kitchen Gardens. He was assisted by a significant number of staff – two foremen gardeners (Isaac Beechey and Walter King), three Under Gardeners (William Long, Alfred Halwell and William Wilkinson), as well as casual labourers including twenty men, ten boys and a woman. Without the pressure of the family in residence, he conducted experiments in horticulture, varying pruning, training and grafting techniques in order to increase production in the Kitchen Garden where fruit trees covered every inch of wall and the ground provided '*every culinary requisite and delicacy of the dessert… in perfection and abundance*'.[71]

At the Royal Horticultural Society Show of 1880, Crump submitted a new variety of melon, called the Blenheim Orange Melon, winning a First-Class Certificate and '*the

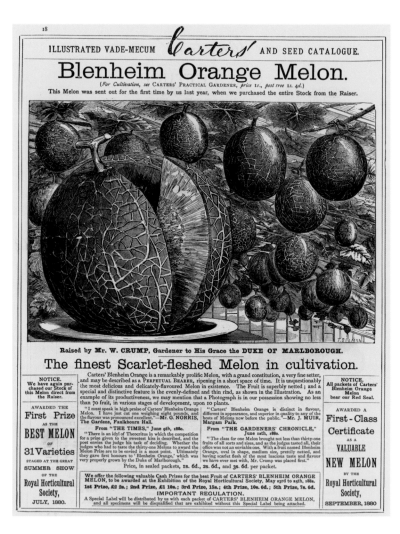

The advertisement for Crump's Blenheim Orange Melon in Carters' 1882 Seed Catalogue. ↑
© RHS

George Charles, 8th Duke of Marlborough (1844–92). ↑

First Prize… for a medium sized oval delicately netted example of Blenheim Orange, a thin rind few-seeded variety of excellent flavour'.[72] Compared with the thirty entries submitted, Crump's Blenheim Orange Melon was superior not only because of its excellent texture and flavour, but also because the plant was considered more productive and quick in ripening. In the year following this triumph, Carters (the seed merchants) purchased his entire stock, advertising it as '*Carters' Blenheim Orange – the finest scarlet fleshed melon in cultivation*'.[73]

Surplus fruit and vegetables from Blenheim's Kitchen Garden had regularly been sent for sale on the market. Previous Head Gardeners like Mr Temple had organised a mixed system of household and commercial production under instruction from the Duke, but Crump was apparently the first to earn a commission on the sale of any excess produce sent to market.[74] He handsomely supplemented his income by £30–35 (paid every December) in addition to his annual wage of £100.[75]

Glasshouses had become an essential part of garden production and maintenance, which increased the rising employment costs for gardeners and labourers. In addition to the fashion for carpet bedding, the requirements for floral displays inside the house made huge demands on Blenheim's gardeners to provide a sufficient quantity of flowering plants. Grown in the 'stove' and in a newly established cucumber house, these included begonias, cyclamens, primulas, *Salvia gesneraeflora*, ferns, crotons, palms, marantas and gardenias; varieties more likely to have been chosen by the Duchess rather than by Temple or Crump. However, estate accounts reveal the vast quantities of seeds purchased from specialised nurseries like Veitch & Co, Methuen & Sons, Sutton & Sons and J.S. Ware.[76]

By the later Victorian period a new enthusiasm for orchids had developed and these delicate, exotic plants also filled Blenheim's hothouses. Orchids were dramatic but hugely expensive, procured by plant hunters undertaking dangerous expeditions to far-flung corners of the world. In the 1870s, the 7th Duke of Marlborough possessed one of the largest orchid collections in the country, many purchased at auctions held by Protheroe and Morris.[77]

Another supplier was Frederick Sander, the founder of a large nursery in St Albans who employed as many as twenty orchid collectors in diverse locations in South America and Asia. Sander developed a lucrative business relationship with the 7th Duke who spent many thousands of pounds.[78] When Sander undertook the publication of his monumental work, *Reichenbachia, Orchids Illustrated and Described*, he included an orchid named *Duke of Marlborough Cattleya labiata mendelii*. The plate for the book was drawn from the specimen in the 7th Duke's collection which had received a First-Class Certificate from the RHS at South Kensington.[79]

George Charles, 8th Duke of Marlborough, was as passionate about orchids as his father. Within a year of his accession to the title he decided to construct an impressive new array of hothouses, the centrepiece of which was a magnificent orchid house, 100 feet (30 m) long and 24 feet (7.3 m) wide. Although his principal interest lay in agricultural and scientific developments, the Duke was also keen on palms and ferns. A palm house, two rose houses, a fernery, several forcing houses and forcing pits were arranged around the orchid house. The rose houses and palm house were completed by 1885, in which year the orchid house was still being erected.[80]

In addition, three Gardeners' Bothies (houses providing basic accommodation for unmarried labourers and apprentice boys) were built facing the north wall of the Kitchen Garden, close to the old wood store, which by this time was used for coal.[81] Coal-fired boilers installed in pits below ground produced hot water which would rise and circulate around the greenhouses in large open pipes covered with perforated decorative iron grillwork. The apprentices, or Bothy boys, usually performed the dreariest tasks – stoking the boilers and carrying coal, adjusting the ventilation in the glasshouses and, most tedious of all, weeding.[82] Gardening activity was predominantly concentrated in the greenhouses of the Kitchen Garden where operations were regulated by the ringing of a garden bell.[83]

Cattleya labiata mendelii was one of the grandest South American orchids, growing naturally in the Andes at an elevation of about 3,500 feet (1067 m). ↑ It flowered twice a year, producing outstanding contrasts of colour in an exquisitely frilled lip, white in the upper half and deep magenta in the lower. *Cattleya* was a comparatively new genus, founded by Dr Lindley and dedicated to William Cattley of Barnet, an early-19th-century patron of horticulture who was an ardent collector and enthusiast of rare plants and one of the first amateurs to form a collection of exotic orchids. When Cattley died, his collection passed into the hands of Mr Knight, the owner of the Royal Exotic Nursery in Chelsea, later taken over by James Veitch and Sons. The first living plants had been commercially imported by Messrs. Backhouse of York but soon the increased quantities of collecting resulted in the plant being only sparingly found in its wild state.

The Main Bothy, a 19th-century lodging house for young apprentice gardeners and labourers. ↑ Gardening staff lived a relentless life, working long hours, six days a week, earning a wage of roughly a shilling a day. There were three Bothies at Blenheim; the main Bothy was occupied by seven men, the second by four men, and the third was a family cottage. Women, usually widows, were employed to cook and clean in the two Bothies occupied by unmarried men.

However, to fund these developments, to purchase new farming equipment and to maintain his expensive lifestyle, the 8th Duke took the unfortunate step of emptying Blenheim Palace of its treasures. The trouble had already begun in his father's time when the dramatic fall of land values, compounded with the agricultural depression of the 1870s, resulted in a dwindling income from this traditional source.[84] By successfully petitioning Parliament, the Blenheim Settled Estates Act of 1880 finally broke the entail that tied the Marlborough heirlooms to the estate. The 7th Duke had knowingly opened the floodgates to facilitate the sale of the famous Marlborough Gems and the Sunderland Library in his own time, and enabled his son immediately afterwards to put over four hundred works of art and other valuable heirlooms under the auctioneer's hammer.[85]

It was ironic that these severe and irreversible losses were not caused by the spendthrift 3rd Duke or the feckless 5th Duke, but by two high-minded Victorian aristocrats.

The 8th Duke only took on the care of his great ancestral home for nine years before his own death, a relatively short time in which irreparable damage was done. He was the only Duke whose obituary did not read too kindly: *'Of late years he spent numerous sums at Blenheim in an attempt to restore some of the former magnificence, for the decadence of which he was mainly responsible. This he was enabled to do by means of the large fortune brought him by his second wife, Lilian Warren of New York'.*[86]

Although the estate had been partially rescued with American funds in the late 1880s, the money was mostly spent on making utilitarian modifications. Ultimately, it would be another significant American fortune in the form of a generous settlement granted to Charles, 9th Duke of Marlborough, by his future father-in-law, which would make an immense and lasting difference to both the Palace and its garden landscape.

The construction
of the Water Terrace
Gardens on the west front
of Vanbrugh's building was a
remarkable achievement, providing a
worthy frame to the Palace and giving
it greater architectural importance.

9 *Recreating Grandeur*
ACHILLE DUCHÊNE &
THE 9TH DUKE'S TERRACE GARDENS

In September 1895, Charles, 9th Duke of Marlborough, proposed to Consuelo Vanderbilt in the splendid surroundings of the Gothic Room at Marble House, her family's Newport home. A substantial marriage settlement of $2.5 million in capital stock, (on which interest at 4% was guaranteed), provided the Duke with an annual income of at least $100,000, whilst Consuelo separately received a comparable sum from her father, William Kissam Vanderbilt. Through this marriage, new American money was not simply transferred to an old English title but the future of Blenheim itself was assured.

After the wedding in New York, the young couple travelled on an extended honeymoon while the renovation of their private apartments was undertaken at Blenheim. By Christmas 1895, the Duke and Duchess reached Rome. Exhausted after the transatlantic crossing and their travels through Spain in freezing weather, they prolonged their stay in the Italian capital, which was then also home to the American sculptor, Thomas Waldo Story. The connection between the Vanderbilts and Waldo Story's family dated back to the Duchess's childhood in America where they were part of the same social circle, before Waldo Story's father, William Wentmore Story, moved to Italy.[1] Consuelo renewed this old acquaintance, and the Marlboroughs commissioned several works from Waldo Story, including a bronze fountain for the Italian Garden at Blenheim Palace.

Charles Richard John 'Sunny', 9th Duke (1871–1934) ↓ and Consuelo, Duchess of Marlborough (1877–1964). ↘

Based on the surviving photographs of models prepared by the sculptor, it would appear that two proposals were considered for the fountain. One was for a circular gadrooned basin supported on a base of dolphins with putti, possibly inspired by a seventeenth-century design *Amours sur des Cygnes*, by Charles Le Brun for an intended fountain at Versailles.[2] However, another more complex design was chosen, consisting of an ornamental basin supported on a sculpted base of mermaids and entwined dolphins. A Naiad (water-nymph) with flowing hair rose from a bed of lilies in the centre of the basin, holding a coronet in her upraised arms.[3]

The marble and gilded bronze fountain was made at Waldo Story's studio in Rome.[4] The bronze casting was probably carried out by Nelli Brothers, a firm habitually employed by the sculptor for this process.[5] However, one significant detail – the coronet held by the Naiad – was still undecided when the fountain was completed. Two different crowns were cast for evaluation. Photographic records show an imperial crown when the fountain was first set up but this was soon replaced with the ducal coronet.

The fountain was delivered in 1899. Estate accounts reveal that in October several men were paid to cart the soil from the central flower bed of the Italian Garden in preparation for its fixing.[6] The placement of the fountain was reported soon

Le Brun's *Amours sur des Cygnes*, a design for a fountain at Versailles.
© Private Collection

The sculptor Thomas Waldo Story (1855–1915). ←
© Private Collection

Clay models for the proposed fountain at Blenheim Palace. The one on the left ↙ which echoes Le Brun's design for a fountain at Versailles, was rejected in favour of the one on the right. ↓
© Private Collection

The completed fountain with the imperial crown, outside Waldo Story's studio in Rome. ↑
© Private Collection

The actual-size model of the mermaid and dolphins (prior to casting) for the base of the fountain. ↓
© Private Collection

afterwards in *The Gardeners' Chronicle*: '*During last autumn a fountain, with basin, has been erected on the site of the central bed, which will doubtless in the future enhance the beauty of the tout ensemble*'.[7]

At this stage the Italian Garden was still planted more or less as it had been during the 8th Duke's time. The Head Gardener, Thomas Whillans, appointed by the 8th Duke in 1887, continued to be employed by the 9th Duke, at an annual wage of £190.[8] Every March, Whillans supervised the preparation of the beds for new planting: '*No mixing is allowed but masses of distinct colours are formed with various suitable plants which must obviously be provided in enormous numbers*'.[9] Through these displays the Head Gardener was expected to reveal his proficiency in botany and in art by producing the most decorative presentation possible. In 1899, Whillans' planting list for the Italian Garden included '*8,000 pelargoniums, 2,000 Begonia semperflorens, 12,000 alternantheras, 10,000 lobelias, 2,500 ageratums, 2,000 iresine, 1,400 tuberous begonias, 1,000 Centaurea ragusina candidissima and 800 yellow calceolarias*'.[10] These, as well as quantities of chrysanthemums, clematis, hydrangeas, hyacinths, rhododendrons, lilac, gladioli, tulips, azaleas, roses and exotic orchids, were all grown in the glasshouses of the Kitchen Garden.[11]

However, the 9th Duke decided to dispose of the large palms which his father had placed within the floral beds and in tubs along the central path of the Italian Garden. In 1904, Sander and Sons, the renowned St Albans-based plant and orchid suppliers, were asked to sell all the palm trees. The 9th Duke similarly dispatched many rare orchids, passionately and expensively collected by his father and grandfather, putting a large part of the stock on the market by 1900.[12] Reversing this decision in November 1907, the Duke restocked the orchid house with thousands of new plants including varieties of cattleya, dendrobium, odontoglossum and laelia.[13]

The earlier obsession with orchids was transformed into a craze for carnations, grown in their thousands for the

9th Duke. The Head Gardener, Thomas Whillans, cultivated a new variety of large yellow carnation with soft, crumpled petals, called *Duchess Consuelo*.[14] Whillans received a commission on the sales of seedlings, while the Duchess often gifted them to friends and to plant enthusiasts.[15] During this time, the Kitchen Garden and the glasshouses were taken off the general visitor route through the grounds and could only be viewed by application to the Head Gardener.[16]

Apart from carnations, the 9th Duke was also partial to lilies, and new varieties of water lilies were introduced *'to give richer colour and greater charm to the lake'.*[17] They were similarly established in the pond within the 5th Duke's arboretum near the 7th Duke's exedra (called the *roundabout*), where glades of alternating box and cypress hedges provided the setting for a charming bronze sculpture of four putti.[18] Lilies filled Waldo Story's fountain pool in the Italian Garden: they were planted in the central beds in the circular Rose Garden (acting as a foil to the clusters of colourful summer-flowering roses trained around the slender metal arches at the garden's perimeter). The basin of the fountain in this garden was now covered with glazed tiles to better display a number of newly introduced Japanese double-tailed goldfish.[19]

This old photograph *c.*1900 shows the Naiad with the imperial crown, as well as the topiary created by Thomas Whillans, the 9th Duke's Head Gardener. ↑
© Private Collection

Waldo Story's fountain in the Italian Garden. The Naiad holds a ducal coronet in her upraised arms. ↑

Even though the 4th Duke's aviary had been removed in the late 1870s, the 9th Duke continued to keep exotic birds (peacocks, ostriches, pelicans, vultures, an ibis and a secretary-bird), often allowing them to roam freely within the pleasure grounds in an area called *the birdwalk*.[20] He also established the practice (which continues today) of planting thousands of daffodils along the grass banks of the pleasure grounds.

But Whillans replaced the rhododendrons and azaleas in the American Garden with clumps of golden yew, *Prunus pissardi* and golden privet.[21] He also created new sculpted topiary in shapes of animals and birds within the Italian Garden.[22] Under Thomas Whillans' care, the grounds offered *'beautiful results in the way of colour effects.'*[23] On his departure from Blenheim in November 1902, he was replaced by Mr Garrett, who, like his predecessors, was in charge of both the pleasure grounds and the production of fruits, flowers and vegetables in the Kitchen Garden.[24] However, many of Blenheim's labour-intensive Victorian gardening practices ended when the 9th Duke decided to completely remodel the gardens surrounding the house, employing the French garden designer and architect, Achille Duchêne.

From a young age, Achille Duchêne worked with his father Henri, an engineer who had turned to landscape gardening.[25] Jointly responsible for the restoration and construction of many French gardens, their style of landscape design was based on the rediscovery and reinterpretation of early formal gardens, creatively adapting the architectural gardening

of the past to suit the tastes of their time. The Duchênes found the contradictions of nineteenth-century gardening, *'a travesty of nature… the indication of real decadence in landscape gardening'*, and rejected the idea that exotic plants from across the world could legitimately feature in European landscapes.[26] Both father and son were inspired by the rules of architecture and decoration rather than horticulture which, in their opinion, could never rise to the level of art. They sought a return to tradition, concentrating on the purity of design in their gardens and the rediscovery of coherence.[27] In the dying years of the nineteenth century, Achille Duchêne was first employed by the 9th Duke of Marlborough on the Sunderland House project.

When the ground lease of Marlborough House in London had reverted to the Crown after the death of the 4th Duke in 1817, the Dukes of Marlborough had had to relinquish their town house in the capital. From then on they had rented many different London houses. However, with an active political career which required him to remain at Parliament for long periods of time, the 9th Duke sought a more permanent base. An opportunity emerged in 1899 when he bought the site of the old Mayfair Chapel in Curzon Street after its demolition.[28] Achille Duchêne was most likely called in to establish a garden for the new house as the accounts mention payment *'for exterior work'*.[29] Beyond this, the exact scope of his involvement in London is unclear.[30] However, over the next three decades, he worked with the 9th Duke on three schemes at Blenheim Palace, reinstating a certain grandeur and elegance focused on the architecture of the building and its axial alignment.

The main entrance courtyard (north court) after 'Capability' Brown had grassed it over. ↓

Throughout the nineteenth century, a reactionary trend had developed against the Brownian model of landscape gardening, condemning the widespread destruction of so many earlier formal garden schemes. In 1828, the famous horticulturist and writer, J.C. Loudon added his voice, advocating that gardens should complement a building's architecture: *'We must in fact adapt our gardens, that at least which adjoins the house, to the building and make them a part of it, appropriate and*

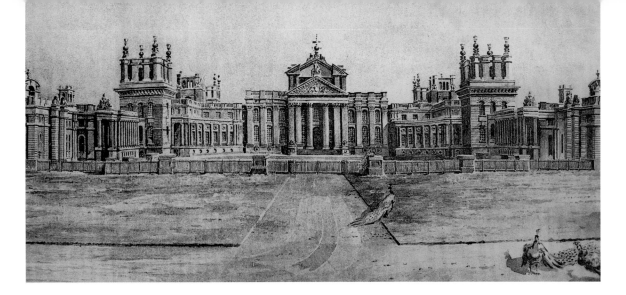

such as in the times when those buildings were erected'.[31] With his strong sense of history, the 9th Duke embarked on the immense and costly task of enhancing Blenheim through the restitution of Vanbrugh's north entrance court and the reconstruction of formal gardens to the east and west, creating a harmonious transition between the wider naturalistic landscape and the rigidly symmetrical architecture of the house.

John Vanbrugh's original design for the Great Court had created an impact through the use of symbolism and triumphal decoration. However, this dramatic effect had been lost for over a century: 'Capability' Brown had brought grass right up to the front steps of the Palace and the 4th Duke had removed most of the statues. Having decided to restore Vanbrugh's scheme, the 9th Duke and Duchêne turned to surviving drawings. Although the original plans showed the rough outlines of the courtyard, they contained insufficient detail for its reconstruction, forcing them to rely instead on the pictorial record provided by eighteenth-century engravings.[32]

The engravings show the courtyard constructed on two levels: a raised terrace paved with stone slabs running adjacent to the front of the building and along the colonnades, and a lower section, paved with square setts within which four rectangular panels of gravel were laid out in a symmetrical grid. Carved pedestals capped with decorative urns featured at junctions and along flights of steps. Statues adorned the top of the building. However, all the old engravings were views looking towards the house, which excluded the northern boundary of the courtyard, where Vanbrugh had intended building a gated colonnade. However, this part of his ambitious scheme had remained on the drawing board and a simple iron railing had been erected instead. For this section inspiration was drawn from an outline sketched in an early proposal (pictured on page 27), imaginatively executed by Duchêne.

Duchêne firmly believed that in following a prescribed scheme to the letter, mere imitation was insufficient; the spirit of the setting also needed to be captured.[33] The architect first turned his attention to reinstating the statues on each side of the pediment above the entrance to the house. As only fragments survived of the originals removed by the 4th Duke, engravings of the eighteenth-century façade were employed

Six terracotta statues, commissioned in 1905 by Achille Duchêne, were placed on either side of the pediment of the north front. ← Badly decayed over time, the statues were removed from the roof and, after restoration, placed in niches at a lower level of the building (to protect them from future erosion). ↘ Cast stone replicas were erected onto the parapet in February 2007. ↘↘

to reproduce the figures. In January 1904, Duchêne sent an outline drawing for *'a warrior'*, with instructions for a mock-up to be raised to judge the effect before it was commissioned.[34] A wooden cut-out was lifted into position in July in an operation involving the installation of moving platforms suspended from the Palace's roof.[35] The experiment must have had some merit, as the five remaining template drawings were similarly sent for trial a year later.[36]

All the drawings were returned to the architect in Paris in August 1905, after which the statues (slightly larger than life-size) were commissioned in terracotta.[37] They were delivered by June 1907 when Richard Angas (the Duke's Agent) received instructions to *'place the figures in the order shown on the old engraving of the front of Blenheim which is in His Grace's possession. I have had the figures reproduced with the same silhouettes…'*[38]

Work on levelling the courtyard had begun in March 1904, using a light steam-powered roller.[39] All the elements of its construction (paved raised terraces, stone walls and steps, granite setts and gravel beds) were then undertaken simultaneously. While York stone was used for the steps and the paving on the raised terraces, the square granite setts (*pavés*) for the courtyard's lower section were ordered from the Paris firm of L. Lang et Fils.[40] The first consignment of *pavés* was delivered by May 1904 from France. Monsieur Lang came to Blenheim in mid-May along with his overseer and a foreman who stayed behind to instruct the local workmen in the laying of the setts. The Duke was concerned about the additional costs involved in

View of the north court.

accommodating the Frenchman for an indefinite length of time and suggested to his Agent that he should be sent back '*after he has laid the eight culverts in the panels… If however, you have any doubts as to the capacity of your English staff to lay the stones, you will have to spin out the Frenchman's work*'.[41] Work on rolling the courtyard and laying the setts continued for over two years.[42]

The large slabs of York-stone paving for the raised terraces were supplied by Robert Roper and Sons from their quarries at Eccleshill near Bradford. Each slab had to be sawn to the right thickness and dimension, the edges tooled to provide close-fitting joints.[43] Roper suggested that they should be laid on a bed of ground lime mortar instead of the usual engine ash.[44] The first two truckloads were sent from Leeds in April and May 1904.[45]

Roper operated his saws day and night with a team of men employed exclusively on the Blenheim order.[46] When work stopped for the winter, the cost of York paving stone supplied from April to October 1904 amounted to over £560. Regular deliveries were started again in March 1905 but then dwindled. The last truckload was sent in October 1906.[47]

North View of Blenheim Palace, by C.W. Radclyffe. Note the pedestals marking the entrance to the kitchen court. ↑

Some of the paving work on the north courtyard was undertaken by H.A. Tolley, a Bladon-based builder.[48] Other local contractors were also employed. The most important of these were the Groves brothers, stone merchants at the Taynton and Guiting quarries. The quarry at Taynton had been one of the many sources of freestone for the building in Vanbrugh's time.[49] Taynton stone was employed again by Duchêne for the courtyard restoration – for the plinths, the ashlar walls and copings.

In March 1904, forty tons (40.6 tonnes) of yellow chippings, specially broken down to size from selected quarried stone, were ordered for the four large inset gravelled panels.[50] The Duke constantly issued instructions from London to his Agent at Blenheim, *'please remember that you will have to roll one of the panels before you put on to it the yellow-stone on which we have decided, but you must not use a heavy roller, otherwise you will spoil all the setts at the side of the panel'.*[51] Suitable blocks of stone were also supplied by Mr Groves for the carved pedestals and urns. They were sculpted to the same dimensions and pattern as those provided by Chambers and Yenn for the 4th Duke. After 'Capability' Brown had grassed over the court, two pairs of pedestals had been placed, near the archways to the kitchen and stable courts. The 9th Duke now had several others made, and positioned exactly as illustrated in the old engravings, some with urns on top.

In the restoration of Vanbrugh's powerful theatrical composition, where the bridge had been built to the same height as the forecourt so that the sprawling panorama of the house remained majestically in view while driving to the entrance, the 9th Duke decided to modify the northern approach. First, the ha-ha to the north of the great court was formed into a large bastion, recalling and celebrating Vanbrugh's predilection for this distinctive shape.[52] The facing stone for the sunken wall was also supplied by the Taynton and Guiting quarries.[53] New North Gates were then commissioned. These were made to Duchêne's design and measurements by L. Bergeotte, a French ironwork specialist, winner of the Medaille d'Or at the 1900 Exposition Universelle in Paris. The gates were finished in mid-July 1906, when the Duke visited Bergeotte's workshop near the Arc de Triomphe, examining them before they were dispatched and installed.[54]

The bastion-shaped wall created by the 9th Duke of Marlborough. ↑
© Private Collection

The final change made to the north approach was in the layout of the road itself. Vanbrugh's original route had been built in a straight line from the Ditchley Gate to the front steps of the house. Subsequently both 'Capability' Brown and Benjamin Read had redirected the road, to meander through the park and around the lake before reaching the entrance court. The 9th Duke altered the road once more. Retracing Vanbrugh's initial route for much of its course immediately north of the Column of Victory, its direction was then turned in a sudden sharp bend before joining Brown's route around the lake once again.[55]

Additionally, from 1896 to 1914, the northern avenue was completely replanted with English elms.[56] However, the shape of the central section was changed from Vanbrugh's original elliptical layout to a large diamond-shaped feature instead, *'enabling the passer-by to look down two sides of the square in his progress. These trees have been planted with great care and at considerable cost… It would be a pity if any of them were ever cut down as the idea of the double avenues is to protect the trees from the wind… These avenues are eight in number, i.e. 4 double row avenues… meant to grow together giving at a distance the effect of one line of trees instead of two.'*[57]

The North Gate was made in Paris by L. Bergeotte in 1906. ↓

In 1901, the 9th Duke transplanted limes and elms in the eastern avenue along the route to the Hensington Gate. The limes were removed after fifteen years to establish the avenue entirely with elms. Actively managing timber as a cash crop, between 1893 and 1931 he planted (and sometimes transplanted) over half a million trees and shrubs throughout the estate, imposing new belts and clumps on the Brownian landscape and greatly increasing the numbers of trees with coloured foliage, such as purple beech (which had been introduced into Blenheim Park by the 6th Duke).[58]

This aerial view of Blenheim Park reveals many interesting features, notably the 9th Duke's redirected road and replanted North Avenue with its distinctive diamond-shaped central feature. The uneven inside edge of 'Capability' Brown's perimeter belt can be seen in the distance. ↑

Delighted with the results Duchêne had produced in restoring Vanbrugh's north court, the Duke paid tribute to his accomplishment, 'you rebuilt that Court Yard and so well did you do it that no one has ever suspected that it did not form part of the original building'.[59] However, apart from the courtyard project, the architect was also kept busy in creating a new layout for the Italian Garden along the east front of the building.[60]

Since Waldo Story's fountain had been placed within the central flower bed of the Italian Garden in 1899, no other changes had been made. In January 1904 a copy of the original Italian Garden plan was made, to furnish Duchêne with the dimensions and layout of the ground he was to modify.[61] Duchêne completely altered the garden. A new circular pool was created around the fountain, providing a focal point for four large symmetrical *parterres de broderie*. In each parterre quarter, a series of interlacing patterns was formed with low, clipped box hedges offset by red sandstone gravel.[62] Retaining a long stretch of sculpted yew topiary near the Orangery, a similar line of hedging was established on the opposite side, previously open to the south lawn. Having strengthened the formality of his design through the existing interplay of levels, Duchêne held it together with enclosing walls of clipped hedges on three sides. However, while straight lines framed the garden, the patterning within the parterres comprised complex symmetrical curved and elliptical scrolls, including the swelling form of the *cosse de pois*, a distinctive early baroque motif. Each parterre quarter was seasonally planted with flowering shrubs. Soldani's bronze statues provided the finishing touch when they were brought out once more from the Great Hall of the Palace into the corners of the renewed Italian Garden.

The newly laid-out Italian Garden with formal symmetry in the *parterres de broderie*, designed by Achille Duchêne. ↗→
© Private Collection

Consuelo, Duchess of Marlborough, had always considered that her marital home possessed a certain stately grandeur. Blenheim impressed one, she said, *'by its immense size and by the beauty of its situation and surroundings'.*[63] However, by 1908 when the Italian Garden was completed, Consuelo was no longer at Blenheim to admire the new view from the windows of the private apartments.[64] Since their marriage had failed, the Duchess had moved to Sunderland House.[65] Although this was perhaps the most significant personal adjustment made by the family, it was not the only one. With the outbreak of the First World War it became apparent that country house life would change irrevocably.

The Duke had 1,000 acres (405 ha) of parkland pasturage ploughed up to grow wheat. The use of steam-powered mowers ceased, but sheep ensured the lawns were kept short. Cabbages were planted in the flowerbeds. Timber was sold from the woods around the estate. Every non-essential project was stopped.

The war also heralded the end of the deer in the park. Their numbers had already dropped from 5,000 in the early eighteenth century to around 3,000 by 1781. The 6th Duke had regularly slaughtered many animals, distributing the venison among labouring villagers and the poor. Now, through the war years, the entire herd was eliminated *'in the interests of food supply'.*[66] To relieve the shortage of meat, the Duke put 500 head of cattle at the disposal of Lord Rhondda, the Food Controller. *The Times* reported that *'the national food problem may not have been greatly lessened by these practices, but it was a patriotic gesture'.*[67]

The Italian Garden in spring

The Italian Garden is now planted with daffodils in the spring. Every summer, orange trees are brought out, greenhouse cultivated fuscias are put into terracotta pots, and geraniums and pink roses planted in the beds. When the garden was remodelled in the early 20th century, the floral displays were more abundant.

A man of cultivated taste and a connoisseur, the 9th Duke continually strived to improve his ancestral home. 'Blenheim', he wrote, 'as Marlborough's descendants have maintained it, is the most splendid relic of the age of Anne, and there is no building in Europe, except Versailles, which so perfectly preserves its original atmosphere, and so adequately enshrines the memory of the man for whom and for whose victory it was called into being.'[68] His personal contribution in enhancing its unique character was not insignificant. In 1924, the Duke ambitiously planned to transform the scene to the west of the house from an uninspiring lawn sloping down to the lake into a magnificent scheme of terraces, boldly connecting the architecture of the Palace with the water and deliberately linking Vanbrugh's building with Brown's landscape. Consuming his time and energy for almost a decade, this project would be his most splendid legacy.

He turned once more to Achille Duchêne for an inspiring design. It was clear from the outset that the irregularity of the terrain became an integral part of Duchêne's layout. Plans were discussed and revised several times by April 1925, when the architect produced a scheme for six terraces leading from the Palace to a landing stage on the lake.[69] The sight lines from the house and each of the terraces were directly aligned with the lake. As excavation and building work progressed, the complicated geology of the site required many adjustments to be made, but with each new proposal, the primary intention, to create a scheme of water suspended over water, was maintained.

The 'crooked lawn' to the west of the house (c.1924) ↑ before it was dramatically transformed into the Water Terrace Garden. ↓ Falling sharply down to the bank of the lake, the sloping ground necessitated complex design, elaborate engineering and difficult earth-moving operations. Duchêne's description of his composition underlines the importance of 'Capability' Brown's lake to the scheme: 'The technical aspect was so closely studied as to enable a person viewing the terrace gardens either from the house or from the gardens themselves, to believe that each terrace terminated in the lake'. It took six years for the terraces to be completed; the Duke cautioned against assuming 'that this work was simple. That any architect could have done it. The result is the combination of Brains, knowledge of technique and culture of two men working in harmony'.

In contrast to the work on the north court where heavy machinery had been employed, the difficult sloping terrain to the west was judged to be too narrow with too many outcrops of limestone. Initially, all the digging and levelling was proposed to be done using manual labour and horse-drawn carts, but the chosen contractor, Aubrey Watson Ltd., agreed to provide a steam navvy for the excavation, the excess earth being carried away in tipping wagons to locations within the park.[70] Accommodation for over thirty men was arranged in rooms above the stables.[71] After contracts were signed at the beginning of September, ground was broken on 12 October 1925.[72] However, although the initial works progressed smoothly, subsequent complications on site resulted in continual modifications to the architect's design, causing frustration all around.

There is no doubt that Duchêne was as eager as the Duke for the project to be a success.[73] Their relations were always cordial, their mutual respect increasing over the years even though the two men did not always see eye to eye. Their surviving correspondence includes details of the building work, as well as their own particular views on the art

The 9th Duke's second wife, Gladys Deacon (1881–1977). ↑
© Private Collection

of decoration and the effect they were aspiring to achieve in creating the terraces. They had been to Versailles together, to examine the effects of the water and lines of vision.[74] Duchêne also made regular visits to Blenheim Palace, occasionally to explain technicalities to the site engineers, but more often to discuss details of his decorative schemes and drawings with the family. He got on well with the Duke's second wife, the beautiful and intelligent Gladys Deacon, who took an active interest in the progress of the new garden, conversing with him fluently in French.

Duchêne produced an inspirational and compelling design which more than adequately tackled the Duke's concerns in integrating both the garden and the baroque architecture of the house with the romantic backdrop of Brown's lake and contoured landscape: *'The problem for Monsieur Duchêne is to make a liaison in decoration… between the façade of Vanbrugh and the water line of the Lake made by Brown. To reconcile these conflicting ideas is difficult. The difficulty is not diminished when you remember that the façade of the house is limited and the line of the Lake is limitless.'*[75] It was apparent by the end of the year that Duchêne had skilfully addressed this main concern, *'I must congratulate you on the work which has been done on the Terrace. It is certainly a stroke of genius on your part bringing the water line up to the first Terrace. I certainly should not have thought of this idea myself and I doubt any English Architect would have thought of the idea.'*[76]

Although the Terrace closest to the house (Terrace 1) was proving to be a success, the Terrace farthest away (Terrace 6) presented real problems. In December 1925 the water in the lake was partially let down in order to establish how the foundations for the landing stage would be built.[77] Earth from the excavation of Terrace 1 had been dropped into an unidentified *'hole by the lake in no man's land'*.[78] However, on contact with the water it

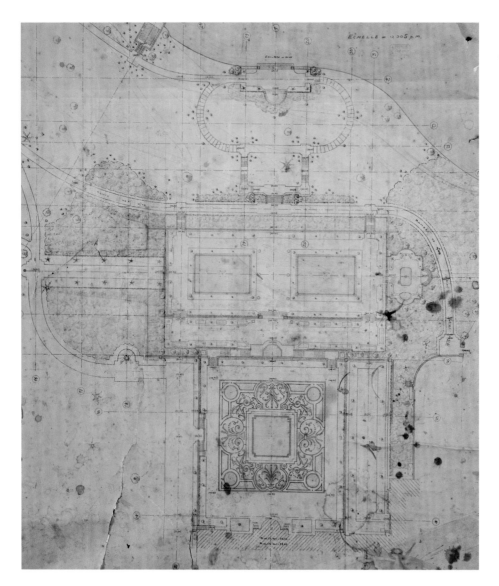

Duchêne's initial plan for a scheme of six terraces. ←

turned into a syrupy mess providing anything but a strong foundation.[79] The difficulty was compounded as the natural bed of the River Glyme ran along the shoreline of this section of the lake, making it the area of fastest flow.

Not wishing to diminish the scheme in any way but afraid that the earth needed to build the landing stage would slide into the middle of the lake, the Duke requested Duchêne to consider revising his plans, encouraging him to *'try and inspire in them a feeling of joyousness, for joy means the birth of everything; of spirit, of hope and aspiration. With that tinge of melancholy in your temperament you are inclined to be sombre and therefore severe. Vanbrugh has faults but 'panache'. Monsieur Duchêne is faultless but he must also remember to be human'.*[80]

Achille Duchêne (1866–1947). →

The south wall of the upper terrace, constructed 'in solid cement'. →→

With the architect still grappling with the problem of extending the terraces beyond the lake shore, work continued on the upper terrace. In January 1926 a wall 'in solid cement' was constructed along its southern edge to frame the terrace on one side, with short flights of steps connecting it to the south lawn. Clipsham stone was chosen for the wall facings as it was considered a good match with the Palace's west front (although to contain costs the Duke had initially suggested using old stone).[81]

An unusually harsh winter with heavy snowfall and severe weather conditions not only caused delays to the work but also impeded travel. Duchêne, who was expected from France at the very beginning of 1926, could only arrive on site in February. In the meantime, two proposals – to support the terrace and landing stage in the lake by sinking wooden piles, or by building reinforced concrete walls – had been considered and rejected. While admitting that his ambitious scheme for six terraces was no longer feasible, the architect remained resolute. Reviving an earlier idea, it was now agreed that only two terraces would be constructed within the existing ground to the lake shore. However, despite the quick decision, this was a major revision to the project and certain problems still needed to be overcome. All the sight lines required adjustment so as not to affect the visual impact from the windows of the house. Duchêne also insisted on making the outer edge of the second or lower terrace parallel with the Palace. For this reason, and to contain landslips, he considered reinforcing the bank of the lake with a wall. Constructed just beyond the existing shoreline, the wall would be supported with excavated earth (tipped over it on the lake side), forming a sharp gradient down to the water.[82]

However, the Duke objected to altering the lake shore in any way. Describing 'Capability' Brown as *'a consummate Artist'*, he judged the contours and banks of the water to have been executed with all *'the skill of the romantic period'*.[83] Duchêne rose to the challenge by removing enough earth along the lake shore to draw it back by about six feet (2 m), then building a toe wall and tipping earth over it to the original outline. To all outward appearances, Brown's lake shore remained untouched. Additionally, with dramatic results, he significantly dropped the level of the lower terrace.

IF YOU STUDY THIS PICTURE AND COMPARE IT WITH THE FINISHED WORK ON THE TERRACES, YOU WILL REALISE THE IMMENSE INFLUENCE I HAD OVER THE ARCHITECT IN MAKING THE EFFECT OF THE TERRACE CLASSICAL IN APPEARANCE, AND HOW I SUCCEEDED IN DESTROYING THE FRENCH MIDDLE CLASS VIEW OF A FORMAL GARDEN.
MARLBOROUGH

In building the terraces, twenty five thousand cubic yards (19,114 m³) of earth were moved and a range of materials (including stone, concrete and reinforced cement) were used. The Duke made daily inspections whenever he was at Blenheim and often raised objections when things were not progressing as they should. The engineer, Fred Rowell, and the foreman, Mr Tompkins, found their work carefully scrutinised and repeatedly criticised. The Duke's uncompromising remark that *gardens were not like railway embankments* made the difference in approach unmistakable: for the contractors the construction was a complex engineering project, but for the Duke it was an *'artistic earthwork'*.[84] Through the skill of his architect, the 9th Duke of Marlborough was able to create a strikingly original new garden. Achille Duchêne constantly reworked every proposal, striving to attain perfection in his design.[85]

Contrary to popular belief, and despite being included in a drawing of the terraces, Duchêne rejected the idea of fountains for the basins. While admitting that they might provide a certain architectural element, he considered the fountain feature to be irrelevant to Blenheim's landscape.[86] Acutely conscious of the view beyond the garden, Duchêne proposed that the water basins of the upper terrace be surrounded by greenery in the form of box hedges or lawn so that the basins would mirror the lake and the greenery echo the undulating foliage on the opposite bank.[87] This firmly adhered to his precept of keeping tradition alive *'by renewing its expression.'*[88] By the end of February 1926, the architect had further developed his ideas for the upper terrace, changing the basin from a large square shape with small round pools in each corner, to a more complex design incorporating different levels within the square.[89]

Duchêne's revised proposal for the Water Terraces, to which many further adjustments were made. On the lower terrace, the shape of the basins was altered and obelisks added. The design for the niches in the retaining wall was dramatically modified, but the most significant amendment was made to the pools of the upper terrace. ↑

Earth being removed after the retaining wall was constructed. ↑

Regardless of its form, and whether it consisted of still pools or had animated effects, the creation of water was, according to Duchêne, the most difficult part of any design.[90] The technicalities of piping a sufficient flow to and channelling the discharge of water from the basins also needed to be addressed. Duchêne contacted the men in charge of the waterworks at Versailles and at Vaux-le-Vicomte.[91] A Monsieur Mercadier visited Blenheim in May and again a month later.[92] It was thought at first that the estate reservoirs would provide an adequate source of water to supply the basins. However, as some of the pumps and hydraulic equipment functioned through centrifugal force, the water had to be completely clean and silt-free.[93] Duchêne was uneasy about clouding which might adversely affect the perfection of the terrace pools, where clarity of water was essential.[94] The Duke therefore suggested supplying pure spring water directly from Rosamund's Well, which, by extending the hydraulic system, could be carried through pipes across the lake and along the valley at the rate of 4,840 gallons (22,000 litres) a day.[95] Although Duchêne subsequently brought in an expert in hydraulics, the £2,500–£2,700 price tag was not the only reason why the Duke postponed installation.[96] More importantly, the Duchess had expressed a view that the basins were too small in proportion to the façade of the house, which made it apparent that the design would have to be modified.[97]

While awaiting these amendments, work began on the lower terrace, a few trees being removed before the ground was staked out.[98] The increased drop of this terrace necessitated the building of a substantial retaining wall. Duchêne's design also ingeniously allowed the lower terrace to be visible or disappear, depending on one's viewing location within the garden. Work on building the retaining wall began in March 1926, the excavation down to foundation level taking about a month. Activity on site increased substantially that summer.[99] Constructed in reinforced concrete to a thickness of 15 inches (38 cm), the wall had to sufficiently withstand the pressure of the upper terrace.[100] Once this was achieved, the remaining earth of the slope down to the lake was removed and carted away.

Initially, the architect suggested that the wall should be entirely faced in stone with three decorative niches in the centre.[101] In order to support the stone facings and ornamentation, iron ties had been embedded along its entire length. After discussions with the Marlboroughs, the decoration was expanded to five niches intersected with caryatids[102] and soon afterwards Duchêne requested that the *'photographs of the caryatids'* should be urgently sent to him.[103] Even though there is no specific mention of the caryatids in question, it is difficult to imagine that the design would echo anything other than the decoration on the upper level of the semi-circular bow window of the Palace. Once again, it is apparent that the entire design was developed around sight lines: the upper level of the Palace was the only part of the building visible when standing in front of the retaining wall.

The niche and caryatid decoration of the retaining wall directly reflects the upper section of the west front of the Palace. ↑↓

Unlike its eastern counterpart, the bow window on the west front of the Palace incorporates six caryatids, a pair on either side of each of three round-headed windows. This scheme is reflected in the retaining wall where six caryatids flank five niches. In addition, the stonework surround of each niche is almost directly copied from the round-headed windows on the top row of the rusticated towers flanking Vanbrugh's building.

The lead sphinxes on the lower terrace were modelled by Henry Ward Willis in the early 20th century. The face on each sphinx represents the portrait bust of Gladys Deacon, second wife of the 9th Duke. Gladys was a great beauty with blonde hair and startlingly blue eyes. Striving for a perfect Grecian profile, she experimented with early plastic surgery but suffered ill effects when a paraffin wax injection into the bridge of her nose slipped into her chin. The wax had to be cut out in four places along her jaw, ruining her looks. Gladys loved the gardens at Blenheim and played a part in the building of the Water Terraces, where she is fittingly represented. ↓

However, although Duchêne had assured the Duke that his design would be in the spirit of Vanbrugh, his initial proposal lacked sufficient meaningful undertones and did not entirely satisfy the Duke's exacting tastes.[104] Subsequently altered to include six figures whose muscularity supported the parapet, the caryatids provided movement (an essential ingredient of baroque decoration), while conveying an impression of strength and a resonance of heroic grandeur appropriate to Blenheim Palace.

By mid-June 1926, the ornamentation was expanded to include lead sphinxes flanking a short flight of steps near the niches.[105] Rather mysteriously, instead of a conventional human face, the Duchess's features were reproduced on the heads of both figures. More used to Parisian diversions, Gladys often relieved the tedium of her life by occupying herself in the gardens. Over the past two years, she had modified the 5th Duke's Rock Garden on the rising ground behind the cascade, enlarging the garden over the dam embankment by extending the sequence of boulders along the shore of the lake to end in a small grotto.[106] On one occasion when she went down after unusually wet weather, she discovered water from the lake overtopping the embankment. Calling for assistance, disaster was narrowly averted but the boulders over the embankment had to be removed and only the grotto remained. A keen amateur photographer, the Duchess's record of the work on the Water Terraces is not merely an invaluable source of information today, but was useful even in her own time: she sometimes sent photographs to Duchêne in Paris, enabling him to follow the progress of the project.[107]

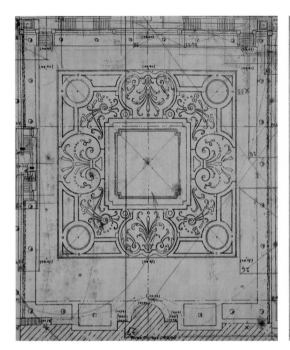

The draughtsmen in the architect's Paris office produced such detailed plans that the contractors often faced difficulties in following them exactly.[108] Additionally, their scaled metric measurements had to be tediously converted into imperial ones for the workmen. Much of the correspondence with the Duke focuses on the minutiae of these drawings, a good example of which is the half-page explanation of the precise proportions of rustication for the wall.[109] Nothing was left to chance. Even though he controlled the project from a distance, Duchêne expected perfection. He repeatedly stressed the importance of his design being *followed to the letter*.[110] Having produced a scheme of great originality and imagination which represented the character of the location, he saw it as his responsibility to ensure its meticulous execution so that there were *'no surprises'*.[111] Urging the Duke to have confidence in his experience as the best guarantee of a successful outcome, he refused to allow any unauthorised changes.[112] Like Vanbrugh and Hawksmoor before him at the time the Palace was first constructed, Duchêne was remarkably proprietary about his Water Terraces.[113] However, in contrast to the two earlier architects, he was rather better paid, receiving 10% of the total costs of construction, plus fees for journeys from France to England when personally attending the site.[114]

Exact planting schemes in and around the terraces were also discussed and decided together. Box hedge *broderies* for the upper terrace would be enhanced

Duchêne's plans for the upper Water Terrace – original ↖ and revised. ↑

A mature Irish yew being transported from the pleasure grounds for transplanting in the Water Terraces. ↓

The construction of the basin pools ↑ and the planting of the upper terrace. ↗ Refined tracery and narrow box broderies were maintained at an optimum height of about 6 inches (15 cm) for the delicate swirling patterns to be properly admired.

with coloured sand or gravel.[115] A narrow, flanking terrace adjacent to the chapel was to be planted with a vertical screen of yews to hide the jumble of utilitarian buildings in the stable courtyard which backed onto it.[116] Similarly, for the lower terrace, a tree-planting scheme of fast-growing varieties interspersed with hardwood saplings was recommended, to ensure an immediate (and future) shielding canopy.[117]

Finalising a unique diagonal design for the water basins of the upper terrace by mid-March 1927, Duchêne proudly considered it worthy of the *'place d'honneur'* in his garden compositions.[118] The design consisted of a large square containing an interconnected series of pools at staggered levels. Water supplied through four slightly elevated corner sections would flow over low stone walls into four intermediary basins on ground level, before finally pouring into a circular, sunken central pool.[119] The repetitive effect of the falling water through each level provided a dynamic element to the design, which, with the impressive concentration of water in the large central pool, played a fundamental role in determining the overall appearance of the terrace. But while Duchêne believed this moving water would give life and animation to the gardens, the Duke was not convinced, *'Bear in mind however, that the situation is grandiose. Limpidity of water is pleasing and possesses a romance. You have got this effect in the basins and in the large area of Water contained by the Lake. Be careful not to destroy this major emotion which Nature has granted to you for the sake of what may possibly be a vulgar display of waterworks which can be seen at any exhibition or public park. Turn all these matters over in your mind when you are at rest in the evening for it is only by thought, constant thought, and mature reflection that artists have left their great works for the enjoyment of posterity.'*[120]

The basin pools were dug out in 1929 and provisionally filled with water to test the effect.[121] Two years later, when construction was completed, the interiors were coloured with a bluish-green tint to enhance the clarity of the water.[122] The basin pools were framed with low box *broderies* and grass borders extending along the outer edges of the

parterre held the design together.[123] The Duke appreciated what had been achieved with the understanding of one who clearly knew the difficulties which had been faced and overcome: he was magnanimous in his praise of the architect, *'Pray tell Monsieur Duchêne that the ensemble… is magnificent… The proportion of the house, the Terrace and the Lake is perfect.'* [124]

To finalise the decorative scheme and, at the Duke's request, Duchêne provided four lead statues (from France) for placement in the corners of the upper terrace. Each statue represented an antique Venus. Better known as the goddess of love and beauty, Venus was also the guardian of gardens, signifying fertility and rebirth. The cult of Venus reached its height in the eighteenth century when it became extremely fashionable to introduce this figure into gardens. The four classical versions chosen for the upper Water Terrace were the Venus de Milo, the Venus of Capua, the Venus Colonna and the Townley Venus.[125]

The basins of the upper terrace were planned on a diagonal axis. ↑ Adhering to the design, the statues were placed at an angle in each corner. ↓ →

Left to right: the Townley Venus, the Venus de Milo, the Venus of Capua and the Venus Colonna. ↑

In following the evolution of the creative process in transforming a grassy slope into a beautiful garden, it is clear that for the Duke a return to history was not an end in itself but an invaluable tool in the completion of the project. The garden needed to satisfy his mind as much as his senses; it needed proper consideration, *'study, knowledge and experience… the sole guide by which a satisfactory result can be achieved'*.[126] This was amply illustrated in the execution of the lower terrace.

The Duke had long had misgivings about its design. Uncertain of being able to supply water to the basins in an area where the geology revealed extensive ridges of limestone, he was reassured by Duchêne that it would be sufficient if the basins were fairly shallow. However, he remained unenthused by the architect's proposals for broad grass edgings containing flowerbeds.[127] Growing impatient and frustrated, the Duke now took matters into his own hands.

A few years earlier he had requested his architect to work *'more in the spirit of Bernini than of Mansard or Lenôtre. On Terrace No. 2, where two basins will one day be dug, I think we can get a magnificent effect by the employment of two obelisks which I have got in the gardens, and which could be built up on half-cut stone, something like the Trevi fountain… The value of the obelisks is this, that they give you the architectural transition between a lateral line of stone and the perpendicular effect of the trees. Pray, therefore, do not despise them. The French have never appreciated a perpendicular architectural effect to create transition between their heavy lateral lines and the perpendicular trees they plant with them'.*[128] However, Duchêne did not approve, concerned that the obelisks exceeded the level of the retaining wall and would therefore be visible not only from the house but also from the upper terrace, spoiling the perfection of his creation.[129] His entire compositional approach had been focused on ensuring *'that the line of vision leading from various points of view does not chance on a motif which, being above or below the line of vision, is partly cut off. It is essential that such motifs should be seen, from these points, in their entirety or, if this is impossible, that they should be completely blocked out'.*[130] But the Duke was immovable regarding the placement of the obelisks on the lower terrace, not wanting to turn *'poetry into prose'.*[131]

This decision necessitated certain adjustments, first to the staircases connecting the upper and lower terraces,[132] where Duchêne decided not to close the view with a wrought iron hand-rail as previously intended.[133] Then, box hedges dotted at intervals were clipped in the shape of round balls, imitating and reflecting Vanbrugh's martial decoration on the roof of the Palace.[134] By August 1927, without consulting Duchêne, the Duke positioned two large lead statues of gladiators in the eastern corners of the lower terrace. He also commissioned Winged Victories for the tops of six cylindrical columns which he placed in front of the niches.[135] Regarding this idea as emblematic of the 1st Duke's military career and talent, the 9th Duke was convinced that his additions provided *'a certain air'* and were a definite improvement on the row of clipped trees proposed in the architect's plan.[136] This decorative arrangement continued the trend established earlier by Sarah, Duchess of Marlborough, in making Blenheim a lasting memorial to the 1st Duke's achievement.

In order to better judge the overall effect of the lower terrace, in July 1927 a model was made of the wall with niches.[137] It may be remembered that the Duke wanted the caryatids to be carved *'in true Italian style'* and that changes were made to their form and projection when the original designs were considered lacklustre and *'not in harmony with the baroque of Vanbrugh'.*[138] In contrast to

One of the six Winged Victories on the lower Water Terrace. ↑

The lower Water Terrace. ↓

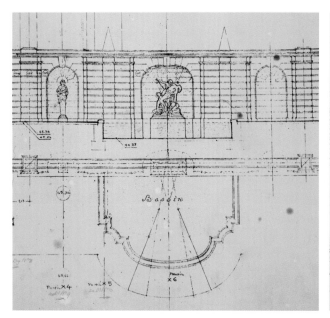
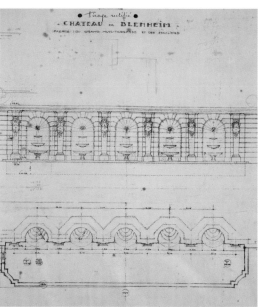

the high value he placed on the stillness of water in the upper terrace, the Duke unambiguously sought movement in the decorative niches of the lower terrace.[139] As a result, Duchêne provided a tiered wall fountain within the bay of each niche. The initial design channelled water through a mask head in the niche wall to cascade over three semi-circular basins of increasing size, but the mask heads were subsequently eliminated and the semi-circular basins transformed into large curved shells, once again adopting a distinctly baroque motif to satisfy the Duke. As this ornamentation was intended to compensate for the increased drop in levels between the two terraces, Duchêne further proposed placing *vases on top of the wall as was so often done in Louis XIV's reign*.[140] Everything was meticulously calculated but without ever giving the impression of effort or artfulness.

Work continued from January to May 1928 on the base of the niches, the masons progressing to a certain height before stopping to await Duchêne's arrival in June.[141]

Two of Duchêne's preliminary drawings for the niches. ↖ ↑

Installation of the shells within the niches ↙ ↙ and the vases on top of the wall. ↓

The three states
of carving →
and a sculptor
at work on the
caryatids in 1929. ↓
The plaster cast
which served as
the prototype can
be seen behind him.
The casts were tried
in situ before the
stone was carved.

The Duke wanted the shells to be made in France, under the architect's supervision.[142] However, the material in which they should be made was still undecided. One proposal was to make them in cement.[143] Another estimate was provided by Jules Visseaux to carve them in Chauvigny stone. Finally, Visseaux moulded them in artificial stone,[144] allowing a ten-week drying period before they were transported to England.[145]

The Parisian statuary firm headed by Jules Visseaux was involved to a great extent in the decoration of the niches, not only in making the shell basins but also in carving the caryatids.[146] With Duchêne's design modifications concluded, Visseaux prepared a life-size plaster model of a niche with two flanking statues.[147] The architect had the model photographed for the Duke's approval before his visit to Blenheim that summer.[148]

The plaster model later served as the sculptors' prototype.[149] The six caryatids were arranged in two groups of three, each group comprising two male figures with a female in between. The group of three on the right balanced and reflected the one on the left, which required three caryatids to be reproduced in mirror image. However, once the tapered blocks of stone had been measured and set into the wall, the carving was deferred, pending the installation of the shell basins in the niches.[150] Duchêne now decided that a trial should be made on one niche to check the proportions of the decoration. Never one to recklessly rush an expensive decision, the Duke wrote back, *'You must be sure that your measurements are correct. I cannot take any responsibility. You are the Architect, I am the Duke. Be sure therefore that any alterations you make are correct… Be sure to make as much effect with this water as possible. It is quite a lot considering it runs all the time.'*[151]

THE BERNINI FOUNTAIN

The Bernini Fountain is a one-third scale copy in marble of the Fountain of the Four Rivers at the Piazza Navona in Rome. The four figures of river Gods represent the Danube (with arms raised), the Nile (head hidden under cloth), the Plata (a moor) and the Ganges (with an oar). They were interspersed with a palm tree, a lion and a horse (attributes of Asia, Africa and Europe).

On the base of the marble obelisk, the inscription (on each side in Latin, Greek, Spanish and Italian) informs us that the model was carved in Gian Lorenzo Bernini's studio in the last years of his life. It was finished after his death in 1680. It was commissioned by Don Gaspar de Haro y Guzman, Duke of Medina de la Torres and Marques del Carpio, Spanish Ambassador to the Holy See. The coats of arms displayed on the model are his. The fountain was known to be in Madrid in 1683 but after his death, his daughter, the Duchess of Alba, sold many works from his collection in order to settle his debts.

It is unclear exactly how the 1st Duke of Marlborough acquired the fountain but tradition has it that the model was a gift from the Spanish Ambassador at the Papal Court. In 1709/10, it was delivered to the Tower Wharf in London, where it was examined by the architect, John Vanbrugh, and the carver, Grinling Gibbons:
'… *I am glad that I can now assure Your Grace the model of the Fountain of Piazza Novona is of Bernini's doing. I shewed it before it went to Blenheim to Mr Gibbons and the best Connoisseurs here who at first sight owned it to be what it pretended, and think it scarce to be Valued. The four figures make the most Valuable part of it, and there is but one of them has received any damage worth naming.*' It was transported by barge to Oxford Wharf and then in several cartloads to Blenheim. Three journeys were recorded: one in January 1709/10, another load in February, and the third and largest part was carted in April.

In one of many decorative schemes he put forward, Nicholas Hawksmoor suggested building a grotto under the Grand Bridge '*finished with Rocks and Shells and a plentifull command of water and how nobily the little fountain of Cavalier Bernini may be placed in it being too tender to stand without doors in the Frosts and violent weather of this Climate*'. The proposal came to nothing.

The fountain was eventually installed by the 4th Duke with the assistance of the architect William Chambers. In January 1774, the Duke requested Chambers to come to Blenheim as he wanted '*much to have this fountain settled*'. The various parts were put out for examination by the sculptor Richard Hayward, and the structure then erected in a large, oval stone basin within the pleasure grounds, near the cascade. Even though it did not universally impress – the Hon. John Byng found the '*sweet spot*' near the cascade '*disfigured by a pitiful Frenchly-adorn'd fountain close to the great water… a paltry, mean piece of Art, amidst the beauties of Nature*' – it was eulogized in a poem by Mavor:

'*You noble fountain, in the valley plac'd*
Allumes my steps and speaks Italia's taste.
There river-Gods, reclin'd at ease explore
A scene more lovely than their native shore…
The marble Gods enjoy their destin'd seat
The spacious basin open at their feet;
Now the grand whole the eyes of taste detains,
And one more beauty decorates these plains.'

By the twentieth century the fountain had become encrusted and damaged from damp and neglect. The 9th Duke wanted to include it in one of the basins on the lower Water Terrace but the figures had lost fingers, toes and even arms. An expert was sent to Italy to compare the surviving parts against the original, in order that Bernini's work could be fully restored. The fountain was repaired by Farmer and Brindley of London in the 1930s, before it was put up in its new location. In the course of the restoration, the figure representing the Ganges was modified to resemble the original in Bernini's Piazza Navona fountain. This figure previously stretched '*out his hand to a serpent crawling and to a shell*' but after restoration, an oar was placed near its base and a palm tree behind.

The Bernini Fountain was first set in a stone basin near the cascade. ↖↖ It was later removed and repaired ↖ before being tried and fixed into its new position on the lower Water Terrace. ←

The lower Water Terrace

The shell basins finally arrived at Blenheim in summer 1929.[152] Once the weather improved in July, Visseaux sent a sculptor over from France. Using geometrical instruments to transfer the measurements from the plaster models directly onto the stone set into the wall, to begin with only two caryatids were carved. Duchêne had asked for the effect to be assessed before the others were undertaken.[153] Each caryatid copied directly from the plaster model was charged at 4,500 French francs, while each mirror-image statue cost 6,300 French francs because of the extra work involved.[154]

The basins of the lower terrace were dug and completed concurrently with those on the upper terrace. However, for the lower terrace the architect expressed no requirement for intricate box broderie – a much simpler arrangement was executed instead (clipped bushes, broad grass edgings and rectangular beds of flowering shrubs), because *'on the transversal axis other decorative motifs are established, the power and the interest of which gradually decrease as we move away from the house'*.[155] Nevertheless, the lake remained the most powerful link with the lower terrace, connecting and extending the water of the basin pools into the landscape beyond (see photograph on page 136).

The Bernini fountain was restored and installed in the north basin of the lower terrace. As had been done so often before, the effect was tried before being finalised. It was balanced on the other side by a second obelisk, built up on a pink granite base roughly cut to mirror its shape and size. The inscription placed on this obelisk was a tribute to the years of labour devoted to creating the water terraces:

> THESE TERRACES OCCUPIED SIX YEARS IN
> CONSTRUCTION TWENTY FIVE THOUSAND
> CUBIC YARDS OF EARTH BEING REMOVED
> THEY WERE ADORNED BY STATUES FROM
> THE GREEK AND BY WATERS DRAWN
> FROM THE WELL OF FAIR ROSAMUND.
> **TO THE GENIUS OF THE ARCHITECT**
> **BY THE KNOWLEDGE OF THE DUKE**
> CAROLO DUCI FILII AMANTISSIMI

With the completion of the Water Terrace Garden in 1932, the west front of the house was at last in harmony with the rest. The 9th Duke of Marlborough's final garden scheme was a remarkable endeavour and an indisputable triumph.

10 *Changing Gardens*

PUBLIC OPENING &
A FOCUS ON THE FUTURE

The Secret Garden. ←
© Richard Cragg

The 9th Duke did not live sufficiently long to enjoy the new Water Terrace Garden. On his death, just two years after its completion, Winston Churchill wrote of his cousin and closest friend, *'always there weighed upon him the size and cost of the great house which was the monument of his ancestor's victories. This he conceived to be almost his first duty in life to preserve and embellish. He sacrificed much to this… but he succeeded and Blenheim passes from his care in a finer state than ever.'*[1]

During the Second World War 400 boys from Malvern College occupied Blenheim Palace for a year. They had lessons in the Great Court (where a number of utility huts were erected), played football on the south lawn, and helped around the gardens. ↓

John Albert ('Bert'), 10th Duke of Marlborough, moved to Blenheim Palace from Lowesby in 1934. As his father had done during the First World War, the 10th Duke contributed in his turn to the 1939–45 war effort – in its first year, four hundred boys from Malvern College occupied the State Apartments, and subsequently the Intelligence Service (MI5) moved a part of their headquarters to the Palace, which remained their base until 1944. A section of the Ministry of Supply was also located at Blenheim while the park was used by the Home Guard and later housed a division of Canadian soldiers.[2] In 1942, the Food Minister gave the Duke permission to sell pike, perch, tench and eels fished from the lake. The grounds reverted to producing a regular supply of food, with much of the northern park turned to arable rotation land.

Once the paraphernalia of officialdom had been removed, the radical change in the economic and social climate after the Second World War, combined with the increased burden of taxation, caused the 10th Duke to allow tourist traffic into the house on a hitherto unprecedented scale.

When the Palace opened to the public on 1 April 1950, the future was still very uncertain.[3] However, after welcoming roughly 100,000 visitors at launch (at two shillings six pence each) and topping the list of stately home visitors in 1951, the preservation of the historic building and its park was to some extent assured.[4]

Tom Page, the gardener at Lowesby, had accompanied the family to Blenheim and brought a good stock of plants with him. He took charge of the greenhouses with six men, entrusting the pleasure gardens to the care of Fon Hollis and his staff of eight.[5] Once the house opened to the public, visitors were accompanied around the Kitchen Garden on payment of sixpence.[6] Routines were then established that are still followed today: box hedges were trimmed every August, first in the Italian Garden followed by the Water Terraces; yew hedges were clipped in September before the first frosts. The greenhouses were usually stocked with fuchsias, pelargoniums, gardenias, chrysanthemums and orchids but, in line with the Duke's seasonal calendar, begonias were produced during the shooting season; carnations, delphiniums and white peonies for Ascot. Regular supplies of choice vegetables from the Kitchen Garden usually included peas, runner beans, tomatoes, asparagus, sprouts, lettuce, leeks, spinach, potatoes, onions and cabbage. Apple trees were planted in the orchard, soft fruits (morello cherries and plums) trained along the walls, and strawberries were forced.

John Albert ('Bert'), 10th Duke of Marlborough (1897–1972). ↑

Tourists flocked to Blenheim Palace when the 10th Duke opened the house in 1950. ↖
© Private Collection

The annual trimming of hedges in the Italian Garden. ↓
© Private Collection

The 10th Duke overseeing work on his Private Garden. ↑

Gordon Masters, the present Foreman of the Kitchen Garden. ↓

Every September a supply of runner beans, peas and plums were delivered to the chef for deep freezing.[7]

With visitors overrunning the grounds from April to October every year, the 10th Duke had a new garden created to provide him with some private outdoor space. Initiated in 1954 as the result of a legacy, it would occupy him for the rest of his life. The new garden, called the Private Garden, was established to the south-east of the Palace, on a three-acre plot (1.2 ha) bordering the 5th Duke's arboretum. The mature trees gave structure to the arrangement of water and winding paths, as well as the garden's planting. In creating the layout, the Duke was mainly assisted by Bob Deacon although Arthur Wilkinson was given the task of bringing some large boulders across from Duchess Gladys's Rock Garden.[8] According to Deacon, *'when His Grace used to come back from London, he would leap out of the car and head straight for his garden, arriving there even before his standard could be raised at Flagstaff Lodge to announce his return'.*[9] The 10th Duke knew his plants and enjoyed supervising the men. Several woodland species were moved into the garden on his instruction.[10] Soil was brought in from Bladon Heath to promote the growth of rhododendrons and pieris.[11] In February 1961 a fully grown juniper tree was transplanted, and, by 1967, lupins, cytisus, *Azalea mollis*, *Primula acaulis*, meconopsis, polyanthus, forget-me-nots and violas had been planted by the gardening staff.[12]

On the 10th Duke's orders, six white marble termini were repositioned in the exedra (near the Private Garden). The statues had been brought out from the arcades of the Great Hall in the Palace.[13] They included Bacchus, Minerva, Hercules and Pan (made *c.*1772 by the sculptor Richard Hayward), but were later returned to the Hall by the present (11th) Duke.[14] The abundance of flowering shrubs throughout the grounds offered a burst of colour in spring and summer. Roses were usually grown on the lower Water Terrace; roses and irises in the Rose Garden. As far as tree planting was concerned, the 9th Duke's record was a hard act to follow.[15] Nevertheless, beech trees were introduced near

Fishery Cottage and spruce and Douglas fir near North Lodge. The poplars along the Glyme meadow were pruned and the cypresses on the Water Terraces tied (they had to be brought back to vertical since they were leaning at a dangerous angle). From the 1950s belts of softwoods were introduced into the park for purely commercial purposes.

Roughly ten years after public opening, the Model Railway Club requested the Duke's permission to construct a wooden track model railway in the grounds, which when completed in mid-August, was the second longest in Britain.[16] It operated every weekend, to the great delight of younger visitors and train enthusiasts. But in the late 1960s an even greater spectacle was organised: a newly fashionable form of outdoor entertainment – *the son-et-lumière* – was offered to visitors in the evenings. With seating arranged on the south lawn, the show was centred on the south front of the Palace and the Water Terrace Gardens. The Palace was bathed with multi-coloured lighting and the terraces animated with five floodlit fountains.[17] In less than forty years since their creation, the effect of the 9th Duke's tranquil pools had been changed beyond recognition, as much through the evolution of taste as by commercial necessity, and the stone copings of the fountain basins were so rapidly degraded through the changed flows and pressure of water that the weirs had to be remade within a decade. The spectacle ran from 4 July to 26 September 1969, and the première (in aid of the Red Cross) was attended by Princess Alexandra.[18]

Some years earlier the Italian Garden had also needed renovation. The marble basin of Waldo Story's fountain was cleaned and the bronze figures re-gilded.[19]

The rustic bridge and seat (pictured *c.*1900) were removed in the 1960s. ↙

Archie Illingworth taking delivery of the *Robin*. ↓
© Private Collection

**The old trophies →
flanking the front steps
were replaced to a
modified design. →→**

The pipes feeding the fountain were renewed and, to economise water, a new electric
pump was installed by Jack Hirst, the Palace engineer.[20] All the tree boxes were painted in
a uniform colour – *spruce green* (later changed to *conifer green*). Bob Deacon cleared the
nepita beds and Fon Hollis laid new gravel on all the paths, including the Broad Walk
and the Cedar Walk leading to the Private Garden.[21]

Even though a major programme of repairs would continue over two decades, some
garden features were lost: a small rustic seat and bridge which collapsed in the 1960s
were removed from an island near the cascade. Around the same time, a small motor
boat called the *Robin* was delivered to Archie Illingworth (then in charge of visitor
services). Illingworth had persuaded the Duke to allow him to operate the boat on
the lake, which soon became very popular with visitors, running a brisk trade on hot
summer days.[22] In winter the lake would occasionally offer a different kind of activity:
ice-skaters made the most of the particularly cold weather in March 1963 and again in
the winter of 1978–9 when the water was frozen solid.[23]

**The fountains within
the upper Water
Terrace were installed
by the 10th Duke. ↓**

The impact of water penetration and
freezing weather adversely affected all the
stonework, but particularly smaller outdoor
structures and statuary. The trophies
flanking the front steps (installed by the
9th Duke in the course of the courtyard
restoration) had become so badly worn
that they were completely remade.[24] Some
of the work was overseen by the Marquis
of Blandford, who had long taken an active
interest in the restoration programme
initiated by his father, and which he
continued on inheriting the title in 1972.

In this temple Winston S. Churchill proposed to Clementine Hozier 11th August 1908

This Temple was restored by the eleventh Duke of Marlborough to commemorate European Architectural Heritage Year 1975

The Temple of Diana before restoration. ◄◄
© Private Collection

Winston Churchill (1874–1965). ◄
© Private Collection

Winston Churchill proposed to his future wife, Clementine Hozier, in this temple on 11 August 1908: '*At Blenheim*', he said,' *I took two important decisions: to be born and to marry. I am happily content with the decisions I took on both occasions*'. Winston had made an assignation with Clementine to walk in the Rose Garden after breakfast. However, promptness in the morning was always a struggle – even on this day he was late, which put Clementine seriously out. Seeing her discomfiture, the (9th) Duke sent a note to his cousin and took Clementine for a drive around the park. Later that afternoon Winston and Clementine went for a walk in the garden. In her biography of her mother, the Lady Soames takes up the story: '*Overtaken by a torrential rainstorm, they took refuge in a little Greek temple, which looks out over the great lake. Here Winston declared his love, and asked Clementine to marry him. When in due course the rain shower being over, they emerged from the temple – they were betrothed*'.

To mark European Architectural Heritage Year, in 1975 a major restoration of William Chambers' Temple of Diana was undertaken.[25] After the stone columns, the decorative frieze of the pediment, the roof rafters and plaster ceiling had been repaired, two new plaques were placed inside the temple, one marking the restoration, the other informing visitors that Winston Churchill had proposed to his future wife, Clementine, in the temple on 11 August 1908.

In the 1980s, attention turned to Chambers' New Bridge where several balusters, which were damaged or had in the past been unsatisfactorily replaced with reinforced concrete replicas, were reinstated.[26] Repairs of a more temporary nature were also carried out to the lead statue of the 1st Duke of Marlborough on top of the Column of Victory, where the iron armature supporting the Duke's right leg had rusted, splitting the lead casing. Although steeplejacks (operating off high ladders) re-fixed the lead, the scope of the mending was limited and not altogether aesthetically pleasing.[27]

As the guardian of this vast and diverse historical landscape, the present Duke has to take the long view. He recently initiated a Heritage Management Programme in order to preserve the inspirational quality of 'Capability' Brown's '*lake-and-bridge centrepiece*' and to ensure the survival of the principal elements of the historic park.[28] The plan has certain key long-term objectives – mainly to conserve the ancient oak woods in High Park through natural regeneration, and to initiate a continuous programme of select felling and replanting in the perimeter belt, ensuring the '*trees would have a mixed age structure while retaining their overall mass*'. Drawn up on a two-hundred-year cycle, shorter term action plans within the programme would guarantee the maintenance of

John George ('Sunny'), 11th Duke of Marlborough (1926–). →

the historic landscape and the preservation of its aesthetic effect. This followed an earlier Landscape Restoration Plan drawn up (in conjunction with the Countryside Commission) as a result of the large-scale loss of trees in the park through Dutch elm disease and beech bark necrosis. The north avenue was clear-felled and completely replanted over three years from 1977 with four rows of limes;[29] and the east avenue with alternating planes and limes. Although the range of tree species in the park has been widened, the diversity of planting in the gardens is kept at a minimum, to contain costs at manageable levels. Such control is only possible through the mechanisation of most labour-intensive gardening tasks or by their partial elimination. A clear instance of this policy is evident in the Italian Garden, where only the borders of the *parterres de broderie* and terracotta pots continue to be planted with flowers (daffodils in spring, fuchsias and geraniums in summer).

Orange trees in wooden tubs are placed in the Italian Garden as a supplement to the planting. They traditionally feature in the Great Court as well (here being watered by Peter Glenister). ◄◄

Nathan Hewett tidying the area around the grotto. ◄

Undoubtedly the financial pressures of running a large country house estate (which still remains in private ownership) are several and substantial. However, while the present Duke remains principally engaged in the preservation of its historic elements, this has not precluded him from adding to the landscape. Alterations have been made to Blenheim's gardens by every Duke, without exception, but now there is one significant difference: the current usage of the grounds (as a recreational venue attracting hundreds of thousands of tourists every year) has acquired a primacy over fashionable trends or personal tastes. Therefore, when the present Duke made his own contribution by creating the new *'Pleasure Gardens'*, incorporating a butterfly house, a lavender and herb garden, and a maze, he established a large garden complex, which, for the first time ever, was conceived primarily for the enjoyment of Blenheim's visitors rather than its family.[30]

The herb and lavender garden established in front of the butterfly house, which was converted from one of the old greenhouses in 1985. ◄

GARDENERS IN OUR TIME

Trevor Wood joined the gardens' staff in 1981, initially as foreman of the pleasure grounds. He took over as Head Gardener fifteen years later. Today, he is ably assisted by his wife, Hilary, and a staff of ten. Summer bedding is grown from cuttings in the greenhouses every September and planted out in the first week of June of the following year. As in the past, grass cutting and edge trimming are still the most labour-intensive jobs. The grass around the Palace is cut once a week, but the south lawn is mowed twice. The hedge-cutting schedule is fairly fixed too – the box hedges in the Italian Gardens and the Water Terraces are trimmed every June and July, the yew hedges from September to November. The hedges of the maze are the last to be cut, in November, when there are fewer visitors. The work of the entire team of gardeners was recognised in 2008, when Blenheim Palace won the Historic Houses Association/Christie's Garden of the Year Award.

Continuously employed in the gardens since September 1955, the longest-serving staff member is Gordon Masters. Born in Bladon, he joined the gardens' staff as an odd job boy whose duties were no more than hoeing, weeding and digging, to eventually take over from William (Bill) Shingler, foreman of the Kitchen Garden, in spring 1980.

Shingler came to Blenheim in 1936 from an estate at Hexham in Northumberland. Initially accommodated in the Bothy, after marrying he moved to the eighteenth-century Gardener's House. During the war, two land girls called Maisie and Phyllis helped with the lighter gardening, while a couple of German prisoners of war undertook heavier tasks like digging cultivated beds and herbaceous borders and picking fruit off espaliered trees. Estate workers were given a box of vegetables from the Kitchen Garden every week. As foreman of the Kitchen Garden, Shingler was in charge of the boilers which heated the greenhouses (assisted by Cliff Tucker and Jock Burns). He also had to water the greenhouse plants, train peaches and figs to grow up the walls, and look after the vines. The grapes grown at Blenheim have long been prize fruit, repeatedly winning awards for their quality and presentation. On one occasion, on a visit to America, when the 10th Duke was disallowed from carrying grapes into the country, he reputedly ate them at the airport! The 10th Duke inspected the Kitchen Garden every Sunday, accompanied by his Head Gardener, Tom Page. The Duke's younger son, Lord Charles Spencer-Churchill, had his own little patch in the Kitchen Garden which he tended under the supervision of his Nanny.

The present team of gardeners pictured in the lavender garden. Back row, left to right: David Wiggins, Kevin Morris, Matthew Wood, Michael Woodward, Anthony Blowfield and Marc Kelly. Front row, left to right: Christopher Horne, Gordon Masters, Hilary Wood, Trevor Wood. Peter Glenister and Nathan Hewett are not in this photo but pictured opposite.

HOW THE MAZE WAS MADE

The trophies on the roof of the Palace provided the inspiration for the design of the maze.

Levelling and path construction were begun in 1987, before 3,000 yews were planted. The maze was opened to the public in 1991.

Newly planted yew hedges. ↑

Although the origin and purpose of mazes remain obscure, the Marlborough Maze was commissioned in July 1987 as a symbolic hedge maze, reflecting the history and magnificence of Blenheim Palace. It is said to be the second labyrinth created in the grounds, the first being the legendary bower where King Henry II allegedly concealed Fair Rosamund from his wife, Eleanor of Aquitaine, and where, according to the tale, the Queen confronted and eliminated her young rival in 1176.

The opening of the Marlborough Maze was planned to be the highlight in a varied programme of events in 1991, designated *'Year of the Maze'* by the English Tourist Board.[31] The consultants for the project submitted a number of emblematic proposals, but the Duke's final choice was a design inspired by the trophies carved by Grinling Gibbons on the east and west colonnades of the Palace, symbolising the 1st Duke's victory at the Battle of Blenheim.[32] Not for the first time, this signal event was built into the landscape. The lines between family history and national history may be blurred, but for every generation, their ancestor's heroic achievement has remained central to the recognition of their inheritance.

To contain the rectangular outline, the east end of the Kitchen Garden was chosen as the best possible location for the maze. This part of the walled garden had long been neglected and was not being used to its full potential, with only three acres (1.21 ha) (out of eight) being productively planted.[33] Covering 54,390 square feet (5,053 m²), the Marlborough Maze is the world's largest 'symbolic' hedge maze: its shape represents a cannon and cannonballs, trumpets and flowing banners, while at the heart of the maze a large wheel forms the word BLENHEIM.[34]

The original miniature narrow-gauge steam railway, operating between the Palace and the 'Pleasure Gardens'. ↓

Hedge mazes take time to grow and reach perfection.[35] In order to meet the 1991 deadline, work on levelling, weed control, drainage and the construction of paths got under way in autumn 1987.[36] Six-and-a-half thousand feet (2,000 m) of paths were laid by November 1988. More than 3,000 yews (*Taxus baccata*), planted a year later,[37] were chosen because they had the advantage of requiring only one cut a year. Two raised wooden bridges were put in, from where the design could be viewed. The maze site was already linked to the Palace by a small narrow-gauge steam railway which had been operational since 1975.[38]

B.P.R
NEW
FOR
1975

NARROW GAUGE LIVE STEAM RAILWAY OPENS SPRING BANK HOLIDAY WEEKEND AT BLENHEIM PALACE

BLENHEIM PARK STEAM RAILWAY

An extraordinary building in a perfect setting, the centrepiece of the composition here is the combination of 'Capability' Brown's lake and Vanbrugh's bridge. The 11th Duke manages the grounds with care, valuing the historic importance of his ancestral home, now designated a World Heritage Site.

No longer simply the ancestral home of the Marlborough family, Blenheim Palace was by now well established as one of the nation's major tourist attractions. When the maze opened to the public on 18 March 1991, it was visited by 33,000 people within the first five months.[39]

Apart from its historic garden landscape, Blenheim has also benefited from its association with two of England's greatest national heroes – the 1st Duke of Marlborough and Winston Churchill.[40] In recognition of its exceptional offering, the Palace was designated a World Heritage Site in 1987.[41] There were two main reasons for its inclusion on this prestigious list: essentially because it illustrates *'the beginnings of the English Romantic Movement'* through its 'Capability' Brown landscape, but equally, since it was presented by

the nation to honour the 1st Duke of Marlborough in recognition of his victory in 1704, it is a unique English example of an eighteenth-century European princely residence.[42]

In 2004, another significant historical milestone – the tercentenary of the Battle of Blenheim – was commemorated with the 11th Duke initiating the most recent garden project in the Palace's three-hundred-year history. Since his father's death in 1972, the Private Garden had become wildly overgrown and sadly neglected. A restoration was planned for the 2004 celebrations. However, difficulties with the planting layout and the necessity to provide paths wide enough for wheelchair access soon forced a rethink: it would not be accurately remade but reinterpreted to recapture the atmosphere of the original garden.

Over four months, shrubs were removed and the ground completely cleared. A new network of pools and streams was established, followed by the marking out of paths, placing of rocks and mounding of beds for planting. Designed to look appealingly tranquil in every season, a diverse range of flora and fauna was arranged to provide distinct spaces of shade and shimmer. With the heavy work undertaken in record time by a staff of ten directed by the Head Gardener, Trevor Wood, and his wife, Hilary, the three-acre (1.2 ha) plot was planted and finished as an inspired romantic garden.[43] Renamed the Secret Garden, it was revealed to the public for the first time in May 2004, when the 11th Duke's sister, Lady Rosemary Muir, officiated at the opening ceremony.

In his management of the estate, the 11th Duke has worked determinedly to secure the future of his ancestral home, often reminding us that '*although the Battle of Blenheim was won in 1704, the battle for Blenheim continues…*' Long-term survival taking precedence over all other considerations, the cornerstone of his tenure has been to ensure that Blenheim is passed on to future generations in not merely the same, but in a much better condition.

The lives and passions of ten generations of the Marlborough family have formed the story of the rich, multi-layered and changing landscape at Blenheim Palace. However, it is also a lasting memorial to the talent and artistic ability of the men they employed. In every significant period, the Palace and its surroundings have been conceived as a whole. Each architect and gardener were creatures of their own time: the work they did reflected most major changes of taste as well as the particular preferences of their patrons, whose ability to spend ultimately determined the scope of the work they undertook.

The reconstruction of the Secret Garden in 2003–4. ➔ ↗

The Secret Garden in 2009.

As with any perishable art form, it is impossible to experience the grounds in the same way as they would have been in earlier times. Gradually maturing over the years, they become perceptibly different. Not even the most perfectly kept garden or the most carefully conserved landscape can escape the effects of the decaying processes of Nature. But what has survived is as important as what has been lost. Apart from the family's heritage being as important today as it has ever been, many historic influences still linger in the landscape. The ancient oaks recall the Middle Ages, the cedars provide an air of eighteenth-century stateliness, the Water Terraces and Italian Garden rediscover the merits of formal gardening, while the neo-classical garden temple in which Winston Churchill proposed marriage provides a different kind of historic reminder. It is evident that the past extends into the present and becomes so much a part of us that it shapes what we take pleasure in today and what is handed down to be enjoyed in the future.

Autumn and winter views. ↑↗
© Richard Cragg

Aerial view. ↓
© Roger Humphreys

The historical significance of the site will continue through its important link with the 1st Duke's celebrated victory. Constructed on an imposing scale, the house remains architecturally unaltered since its creation, but there is no doubt that the significant remodelling of the park and gardens make Blenheim Palace unexampled in stateliness, giving it a timeless appeal. The beautifully distinctive form of landscape harmony created by 'Capability' Brown has been fundamentally retained and has become such an essential and undiminished part of Blenheim's character that the overriding legacy is undoubtedly his. The 9th Duke tried to enhance it while the present Duke strives to preserve it.

Visitors to Blenheim will always be served a generous portion of history, but for the vast majority, its primary pleasure is purely visual. Through every season, at different times of day, and in spite of the unpredictable English weather, the gardens and park create the most sublime setting for Vanbrugh's heroic building. While there are many country houses which may be considered magnificent places in which to live, the majesty of Blenheim Palace within its surrounding landscape makes it much more than that. A unique work of collective genius, it remains, as intended three hundred years ago, a national monument.

ACKNOWLEDGEMENTS

I owe grateful acknowledgements to several individuals. First and foremost, to His Grace, the Duke of Marlborough, for allowing access to the Palace collection and archive; for permitting quotations from documents, and for consenting to the reproduction of plans, drawings and paintings.

For allowing the use of manuscript and other collections in their custody or ownership, I thank Hugo Vickers, Peter de Brant, Anne Illingworth, Don and Judith Thompson, Christopher Rayson, Julian Munby, Jessie Lane, Henry Groves, Philip Winterbottom, P. Chemineau, Michel Lachiver, Peter H. Anderson, Matthew Roper, Lucy Brady and William Palmer. For allowing particular photography I am grateful to Rosita, Duchess of Marlborough. John Phibbs kindly offered helpful comments, I owe him many thanks. I am also indebted to Professor Kathleen Lawrence who generously shared unpublished research. Professor Sir John Boardman and Dr Claudia Wagner are thanked for their contributions and for several memorable afternoons spent in the gardens. I am grateful to Jean Ball for sharing her childhood memories and for allowing their publication. Thanks are also due to Jon Culverhouse, Laura Valentine, Lucy Waitt, Nick Cistone, Canon Roger Humphreys, Richard Cragg, Revinder Chahal and Nathalie Roy for their help with images; and to Comte Patrice de Vogüé, Roger Turner, Morgan Feely, David Brown and Cliff Davies for responding to enquiries. Credit and thanks are due to Kaarin Wall and Peter Smith who patiently helped in the preparation of this publication.

For their continuing assistance during several years of research, I am most grateful to the staff at the British Library, the Bodleian Library, the RHS Lindley Library, the Paul Mellon Centre for British Art (in particular Emma Floyd), the National Archives, the Sackler Library, the Earl Gregg Swem Library, the House of Lords Records Office, the National Art Library, the Royal Academy Archive and the Centre for Oxfordshire Studies where Steven Rench and Susan Lisk (Sites and Monuments Research) generously gave their time.

This book would have taken longer to finish without the assistance of several colleagues. I thank Roger File for clarifying certain technical matters. I am particularly grateful to John Forster for facilitating the retrieval of material while the cataloguing of the muniments is still in process. Timothy Mayhew, Heather Carter, Christopher Keeler and Paul Orsi were helpful on many occasions. Last but not least, the entire gardens' staff, but especially the Head Gardeners, Trevor and Hilary Wood, for their unreserved help and support and for allowing me to work on this project in the most congenial environment. There is no one else at Blenheim Palace whose skill or effort is so universally admired and appreciated, by many thousands of people, every day.

NOTES

1 Before Blenheim

1 Mrs George Cornwallis-West, *The Reminiscences of Lady Randolph Churchill*, 1908, 57.

2 The Saxons called it Vubeztob (*Locus silvestris*), J. Skelton, *Engraved Illustrations of the Principal Antiquities of Oxfordshire*, 1823, Wootton Hundred, 21–24; Woodstock is also mentioned in the Domesday Book as one of the five Royal forests in the area – '*Shotover, Stowood, Wodestoch, Cornbury and Wychwood*.'

3 Dr. Robert Plot, *The Natural History of Oxfordshire*, 1677, 349; D.H. Farmer, *St. Hugh of Lincoln*, 1985, 35 – I am grateful to Christine Gadsby for this second reference.

4 Daughter of Sir Walter Clifford, called Fair Rosamund from her depiction as 'Rosa Mundi' – Rose of the World.

5 Bodleian Library, Wood 276b f. 43v.

6 The Wyatt Plot, a Kentish Protestant uprising against Queen Mary I in 1554, led by Sir Thomas Wyatt the younger.

7 British Library, Add. Mss. 61,359, f. 16.

8 House of Lords Record Office, 5&6 Anne, No. 3–3. The acreage was extended in the later eighteenth century after the 4th Duke of Marlborough purchased land adjacent to the southern boundary of the park at Bladon.

2 Formal Parterres

1 British Library, Add. Mss. 19,592 f. 12.

2 The river Evenlode was known as the Bladen until the end of the thirteenth century. The village (Bladon) was named after it.

3 When King Henry II visited Woodstock several members of the royal entourage were granted freehold plots of land near the park gates to build their own lodgings. By 1279, 137 houses were standing. A. Ballard, *Woodstock Manor in the Thirteenth Century*, 445.

4 British Library, Add. Mss. 9,123 f. 35.

5 British Library, Add. Mss. 61,353 ff. 3–4.

6 British Library, Add. Mss. 19,602 ff. 73–75; Add. Mss. 24,327 f. 66; Add. Mss. 61,353 f. 91.

7 British Library, Add. Mss. 61,353 ff. 13, 19. In avenues of trees in three rows, the middle row was planted to offset the gaps in the outer two. The geometry of these avenues depended on the linear spacing of the trees as well as the spacing between the lines. This determined the development of the effect of the tree canopy.

8 The medieval church of St Martin was demolished in October 1802 and a new church built, which reopened in June 1804, consisting of a nave and chancel, paid for by the 4th Duke of Marlborough. Bodleian Library, Ms. Top. Oxon. b.220 f. 89/174; J. Skelton, *Engraved Illustrations of the Principal Antiquities of Oxfordshire*, 1823, Wootton Hundred.

9 Vanbrugh was particularly fond of Roman symbolism, which was used repeatedly throughout the house and gardens. Fortifications '*after the ancient Roman Manner*' – S. Switzer, *Ichonographia Rustica*, 1718, II, 174 quoted in C. Ridgway & R. Williams (Eds.), *Sir John Vanbrugh and Landscape Architecture in Baroque England 1690–1730*, 2000, 51.

10 British Library, Add. Mss. 61,353 f. 19; Add. Mss. 61,428 f. 187; Lawsuits 1724, '*concerned in the designe of and carrying on the worke of the gardens*' cf. D. Green, *Gardener to Queen Anne*, 1956, 100.

11 British Library, Add. Mss. 61,428 f. 86. The Duchess of Marlborough acquired a life interest in the Great Lodge when she was appointed Ranger of Windsor Park by Queen Anne.

12 British Library, Add. Mss. 61,429 f. 11.

13 Blenheim Palace, 1719 & 1709 plans; Bodleian Library, Ms. Top. Oxon. a.50 (r) ff. 1a,b; Ms. North b.24 f. 154.

14 Bodleian Library, Ms. Top. Oxon. a.37* f. 1.

15 Blenheim Palace collection (u/c); Bodleian Library, Ms. Rawl. B. 400e, f. 18. Both specifically show the various vistas.

16 Blenheim Palace, 1709 & 1719 plans.

17 British Library, Add. Mss. 19,592 f. 99v–100v.

18 British Library, Add. Mss. 19,592 ff. 99–100; Add. Mss. 19,593 f. 143; Add. Mss. 19,594 f. 68v; Add. Mss. 19,595 f. 13; J. Woudstra, *The planting of the privy garden*, Apollo Magazine, 2005, 66.

19 S. Switzer, *Practical Fruit Gardener*, 1724, 65.

20 British Library, Add. Mss. 19,595 ff. 44, 102v, 114v; Bodleian Library, Ms. Top. Oxon. c.230 ff. 10v, 28v, 38v.

21 Blenheim Palace, 1709 & 1719 plans; Bodleian Library, Ms. Top. Oxon. a.50, 1a–b; Ms. Rawl. B.400e, f. 18; Ms. Top. Oxon. a 37* f. 2.

22 Bodleian Library, Ms. Top. Oxon. A.50,1a; Ms. Rawl. B. 400e f. 18; British Library, Add. Mss. 61,353 f. 13.

23 Mainly elms. British Library, Add. Mss. 19,597 ff. 85, 95v; Add. Mss. 61,354 f. 115.

24 British Library, Add. Mss. 19,592 f. 99v–100v; Add. Mss. 64,082(c), f. 7.

25 British Library, Add. Mss. 18,556 f. 1.

26 British Library, Add. Mss. 61,353 f. 13; D. Green, *Blenheim Palace*, 1951, 241.

27 British Library, Add. Mss. 19,597 f. 31.

28 J. Macky, *A Journey through England*, Vol. II, 1724, 108; *Ibid*, 1732,124.

29 British Library, Add. Mss. 19,592 f. 100.

30 British Library, Add. Mss. 61,353 f. 177 & seq.

31 British Library, Add. Mss. 61,429 f. 120.

32 British Library, Add. Mss. 61,353 f. 191.

33 British Library, Add. Mss. 9,123 f. 54v.

34 British Library, Add. Mss. 61,353 f. 36–7.

35 Bodleian Library, Ms. Top. Oxon. a.50 (R) f. 3. Whichever plan was adopted, being a sunken garden, steps would have been needed. These were recorded as being unfinished in November 1714 – British Library, Add. Mss. 61,354, f. 28v; Add. Mss. 19,603, f. 46–47.

36 Blenheim Palace Muniments, Plans folder.

37 Bodleian Library, Ms. Top. Oxon. d.173 f. 109.

38 British Library, Add. Mss. 9,123 f. 54; Add. Mss. 19,597 f. 105v; Add. Mss. 19,597 f. 110. An amount of £66:10:6 was paid to Thomas Warren, blacksmith for the 'iron rail made for the East Boundary Wall between the peers'; Blenheim Palace Muniments, John Hughes to Sarah Marlborough, regarding the theft of twenty iron spikes 'in between ye Great Iron Barrs of the Palosodioes'. A palisade was an iron fence.

39 The Victoria History of the County of Oxford, Vol. XII, 1990, 452.

40 British Library, Add. Mss. 19,597 f. 23; Add. Mss. 19,602 ff. 77–78.

41 British Library, Add. Mss. 61,353 f. 19.

42 Bodleian Library, Ms. Top Oxon. a.37* f. 14.

43 British Library, Add. Mss. 61,429 ff. 22, 41, 85, 108, 126, 148, 202; Add. Mss. 61,430 ff. 67, 113; Add. Mss. 61,431 ff. 7, 51, 85.

44 Bodleian Library, Ms. Top. Oxon. d.173, f. 113; Ms. Top. Oxon. c.218, f. 47.

45 New houses – Blenheim, Marlborough House, Wimbledon Park House. Renovations – Holywell House (partly rebuilt), Windsor Lodge, Old Wimbledon House (later demolished).

46 British Library, Add. Mss. 61,353 f. 70.

47 British Library, Add. Mss. 61,354 ff. 1–2; Bodleian Library, Ms. Top. Oxon. a.37* f. 2.

48 British Library, Add. Mss. 61,353 f. 187.

49 British Library, Add. Mss. 19,597 f. 105v.

50 Aldersea was paid £623:15s, British Library, Add. Mss. 19,602 ff. 101, 104; Add. Mss. 19,595 f. 20. The engine house was built by the stonemason Bartholomew Peisley, British Library, Add. Mss. 19,595 f. 84.

51 British Library, Add. Mss. 61,353 f. 13. The watercourse was 3,000 ft (914 m) long, 15 ft (4.6 m) wide and 3 ft (0.9 m) deep.

52 British Library, Add. Mss. 19,592 f. 92.

53 Bodleian Library, Ms. Top. Oxon. c.218, f. 48, 28 September 1710; British Library, Add. Mss. 61,353 ff. 97–v, 111.

54 British Library, Add. Mss. 19,602 ff. 80–81.

55 British Library, Add. Mss. 19,603 ff. 98–99.

56 B. Dobree & G. Webb, The Complete Works of Sir John Vanbrugh, 1928, Vol. IV, 198–205.

57 British Library, Add. Mss. 19,603 f. 35; Add. Mss. 61,353 f. 163; Add. Mss. 61,354 f. 32; Bodleian Library, Ms. Top. Oxon. d.173, 117. In November 1714, the steps of the east flower garden were still unfinished (British Library, Add. Mss. 19,602 f. 47) and the walls and planting of the Great Parterre were also incomplete (British Library, Add. Mss. 61,354 ff. 5/72–76; Add. Mss. 61,353 f. 246).

58 British Library, Add. Mss. 61,355 f. 7.

59 British Library, Add. Mss. 61,353 ff. 167, 169 & seq. Vanbrugh left in 1716 but Wise was at Blenheim until 1719/20.

60 British Library, Add. Mss. 61,463 ff. 154–5.

61 Bodleian Library, Ms. Top Oxon. c.218, f. 44.

62 British Library, Add. Mss. 61,353 f. 62.

63 British Library, Add. Mss. 61,354 f. 44 & seq.

64 British Library, Add. Mss. 61,353 ff. 181 & seq., 205; Sarah Marlborough had offered Vanbrugh the use of High Lodge – 'Mr Vanbrugh to lye at my own lodge if he pleased where everything is convenient' – which made his actions even more difficult for her to understand or accept (Bodleian Library, Ms. Top. Oxon. d.173, 111).

65 British Library, Add. Mss. 61,353 f. 213.

66 British Library, Add. Mss. 61,353 f. 201.

67 British Library, Add. Mss. 61,354 f. 44; Add. Mss. 61,353 ff. 52 & seq., 58v.

68 A wenn was a lump or wart. British Library, Add. Mss. 61,354 f. 44 & seq.; J. Skelton, Engraved Illustrations of the Principal Antiquities of Oxfordshire, 1823, Wootton Hundred, 24.

69 British Library, Add. Mss. 61,429 f. 171; Add. Mss. 19,602 f. 84 & seq.; Add. Mss. 19,603 f. 60.

70 Letters of Sarah Duchess of Marlborough at Madresfield Court, 1875, 107.

71 Work on the arcaded superstructure and the decoration of the bridge was stopped in 1711. British Library, Add. Mss. 61,353 f. 149–v.

72 The Long Gallery had been covered in 1717 but was still a shell which Sarah ultimately finished with Nicholas Hawksmoor's help. The Chapel was consecrated on 4 September 1731.

73 British Library, Add. Mss. 61,354 f. 116. This work was undertaken by Sarah's gardener, John Hughes, c.1720–8.

74 Bodleian Library, Ms. Top. Oxon. d.173 ff. 108, 114, 117; British Library, Add. Mss. 19,603 ff. 46–47.

75 Bodleian Library, Ms. Top. Oxon. d.173 f. 107, 114, 117.

76 Bodleian Library, Ms. Top. Oxon. d.173 f. 108.

77 Bodleian Library, Ms. Top. Oxon. c.218 f. 40.

78 British Library, Add. Mss. 19,603 f. 46–47; Add. Mss. 61,354 f. 82; Bodleian Library, Ms. Top. Oxon. d.173, f. 117.

79 British Library, Add. Mss. 61,353 f. 246.

80 British Library, Add. Mss. 19,597 ff. 76, 85, 93v; NAL, 86NN.2.

81 House of Lords Records Office, Acts 3 & 4 Anne, No. 14–6; 5 & 6 Anne, No. 3–3.

3 Finishing Flourishes

1 Bodleian Library, Ms. Top. Oxon. a37* ff. 1–2; C. Campbell, Vitruvius Britannicus, 1725, Vol. III , Plate 71.

2 Bodleian Library, Ms. Top. Oxon. c.218 f. 55.

3 British Library, Add. Mss. 61,354, f. 115. The lower causeway was the one adapted.

4 Bodleian Library, Ms. Top. Oxon. d.173 ff. 134–5, 168.

5 Bodleian Library, Ms. Top. Oxon. c.351, f .221; NAL, 86NN.2. One contemporary record mentions the cascade as having twelve steps, but this seems unlikely.

6   J. Bond & K. Tillier (Eds.), *Blenheim Landscape for a Palace*, 1987, 80.

7   S. Switzer, *An Universal System of Water and Waterworks*, 1734, Book I, 14; NAL, 86NN.2.

8   Bodleian Library, Ms. Top. Gen. d.14 f. 14v; NAL, 86NN.2; J. Boydell, North West View of Blenheim, 1752; The canal construction was completed by the masons William Townsend and Bartholomew Peisley in September 1724, British Library, Add. Mss. 61,355 f. 13–14v. Bartholomew Peisley junior worked on this scheme, while his father, also named Bartholomew, built the Grand Bridge and the clock tower with John Townsend.

9   British Library, Add. Mss. 61,355 f. 12v–14v; Bodleian Library, Ms. Top. Oxon. d.173, 176; Gough Oxon. 17(1), B, 115.

10   This was used by the male staff for bathing and washing. Female servants were allowed to bathe and wash indoors. At the time these arrangements were in place, the house was only used by the family during the summer months.

11   Bodleian Library, Ms. Top. Oxon. d.173, 176; NAL, 86NN.2,112.

12   Proposal dated May 1722. D. Green, *The Bernini Fountain at Blenheim*, Country Life, 27 July, 1951.

13   NAL, 86NN.2,111.

14   *Letters of Sarah Duchess of Marlborough at Madresfield Court*, 1875, 166.

15   British Library, Add. Mss. 61,354 f. 115; Bodleian Library, Ms. Top. Oxon. d.173, 146.

16   NAL, 86NN.2; *Oxoniensa*, Vol. XXXI, 1966, 145.

17   British Library, Add. Mss. 61,353 f. 240.

18   Bodleian Library, Ms. Top. Oxon. d.173 f. 210.

19   *Transactions of the Birmingham Archaeological Society*, 1887, 10.

20   The petition was made in October 1722. *Transactions of the Birmingham Archaeological Society*, 1887, 9; *The Victoria History of the County of Oxford*, Vol. XII, 1990, 465.

21   British Library, Add. Mss. 61,353, f. 240.

22   The Woodstock Gate cost £512 to build, cf. D. Green, *Blenheim Palace*, 1951, 158.

23   D. Green, *Ibid*, 1951, 162. Fig. 72.

24   Blenheim Palace Muniments, Hawsmoor Drawings No. 6F, 11F, 12F, two more unnumbered; Bodleian Library, Ms. Top. Oxon. a37*f. 12.

25   Blenheim Palace Muniments, Hawksmoor Drawing No. 6F; quotation, D. Green, *Blenheim Palace*, 1951, 277.

26   Blenheim Palace Muniments, Hawksmoor Drawings.

27   Blenheim Palace Muniments, Hawksmoor Drawings, a variant of No.11F.

28   Jeri Bapasola, *Threads of History – The Tapestries at Blenheim Palace*, 2005, 64–5.

29   British Library, Add. Mss. 61,457 f. 38.

30   British Library, Add. Mss. 61,440 f. 64, Add. Mss. 2,540 f. 457; Add. Mss. 61,437 f. 24.

31   H. Colvin, *A Biographical Dictionary of British Architects 1600–1840*, 3rd edition 1995, 490.

32   British Library, Add. Mss. 61, 469 f. 42; Stow Mss. 750, f. 434.

33   British Library, Add. Mss. 38,056 ff. 20–1.

34   British Library, Add. Mss. 61,354, f. 115. The foundations were 7 ft (2.1 m) deep.

35   *The Georgian Group Journal*, Vol. X, 51.

36   *Transactions of the Birmingham Archaeological Society*, 1887, 12–13. Flitcroft delivered the marble in 1730.

37   The west face describes the Act of 1706 which allows the succession through the female line, as well as the bestowing of an annual pension of £5,000 for life. The east and north faces detail the Act of 1704 settling the Manor of Woodstock on the Duke and his heirs.

38   *Oxoniensa*, Vol. XXXI, 1966, 142, 144.

39   Charles Bridgeman was at Wimbledon from 1732 until his death in 1738. G. Scott Thompson, *Letters of a Grandmother 1732–1735*, 1943,169; F. Harris, *The Best Workmen of All Sorts, The Building of Wimbledon House 1730–42*, 1992, 88; R. Milward, *A Georgian Village*, 1985, 43.

40   British Library, Add. Mss. 61,478 ff. 9–12,17–18,31–34,43–44,47–48; P. Willis, *Charles Bridgeman and the English Landscape Garden*, 1977, 46–7; F. Harris, *Charles Bridgeman at Blenheim*, Garden History, Vol 13, No 1, 1–3.

41   *Birmingham & Midland Institute Transactions*, 1884, 15.

42   *Letters of Sarah Duchess of Marlborough at Madresfield Court*, 1875, 145.

4 An Important Transition

1   British Library, Add. Mss. 75,432.

2   British Library, Add. Mss. 61,666 f. 58.

3   Jeri Bapasola, *Faces of Fame and Fortune: The Marlborough Family Portraits at Blenheim Palace*, 2006, 27–32.

4   In 1741. G. Lipscomb, *The History and Antiquities of Buckinghamshire*, 1847, IV, 534.

5   British Library, Add. Mss. 75,432 f. 3; Add. Mss. 75,433 ff. 17, 22,23.

6   The temple was in existence by 1743. On 20 May Lady Hertford wrote to her son Lord Beauchamp: 'We went in the Landau this morning to Langley. We were in the Temple, which I think is very pretty, and the prospect from it of Windsor Castle is I think, a great addition to its charms'. Lady Newdigate describes it in 1748 in her Journal: 'Langley Park, a seat of ye Marlboroughs… a small pretty park in such stands a very elegant temple newly built it is circular stands on eight arches ye room above an octagon ye dome and sides of which are very richly worked in stucco in very high taste. There are three recesses which open to beautiful prospects, ye principal one looks directly upon Windsor Castle which is four miles off, so that on a clear day every part of ye building is easily seen this room is about 20 ft in height and some 18[feet] in diameter'; G. Jackson-Stops, *The Georgian Group Journal*, 1994, 20–29.

7   Mr Salmon, *The Present State of the Universities and of the five adjacent counties*, 1744, 9–10.

8   Mr Salmon, *Ibid*, 5.

9   J. Macky, *A Journey through England*, Vol. II, 1724, 105; *Ibid*, 1732, 121.

10   Blenheim Palace Muniments, G1/10 – 'An account of what yet remains to finish Blenheim'; Bodleian Library, Ms. Top. Oxon. d.173, f. 120; NAL, 86NN.2; British Library, Add. Mss. 19,592 ff. 28v, 42v, 51, 81v, 83, 94; Add. Mss. 19,595 ff. 7v, 102v, 108,114v.

11   British Library, Add. Mss. 75,432 f. 1.

12   British Library, Add. Mss. 75,432 f. 15.

13   House of Lords Records Office, *An Act for providing a maintenance for the Marquis of Blandford during the life of his father the Duke of Marlborough and for rebuilding the Duke's house at Langley, in the county of Bucks*, 1756; British Library Add. Mss. 75,435, f. 39; Add. Mss. 61,668 f. 5.

14   £2,000 allocated annually over five years. The contract for Langley was awarded to Stiff Leadbetter, who had previously worked as a carpenter for the 3rd Duke's uncle, Francis, Earl Godolphin. Leadbetter was paid £5,500 over two years for improvements to the house and the provision of a new orangery. British Library, Add. Mss. 75,435 ff. 25, 33, 46, 59, 67, 70; Add. Mss. 75, 434 f. 168; Add. Mss. 61,668 ff. 100–1. A further payment of £1,140 was made in 1760.

15   British Library, Add. Mss. 61,668 f. 5; Add. Mss. 75,434 f. 180. The large payment of £30,000 was made on 16 April 1756.

16   *A Pocket Companion to Oxford or Guide through the University*, 1759, 115; Bodleian Library, Gough Oxon. 17 (1).

17   Bodleian Library, Gough Oxon. 17 (1), 105,115; Collection CCA, DR1985:0416; Garden History, Vol 15, No.2, 107.

18   Bodleian Library, Ms. Eng. Misc. e. 498, f. 68v. Between 1731–68, the number of plants cultivated in England doubled. The Lombardy poplars at Blenheim were reported to be the oldest in England. When William Gilpin visited in around 1781, he estimated the specimens in the park were approximately 28 years old which implies they were planted in the early 1750s; they were located near Seven Arches Bridge. Slatter (Pub.), 1846, 78.

19   Bodleian Library, Top. Oxon. d.173, f. 172.

20   *The New Oxford Guide or Companion through the University*, 2nd edition, 105; Bodleian Library, Gough Oxon. 17 (1).

21   British Library, Add. Mss. 75,435,ii,13. Further payments were made for Langley in 1759 (£2,000) and 1760 (£2,500). It is likely that the dowager Duchess occupied the house only briefly before her death in October 1761.

22   British Library, Add. Mss. 75,435, ii, f. 3. Charles Arbuckle was paid £10:10s on account in January 1759. His final account for work carried out (including new wallpaper and chairs supplied to High Lodge) was submitted in 1764, which led to the assumption that High Lodge was renovated then. However, the account submitted runs into five pages and includes work at Blenheim, at Marlborough House, at Langley, as well as High Lodge for a total cost of roughly £450. It is therefore more likely that Arbuckle was engaged from 1759 till 1764, when the account was settled. British Library, Add. Mss. 61,678 ff. 90–5.

23   D. Stroud, *Capability Brown*, 1975, 130.

24   British Library, Add. Mss. 69,795 f. 4.

25   Jeri Bapasola, *Faces of Fame and Fortune: The Marlborough Family Portraits at Blenheim Palace*, 2006, 43–51. The building was commonly called Blenheim Palace from the nineteenth century onwards. Before then, it was known as Blenheim House, Blenheim Castle or usually, just Blenheim.

26   Ashworth was assisted by Richard Smallbones from 1725 onwards. Smallbones eventually took over from him; Jeri Bapasola, *Household Matters – Domestic Service at Blenheim Palace*, 2007, 32. Ashworth hanged himself at Coombe in 1759, but the family connection with Blenheim endured through his niece who married Dr Mavor, a local preacher who moved to Woodstock. Dr Mavor was tutor to the 4th Duke's young children and later wrote the first popular guidebook to Blenheim, which ran into several editions. See fn. 19, Chapter 6.

27   British Library, Add. Mss. 61,678 ff. 90–5.

5   'Nothing Equal to This'

1   C. Hussey, *English Gardens and Landscapes 1700–1750*, 1967, 40.

2   D. Stroud, *Ibid*, 1975; R. Turner, *Capability Brown and the Eighteenth Century English Landscape*, 1985; P. Willis, *Capability Brown in Northumberland*, 1983; J. Clifford, *Capability Brown*, 1974; E. Hyams, *Capability Brown and Humphry Repton*, 1971; T. Hinde, *Capability Brown, The Story of a Master Gardener*, 1986

3   British Library, Add. Mss. 69,795 f. 4.

4   Bodleian Library, Top. Oxon. d.173, 206.

5   The Royal Bank of Scotland Group Archives, DR/427/48 – I am grateful to Philip Winterbottom, RBS Group Archives Manager, for access.

6   D. Stroud, *Ibid*, 1975.

7   Blenheim Palace Muniments, *A Plan for the intended Alterations of the Water at Blenheim belonging to His Grace the Duke of Marlborough*.

8   Bodleian Library, Top. Oxon. d.173, f. 174.

9   J. Bold & E. Chaney (Eds.), *English Architecture Public and Private*, 1993, 174.

10   Blenheim Palace Muniments, *'A Plan for the intended Alterations of the Water at Blenheim belonging to His Grace the Duke of Marlborough'*. This was the first of three boathouses built at Blenheim. The boathouse is also mentioned by Richardson (Bodleian Library, Top Oxon d.173, f. 176–8) but he incorrectly states its location as under the south arch. As this manuscript is referenced by Colvin and Rowan in J. Bold & E. Chaney (Eds.), *Ibid*, 1993, 159–175, the error is repeated.

11   Bodleian Library, Top. Oxon. d.173, f. 176; possibly the ruins remaining to the west of Rosamund's Well after the bridge was completed and no more rubble needed, Ms. Top. Gen. d.14 f. 14v.

12   Blenheim Estate Office.

13   The top water level of the Bladon dam is at the tail water level of the lake dam.

14   G.M. Binnie, *Early Dam Builders in Britain*, 1987, 67–8.

15 Blenheim Estate Office. The cascade dam is 522 ft long (159 m), the crest measures 25 ft wide (7.6 m) on average. The foundations are at a depth of 24 ft (7.3 m) below the crest. I am grateful to Roger File for access to technical information.

16 The earliest repairs were carried out by the 6th Duke, see Chapter 8. Subsequent repairs were recorded in 1885 for *works executed by Jerrams renewing clay walls etc. by the cascade*. This was presumably when the clay core was widened to approximately 15 ft (4.6 m).

17 G.M. Binnie, *Ibid*, 1987, 61.

18 *Journal of Garden History*, Vol. 29, No 1.

19 Bodleian Library, Ms. Eng. Misc. e.488(1), f. 21. I am grateful to John Phibbs for this reference.

20 D. Adamson (Ed.), *Rides Around Britain*, 1996, 59; Earl Gregg Swem Library, Thomas Jefferson's Memorandums; C. Bruyn Andrews, *The Torrington Diaries*, 1934, Vol. I, 236.

21 Two causeways were built across marshy meadowland linking the old royal manor to Woodstock and the road to Oxford. These causeways were possibly built in 1256 when royal building accounts mention alder supports being used for construction over marshland. (*Arboricultural Journal*, Vol. 5, 1981, 206).

22 L. Brown, *A Plan for the alterations from Pritchard's gate to the new gate*, Woodstock Town Hall, gifted by the 10th Duke of Marlborough. I am grateful to Peter H. Andersen, Town Clerk, for access to the drawing and for permitting its reproduction.

23 Blenheim Palace collection.

24 Blenheim Palace Muniments, G1. In 1776 these are listed as: the Bear, Marlborough Arms, the Compasses, the Dog and Duck, Woodstock Arms, Jos. Truss's, the Star, Six Bells, the Bull, Wilkes's and the White Horse.

25 British Library, Add. Mss. 69,795 f. 13. Charles Cadogan (1684/5– 1776), second Baron Cadogan of Oakley, younger brother of William, 1st Earl Cadogan (1675–1726), quartermaster general in the 1st Duke of Marlborough's army and a most trusted subordinate. The 2nd Baron Cadogan had a house in Bruton Street, London, and inherited his brother's country estate, Caversham Park.

26 W.S. Lewis (Ed.), *Horace Walpole's Correspondence*, Vol. X, 309.

27 W. Mavor, *New Description of Blenheim*, 1806, 59.

28 The lake is nearly 1.5 miles (2.4 km) long.

29 H. Slatter (Pub.), *A New Guide to Blenheim Palace*, 1835, 14.

30 W. Mavor, *Launching the Sovereign*, 1787.

31 Jeri Bapasola, *Household Matters – Domestic Service at Blenheim Palace*, 2007, 33.

32 British Library, Add. Mss. 61,674 ff. 75, 77; The Hon. John Byng also enjoyed fishing on the lake, see C. Bruyn Andrews, *Ibid*, 1936, Vol. III, 165–7.

33 S. Shields, *Lancelot Brown's early work at Grimsthorpe and Stowe*, Garden History 34:2, 2006, 183.

34 British Library Add. Mss. 69,795 f. 13-v ; D. Stroud, *Ibid*, 1975, 59–60; D. Jacques, *Georgian Gardens The Reign of Nature*, 1983, 81.

35 RBS Group Archives, DR/427/56, 62, 64.

36 British Library, Add. Mss. 61,674 ff. 7, 9.

37 RHS Lindley Library, Lancelot Brown's account book, ff. 23–4. Work usually slowed down or stopped during the winter months.

38 RBS Group Archives, DR/427/68.

39 RBS Group Archives, customer account ledger DR/427/48, account of Lancelot Brown.

40 It should also be pointed out that Brown only made the payment to Read in March 1774, once he had received his 'Balance and all Demands' from the Duke. RHS Lindley Library, Lancelot Brown's account book, f. 24.

41 British Library, Add. Mss. 61,680 f. 65.

42 Jackson's *Oxford Journal*, No. 2152, 26 July 1794, 3. Read died *after a long indisposition*.

43 C. Bruyn Andrews (Ed.), *Ibid*, 1934, Vol. I, 324; 1936, Vol.III, 169.

44 *The Victoria History of the County of Oxford*, Vol. XII, 1990, 465, fn. 56.

45 British Library, Add. Mss. 18,556 f. 1.

46 Memorandum dated 12 February 1788. I am grateful to a private collector for access to this document and for permission to quote from it.

47 The exact location of this structure is not known.

48 British Library, Add. Mss. 18,556 f. 2.

49 British Library, Add. Mss. 71,602; Add. Mss. 18,556 f. 2; Woodstock Town Hall, L. Brown, *A Plan for the alterations from Pritchard's gate to the new gate*; Blenheim Estate Office, *Survey of the Magnificent Improvements* by T. Richardson and C. Dean.

50 D. Adamson (Ed.), *Ibid*, 1996, 59.

51 D. Stroud, *Ibid*, 1975.

52 Sir Henry Steuart, *The Planter's Guide*, 1828, 223.

53 British Library, Add. Mss. 61,680 ff. 55– 9.

54 British Library, Add. Mss. 61,680 ff. 64– 75.

55 D. Adamson (Ed.), *Ibid*, 1996, 124; C. Bruyn Andrews, *Ibid*, 1934, Vol. I, 323.

56 C. Bruyn Andrews, *Ibid*, 1936, Vol. III, 160.

57 C. Bruyn Andrews, *Ibid*, 1936, Vol. III, 159; D. Adamson, Ed., *Ibid*, 1996, 384–5.

58 T.G. Jackson, *Wadham College*, 1893, 216 Convention book 7/4/1796. I am grateful to Cliff Davies for supplying this reference.

59 British Library, Add. Mss. 61,680 ff. 76– 7.

60 Blenheim Palace Muniments, *A Plan for the intended Alterations of the Water at Blenheim belonging to His Grace the Duke of Marlborough*.

61 British Library, Add. Mss. 71,602; OSD 162,9.

62 Blenheim Estate Office, *Magnificent Improvements Plan* by T. Richardson and C. Dean.

63 There were two possible types of visits – the circuit ride (undertaken by carriage) which included the wider landscape, and the circuit walk (on foot) which went around the gardens (then called the pleasure grounds) in the vicinity of the Palace.

64 British Library, Add. Mss. 71,602; Blenheim Palace Muniments, Thomas Pride, *A Plan of the Manor of Woodstock belonging to His Grace the Most Noble George, Duke of Marlborough in the County of Oxford*, 1772. The survey was carried out in 1771 and drawn in 1772.

65 W. Mavor, *New Description of Blenheim*, 1806.

66 S. Switzer, *Ichnographia Rustica or the Nobleman, Gentleman and Gardener's Recreation*, 1718.

67 *Letters of Sarah Duchess of Marlborough at Madresfield Court*, 1875, 67.

68 In 1781 over 3,000 head of deer were recorded in the park, B. Cozens-Hardy (Ed.), *The Diary of Sylas Neville 1767–1788*, 1950, 281.

69 Bodleian Library, Top. Oxon. d.173, ff. 211, 214; D. Adamson (Ed.), *Ibid*, 1996, 387; C. Bruyn Andrews, *Ibid*, 1936, Vol. III, 162–3. Queen Pool was named after Philippa, consort of King Edward I.

70 Blenheim Estate Office, *Survey of the Magnificent Improvements*; Blenheim Palace Muniments, Thomas Pride, *A Plan of the Manor of Woodstock*, 1772; British Library Add. Mss. 71,602.

71 Earl Gregg Swem Library, Thomas Jefferson's Memorandums.

72 Blenheim Palace Muniments, Thomas Pride, *A Plan of the Manor of Woodstock*, 1772.

73 British Library, Add. Mss. 61,672 f. 119. The new stairs referred to here were probably the steps leading out from the East Drawing Room of the private apartments. This room had previously been the 1st Duke's bedchamber.

74 Bodleian Library, Top. Oxon. d.173, 191.

75 *The Victoria History of the County of Oxford*, Vol. XII, 1990, 466.

76 T. Hinde, *Capability Brown, The Story of a Master Gardener*, 1986, 51; G.M. Binnie, *Ibid*, 1987, 65.

77 W. Mavor, *A New Description of Blenheim*, 1793, 88; J.N. Brewer, *The Beauties of England and Wales*, 1813, Vol XII, ii,416; C. Bruyn Andrews, *Ibid*, 1934, Vol. I, 235; W. Gilpin, *Observations on Cumberland and Westmoreland*, 1786, Vol. I, 29–30; Bodleian Library, Ms. Eng. Misc. e.488(1) f. 23; Ms. Eng. Misc. f. 180 f. 5.

78 RBS Group Archives, DR/427/60, 62, 64: 1770 (February–April), 1771 (March–July), and 1772 (February–October). However, the largest single sum (£260 in December 1772) may have also included a pay-out incurred at Croome where Read returned to repair a leak in Lord Coventry's dam, D. Stroud, *Ibid*, 59–60; D. Jacques, *Ibid*, 1983, 81.

79 British Library, Add. Mss. 61,672 f. 119.

80 Jackson's *Oxford Journal*, Vol. 988. In 1772 the Marlborough tiger was put on show as part of '*a collection of living curiosities*' in Oxford along with a zebra, a leopard, a porcupine, a lion and other rare animals; D. Adamson (Ed.), *Ibid*, 1996, 124; C. Bruyn Andrews, *Ibid*, 1934, Vol. I, 324.

81 Bodleian Library, Ms. Eng. Misc. f. 180 (1), Gilpin's Journey in 1772. I am grateful to John Phibbs for drawing my attention to this manuscript.

82 British Library, Add. Mss. 41,133 ff. 1, 39.

6 Introducing Classicism

1 British Library, Add. Mss. 61,680 f. 113, H. Colvin, *Dictionary of British Architects 1600–1840*, 1995, 241, 603; J. Harris, *Sir William Chambers Knight of the Polar Star*, 1970, 56, 224. Plans and elevations for the building were sent to the Gentlemen of Woodstock Corporation by 25 January 1766. Jackson's *Oxford Journal*, Vol. 665, 3. Estate accounts show roughly £500 being spent from autumn 1767 to 1768. British Library, Add. Mss. 61,678 f. 100.

2 British Library, Add. Mss. 61,674 ff. 21, 35; *The Victoria History of the County of Oxford*, Vol. XII, 1990, 20; Blenheim Palace Muniments, Shelf G1/Box 4; Register of Documents 1748–1816 ff. 45,70,177; *Journal of the Furniture History Society*, Vol. XXX, 119. The house was built by John Hooper (mason), furnished from Lady Day 1769 and let to Walker for 50 years.

3 British Library, Add. Mss. 41,133 f. 5.

4 L. Brown, *A Plan for the alterations from Pritchard's gate to the new gate*, Woodstock Town Hall; Blenheim Palace collection, L. Brown, *Design for a gate*.

5 Sir W. Chambers, *A Dissertation on Oriental Gardening*, 1772, v.

6 British Library, Add. Mss. 41,133 ff. 98, 106v.

7 British Library, Add. Mss. 41,133 ff. 106v, 108.

8 The total area of the park grew to 2,268 acres (918 ha) and the boundary wall now extended about nine miles (14.5 km).

9 Wakeman was in charge of the exotic birds in the aviary and the pheasants reared at the Lince. W. Mavor, *A New Description of Blenheim*, 10th edition improved, 1817, 69; J. N. Brewer, *Ibid*, 1813, Vol. XII, ii, 413.

10 This was probably one of the last major tasks Read undertook before his death in 1794. C. Bruyn Andrews, *Ibid*, 1936, Vol. III, 162–3.

11 Bodleian Library, Ms. Top. Oxon. d. 173, 181. Brown had also removed the paving between the towers and covered the carriageway with lead.

12 British Library, Add. Mss. 41,133 f. 127; Bodleian Library, Top. Oxon. d. 173, 193; D. Adamson (Ed.), *Ibid*, 1996, 386. The valley north of the bridge including the hilly outcrop on which the old manor once stood had been substantially levelled before this time. Vanbrugh had described the landscape as an '*irregular, ragged ungovernable hill*', British Library, Add. Mss. 61,353 ff. 62–3 & seq. Although Sarah, Duchess of Marlborough demolished the building and levelled the ground, it was the 4th Duke of Marlborough who completely dug up the foundations and removed all trace of the buildings when lowering the slope.

13 Bodleian Library, Ms. Top. Oxon. a. 37, f. 121.

14 Earl Gregg Swem Library, Thomas Jefferson's Memorandums. John Adams accompanied Thomas Jefferson on this tour (they were respectively the second and third Presidents of the United States of America). In his own diary, Adams simply describes Blenheim as '*superb*'.

15 The number of permanent labourers typically averaged 30, of which a third were women. British Library, Add. Mss. 61,677, 61,678, 61,680; Bodleian Library, Ms. Top. Oxon. d. 173, 189; John Byng also records 50 people working in the gardens and 100 in the park. C. Bruyn Andrews, *Ibid*, 1934, Vol. I, 323.

16 Earl Gregg Swem Library, Thomas Jefferson's Memorandums.

17 W. Gilpin, *Observations on Cumberland and Westmoreland*, 1786, Vol. I, 31.

18 W. Mavor, *A New Description of Blenheim*, 1793, 61–3; J. N. Brewer, *Ibid*, 1813, Vol. XII, ii, 414; E. D. Clarke, *A Tour through the South of England*, 1791, 394; J. Harris & M. Snodin (Eds.), *Sir William Chambers, Architect to George III*, 1996, 62.

19 W. Mavor, *Ibid*, 1797, 76–77 and *Ibid*, 1800, 63. William Fordyce Mavor (1758–1837) was the author of Blenheim's eighteenth century guidebook which ran into several editions. He was writing master to the 4th Duke's children before taking holy orders and applying to his patron for a church position, duly becoming rector of Bladon-with-Woodstock. Later headmaster of the village grammar school, he was also elected Mayor of Woodstock Borough ten times.

20 Royal Academy Archive, Yenn Papers, A.3.b.

21 British Library, Add. Mss. 41,133 f. 84v.

22 W. Mavor, *Ibid*, 1814, 9th ed. The theatre first opened on Friday 19 October 1787 with the comedy of 'False Delicacy' and 'Who's the Dupe'.

23 Royal Academy Archive, Yenn Papers, A.1.a–c.

24 A large timber store was located near these buildings, supplying fuel for the stoves. W. Mavor, *Ibid*, 1806, 64–5.

25 Chambers' design for this gate to the Kitchen Garden was based on Palladio's Teatro Olimpico in Vicenza, J. Sherwood & N. Pevsner, *The Buildings of England, Oxfordshire*, 1974, 475; the Gate was built by 1772, Blenheim Palace Muniments, Thomas Pride, *A Plan of the Manor of Woodstock*, 1772; Royal Academy Archive, Yenn Papers A.1.a–c.; *The Victoria History of the County of Oxford*, Vol. XII, 1990, 463.

26 I am grateful to Sir John Boardman for his help with these inscriptions.

27 Bodleian Library, Gough Oxon. 17(1)C, f. 102, 1788 *Guide to Blenheim*.

28 *Blenheim in Oxfordshire, the Seat of the Duke of Marlborough*, 1787, 2.

29 British Library, Add. Mss. 61,353 ff. 86, 107v.

30 British Library, Add. Mss. 15,545 f. 133.

31 Bodleian Library, Gough Oxon. 17 (1), III/ 103; Ms. Top. Oxon. d. 173 ff. 197, 199.

32 D. Green, *Ibid*, 1951, 289.

33 British Library, Add. Mss. 41,135 f. 1; Add. Mss. 41,133 f. 121v.

34 Mr Faraday of the Royal Institute analysed the spring water to find '*Free carbonic acid. Carbonate of lime, held in solution. Sulphate of lime, a little.*

Muriate of soda. Carbonate of soda, a small proportion.' A pint of water contained 3.2 grains of salt. H. Slatter (Pub.), *A Description of Blenheim*, 1835, 70; *Ibid*, 1846, 70.

35 Bodleian Library, Gough 17 (1), III/ 103; Ms. Top. Oxon. d. 173, f. 192.

36 E.D. Clarke, *Ibid*, 1791, 395; Bodleian Library, Ms. Top. Oxon. d. 173, f. 191.

37 Bodleian Library, Ms. Top. Oxon. d.173, 193; J.C. Loudon, *The Gardener's Magazine*, Vol. X, No.49, 100.

38 Bodleian Library, Ms. Top. Oxon. d.173, 193; British Library, Add. Mss. 19,597 ff. 96v, 98&v. The lions' heads on the gate were made to Chambers' design – Duke's letter 29 August 1773, RIBA archive, quoted in D. Green, *Ibid*, 1951, 318: '*I return you your enclosed plan for the Gateway here. I think it is very handsome and wish you would order drawings for the ornaments to be made out at large; they certainly had better be made in Town. The only parts we wish to have altered in your drawing are the Trophys under the cornice, we think the Lions heads in your first sketch looked better than the Trophys*'.

39 British Library, Add. Mss. 19,595 ff. 84v–85.

40 Blenheim Palace Collection; Royal Academy Archive, Yenn Papers, A.4.a; J. Harris, *A Catalogue of British Drawings for Architecture*, 1971, 310.

41 British Library, Egerton Papers 2,678, f. 40v–41.

42 Royal Academy Archive, Yenn Papers, A.1.a–c.; A.2.a–b.; A.3.a–c; A.4.a–b; A.5.

43 Bodleian Library, Ms. Top. Oxon. a37* f. 24.

44 W. Mavor, *Blenheim – A Poem*, 1787.

45 British Library, Add. Mss. 41,133 f. 108; J.P. Neale, *An Historical Description of Blenheim with Six Views*, 1823, 5. The present trophies on the front steps are recent replacements.

46 J.P. Neale, *Ibid*, 1823, 15; J.N. Brewer, *Ibid*, 1813, Vol. XII, ii, 413; Payments to Yenn were recorded in 1792 (£250 '*on account of portico*') and June 1793 (£746:18:6 without details), Blenheim Palace Muniments, G1.

47 C. Bruyn Andrews, *Ibid*, 1934, Vol. I, 192, 322; *The Victoria History of the County of Oxford*, Vol. XII, 1990, 465–6.

48 M. Soames, *The Profligate Duke*, 1987, 23.

49 Blenheim Palace Muniments, Register of Documents 1748–1816, f. 142.

50 Jeri Bapasola, *Mr. Spalding's Gift – The Oriental Porcelain Collection at Blenheim Palace*, 2003, 9, 11–14, 18.

51 British Library, Add. Mss. 61,674, ff. 110–16.

52 W. Mavor, *Ibid*, 1817, 64–5 Erected in two sections, each with six compartments.

53 Bodleian Library, Ms. Top. Oxon. d. 173, f. 298 ; British Library, Add. Mss. 61,674 ff. 113–114; Add. Mss. 61,672, f. 202; J.P. Neale, *Ibid*, 1823, 15; W. Mavor, *Ibid*, 10th edition improved, 1817, 65; D. Adamson (Ed.), *Ibid*, 1996, 387.

54 W.S. Lewis (Ed.), *Ibid*, Vol. XXXIX, 435, fn. 7. Mary Delany was famous for her flower collages of cut paper, her embroidery and decorative shell work. Her friendship with the Duchess of Portland brought her into contact with some of the greatest artists and botanists of the eighteenth century.

7 Collecting Plants, Growing Debts

1 British Library, Add. Mss. 61,670 f. 56.

2 M. Soames, *Ibid*, 1987, 64.

3 Blenheim Palace Collection, Blandford *Florilegium*.

4 British Library, Add. Mss. 56,298 f. 18.

5 Royal Botanic Gardens Archives, I.B., 1793–1809, 44. I am grateful to Helen Walch for this reference.

6 British Library, Add. Mss. 33,981, f. 16; Add. Mss. 56,298 ff. 19–20.

7 British Library, Add. Mss. 56,298 f. 19v.

8 M. Soames, *Ibid*, 1987, 79.

9 Whiteknights was re-leased to the Marquis for 21 years in 1808 at a nominal rent of 8 guineas per annum. Blenheim Palace Muniments, Register of Documents 1748–1816, ff. 186, 195; Bodleian Library, Mss. D.D.C1-4, Berkshire Records Office, D/ESv (M) B11; W.R. Dawson (Ed.), *The Banks Letters*, 1958, 217.

10 J.C. Loudon, *The Gardener's Magazine*, Vol. IX, No. 47, 665. Lee and Kennedy also bought American plants at wholesale rates from John Fraser.

11 *Magnolia auriculata* and *Abies fraseri*. Archives of Natural History, Vol. 24, Part 1, 1–18. From around 1789 until his death in 1811, Fraser set up and ran his business on the King's Road near Sloane Square in Chelsea – *Curtis's Botanical Magazine or Flower-Garden Displayed*, 1804, 754v.

12 Mrs Hofland, *Descriptive Account of the Mansion and Gardens of Whiteknights*, 1819, 52.

13 Blenheim Palace Collection, S. Blandford, *Florilegium*, f. 59/88, *Phlox subulata*, June 1797.

14 H. Andrews, *The Botanist's Repository of New and Rare Plants*, Vol. IV, 343, Plate CCCXLIII. Henry Andrews published his *Botanist's Repository* from 1797 to c.1814. He was the son-in-law of John Kennedy, owner of the Vineyard Nurseries in Hammersmith who supplied many plants to the Marquis of Blandford.

15 Within two decades, by 1833. J.C. Loudon, *Ibid*, Vol. IX, No.47, 665.

16 In February 1816.

17 E. Smith, *A History of Whiteknights*, 1957, 23–4.

18 It specifically stipulated that the 4th Duke's renowned collection of antique gems was to be safely kept locked away at his banker's during the 5th Duke's lifetime.

19 Lady Diana Beauclerk was an accomplished artist who produced designs for Josiah Wedgwood and also a set of seven drawings for Walpole's tragedy *The Mysterious Mother*, which he later fitted into the Beauclerk Closet at Strawberry Hill.

20 J.C. Loudon, *Ibid*, Vol. IV, No. 14, 176; Vol. IX, No. 67, 502.

21 The sale raised barely £15,000.

22 J.P. Neale, *Ibid*, 1823, 15; J.C. Loudon, *Ibid*, Vol. IV, No. 14, 176; Vol. IX, No. 47, 664,668.

23 British Library, Add. Mss. 61,680 f. 80 Mr Whitman was employed from 15 February 1817, paid the same wage as the Butler, £50 per annum; Bodleian Library, Ms. Top. Oxon. d. 173, 312; J.C. Loudon, *Ibid*, Vol. IX, No. 47, 664; Vol. VI, No. 29, 655.

24 *Tour in England Ireland and France in a series of letters by a German Prince*, 1833, 86. The visit was actually undertaken in 1827.

25 W. Mavor, *Ibid*, 10th edition improved, 1817, 62.

26 The clumps were surrounded with borders of seedling oaks. *The Perambulation of Oxford, Blenheim and Nuneham*, 1824, 197.

27 W. Mavor, *Ibid*, 1820, 11th edition improved, 65; *The Perambulation of Oxford, Blenheim and Nuneham*, 1824, 194.

28 *The Perambulation of Oxford, Blenheim and Nuneham*, 1824, 194.

29 J.C. Loudon, *Ibid*, Vol. X, No. 49, 101.

30 The western undercroft previously contained the old Stone Gallery and Chinese Closet. The Chinese Closet in the Palace should not be confused with the China Gallery in the park. The former housed the 3rd Duke's collection of Meissen porcelain with some very large porcelain jars belonging to Sarah, Duchess of Marlborough. The China Gallery on the other hand, displayed Mr Spalding's gifted collection of oriental porcelain.

31 Bodleian Library, Ms. Top. Oxon. d. 173 f. 299. The room was furnished with ten chairs, two tables, a barometer and a telescope. The floor was covered with matting, and paintings of aquatic plants adorned the walls.

32 Manufactured by Joseph Dufour et Cie.

33 The Bamboo Room (created in 1835) is now the Water Terrace Café. The Indian Room, the only one to survive with decoration intact, is the Water Terrace Restaurant.

34 Bodleian Library, Ms. Top. Oxon. d. 173 f. 298.

35 W. Eccles, *A New Guide to Blenheim*, 1861, 40.

36 *The Perambulation of Oxford, Blenheim and Nuneham*, 1824, 195.

37 J. C. Loudon, *Ibid*, Vol. X, No. 49, 102.

38 J. C. Loudon, *Ibid*, Vol. X, No. 49, 101.

39 J. C. Loudon, *Ibid*, Vol. X, No. 49, 102.

40 *The Perambulation of Oxford, Blenheim and Nuneham*, 1824, 196–7.

41 *The Perambulation of Oxford, Blenheim and Nuneham*, 1824, 196.

42 Blenheim Estate Office, *Magnificent Improvements Plan*.

43 J. C. Loudon, *Ibid*, Vol. X, No. 49, 102.

44 W. Mavor, *Ibid*, 1800, 76.

45 H. Slatter (Pub.), *A Description of Blenheim*, 1846, 62.

46 H. Slatter (Pub.), *The Oxford University and City Guide*, 1835.

47 W. Eccles, *A New Guide to Blenheim*, 17th edition, 71.

48 H. Slatter (Pub.), *The Oxford University and City Guide*, 1835, 189; *The Victoria History of the County of Oxford*, Vol. XII, 1990, 469.

49 Bodleian Library, Ms. Top. Oxon. d. 173, f. 298.

50 The pool still survives today, near the exedra.

51 H. Slatter (Pub.), *The Oxford University and City Guide*, 1835, 189.

52 J.C. Loudon, *Ibid*, Vol. X, No. 49, 102.

53 J.C. Loudon, *Ibid*, Vol. X, No. 49, 99.

54 This was a Post Office pension which had been granted by Queen Anne to the 1st Duke and his heirs in perpetuity.

55 J.C. Loudon, *Ibid*, Vol. V, No. 22, 551.

56 F. Bamford, Ed., *The Journal of Mrs Arbuthnot 1820–1832*, 1950, 305.

57 British Library, Add. Mss. 38,367 f. 244.

58 M. Soames, *Ibid*, 1987, 202–3.

8 Melons, Roses, Orchids

1 House of Lords Records Office, Victoria Regina, Anno Quinto, Cap. 2. 5 October 1841. Blenheim Palace itself was excluded from the mortgage. The mortgage was advanced by the Clerical and Medical Office.

2 House of Lords Records Office, Victoria Regina, Anno Quinto, Cap. 2., 39; M. Soames, *Ibid*, 222.

3 Blenheim Palace Muniments, Account Ledgers E/A/2, 176; E/A/3, 161,200.

4 House of Lords Records Office, Victoria Regina, Anno Tertio & Quarto, Cap. XLIII, 4 August 1840, 333; Victoria Regina, Anno Quinto, Cap. 2. 5 October 1841, 29–33.

5 J. Timbs, *An excursion to Blenheim*, *The Literary World*, 1840, 328.

6 H. Colvin, *A Biographical Dictionary of British Architects 1600–1840*, 1995, 73.

7 Blenheim Palace Muniments, Account Ledgers E/A/1, 167; E/A/2, 187; *The Victoria History of the County of Oxford*, Vol. XII, 1990, 457 (fn.2).

8 Blenheim Palace Muniments, H/P/3; W. Eccles, *A New Guide to Blenheim*, 17th edition, 6.

9 Blenheim Estate Office, *Magnificent Improvements Plan – Surveyed and drawn under the direction of Mr Dean by I. Thompson and C. Dean and intended to convey an idea of the Magnificent Improvements designed by His Grace George Duke of Marlborough and now in progress of execution.*

10 H. Slatter (Pub.), *A Description of Blenheim*, 1846, 78.

11 Jeri Bapasola, *Mr. Spalding's Gift*, 2003, 18.

12 W. Eccles, *A New Guide to Blenheim*, 1850, 52; W. Eccles, *Ibid*, 1852, 47.

13 Ordnance Survey 1876; Blenheim Palace Muniments, H/P/3.

14 H. Slatter (Pub.), *A Description of Blenheim*, 1846, 24–5. Although on pages 74–5 of this edition Slatter has not amended the text from the previous edition and removed the bronze figures from the gardens, a copy in the Blenheim Palace Library with annotations by the 6th Duke clearly shows them cancelled out.

15 J.C. Loudon, *Ibid*, Vol. X No 49, 99–100.

16 Blenheim Palace Muniments, Account Ledgers E/A/1; H/P/3, 1840 & seq. Repairs by Edward Weekes, glazing by William Brooks.

17 Blenheim Estate Office, *Magnificent Improvements Plan*; C. Bruyn Andrews, Ed., *Ibid*, 1936, Vol. III, 159.

18 A. Graves, *The Royal Academy of Arts – A Complete Dictionary of Contributors*, 1906, Vol. IV, 363–4:1848, No. 474.

19 *Gardener's Chronicle*, 21 March 1964, 250.

20 W. Eccles, *A New Guide to Blenheim Palace*, 1852, 14–5.

21 All the paintings in this room were part of the 1st Duke of Marlborough's collection – the Titians covered three sides of the room, on the fourth Rubens's *Rape of Proserpine* was displayed. (Eccles, 1861, 36).

22 Jeri Bapasola, *Household Matters, Domestic Service at Blenheim Palace*, 2007, 42–4. The 4th Duke had wanted to renew the dairy at Furze Plat Farm. He considered moving it to his new menagerie near the kennels, but thought it might be too far from the house to be practical: Blenheim's dairy maids worked at the house when they were not busy in the dairy. (British Library, Add. Mss. 61,674 f. 44). In April 1789, the dairy was finally moved to the menagerie. (British Library, Add. Mss. 61,674 f. 46). When the 6th Duke made his changes, the dairy moved into the kitchen court. Austin & Seeley supplied a cooling fountain for the settling room in Feb 1843, at a cost of £125:4:0. (Blenheim Palace Muniments, H/P/3/, 1843; Account Ledgers E/A/3, 215).

23 J.C. Loudon, *Ibid*, Vol X No 49, 99.

24 J. Timbs, *Ibid*, 1840, 327.

25 Blenheim Palace Muniments, H/P/3.

26 W. Eccles, *A New Guide to Blenheim Palace*, 1852, 45; *Ibid*, 1870, 43.

27 Blenheim Palace Muniments, Account Ledgers E/A/1; E/A/2, 187, 189; E/A/3, 168; E/A/3, 174, 180.

28 Apart from the annual timber sales, some entire trees, faggots and 'underwood' were sold separately. Blenheim Palace Muniments, Account Ledgers E/A/1, 149–150, 166, 201; E/A/2, 155, 167–8, 184, 186; E/A/3, 173.

29 Blenheim Palace Muniments, H/P/3.

30 The sales of elms alone raised £7,000.

31 Blenheim Palace Muniments, Account Ledgers E/A/2, 155, 184–186; E/A/3, 173.

32 Bodleian Library, Ms. Top. Oxon. c.218, ff. 49–50.

33 In June 1845, £20,000 was raised by selling land to the Oxford–Worcester and Wolverhampton Railway Company. The following year the Great Western Railway Company paid £5,000 for land needed for the development of the Oxford to Rugby line, and in September 1855 £3,475 was received from the Buckinghamshire Railway Company. Blenheim Palace Muniments, Trust accounts 1843–5, ff. 2, 45. Additionally, a large estate in Sussex was sold to a Colonel Wyndham for £22,000 (f. 49).

34 It is possible that alterations were made to 'Capability' Brown's Gothic farmhouse and granary during this time. W. Eccles, *A New Guide to Blenheim Palace*, 1852, 43.

35 W. Eccles, *Ibid*, c.1861, 50–1.

36 N. Hawthorne, *Our Old Home*, 1901, 290.

37 In 1852, the Palace was open on Mondays, Wednesdays and Fridays from 11–1, the park and gardens every weekday. W. Eccles, *Ibid*, 5th edition, 14–15.

38 Blenheim Palace Library, Interesting Records Folder, News cutting, 1840.

39 British Library, Add. Mss. 61,677 ff. 179, 190; *The Times*, Letters to the Editor, 31 October 1856.

40 Blenheim Palace Library, Interesting Records Folder, News cutting, 1845.

41 *The Times*, 27 October 1856.

42 W. Eccles, *Ibid*, 1852.

43 *Illustrated London News*, 1 November 1856.

44 British Library, Add. Mss. 61,677 f. 190; D. Adamson (Ed.), *Ibid*, 1996, 126.

45 W. Eccles, *Ibid*, 1861. The Radcliffe Infirmary in Oxford was a principal beneficiary. (Eccles, 1883).

46 A. L. Rouse, *The Later Churchills*, 1958, 215.

47 The first emus were gifted to the Duke by his brother Lord Alfred. One male emu was subsequently swapped for a female from the Zoological Gardens, and all the other birds in the paddock came from that lot, then F. Buckland, *Log-book of a Fisherman and Zoologist*, 1875, 47–56. Several kangaroos were involved in an incident with the Heythrop Hounds on 3 January 1874 when the hounds got off the scent and two animals were accidentally killed. Another fifteen kangaroos were purchased at £1 each from a supplier called H. Damrach in March 1884, Blenheim Palace Muniments, A/4/1883–5, f. 102.

48 W. Eccles, *Ibid*, 1878, 48; *Rambles and Rides around Oxford*, 1882, 94.

49 Blenheim Palace Muniments, design for the Orangery roof. I am grateful to John Forster for bringing this to my attention.

50 W. Eccles, *Ibid*, 1867, 36.

51 *The Garden*, 21 June 1873, 480.

52 Farming operations on the Blenheim estate were terminated in the early twenty-first century. The entire herd of 350 Fresian cattle was sold by spring 2003 and all the farm machinery sold after the harvest in 2002 when twelve farm staff were also made redundant. The decision was made very reluctantly by the 11th Duke, for purely commercial reasons. It cost the estate 16 pence a litre to produce milk while prices had sunk to around 13–14 pence, making the business untenable and a casualty of the crisis in dairy farming throughout the country. However, the herd of 1,500 sheep was retained, under the care of two shepherds.

53 Blenheim Palace Muniments, Cash Ledger 1871–5, f. 311.

54 Blenheim Palace Muniments, Cash Ledger 1877–81, f. 333.

55 *The Victoria History of the County of Oxford*, Vol. XII, 1990, 466.

56 W. Eccles, *Ibid*, 1861, 38.

57 W. Eccles, *Ibid*, 1878, 45–6. The circular beds were 16 ft (4.9 m) in diameter.

58 *The Gardeners' Chronicle*, Vol. XXVII, 1900, 10.

59 *The Garden*, 1873, 480. The axis led from the bow window to Henry Wise's original eastern avenue of elms.

60 *The Garden*, 1873, 480.

61 William Lee was 37, his wife Mary, 43 years old. They had no children living with them at Blenheim. Lee originated from Retford in Notts. When Lee left, 26-year-old John Austin replaced him. The foreman was Thomas Sutton, the Under Gardener, William Savage. Other known gardening staff were Henry Dorning, Edward Lake, Thomas Slatter (who lived in Middle Lodge with his wife Rebecca) and James Hitchman, the 12-year-old son of the Blenheim Gatekeeper, William Hitchman, who lived with his parents in the small rooms inside Hawksmoor's Triumphal Arch/Woodstock Gate.

62 In February 1873, a few months after his arrival, the Duke dispatched Temple to visit the gardens at Chatsworth, although the specific reason for his visit is not known. Blenheim Palace Muniments, Cash Ledger 1871–5, ff. 256–261.

63 Constructed by M/s. Rosher.

64 The fountain has a Latin inscription on the base – ALIGERI NUMINIS AVSPICIO MANV TRITONIS BALNEIS EXANGUEM AB VNDIS RESTITVTAM '*The winged numen, through the guidance of the hand of Triton, recovered deathly pale from the waves of the basin*'. I am grateful to Dr Claudia Wagner and Sir John Boardman for the translation.

65 Robert Turnbull was from Northumberland and known to be working at Blenheim in 1851, when he was 38 and still unmarried. He was assisted by two Under Gardeners, Charles Tolley (aged 24) and Charles Turner (aged 18).

66 *Journal of Horticulture and Cottage Gardener*, 1874, 277, 334.

67 *Journal of Horticulture and Cottage Gardener*, 1874, 275–7.

68 The early hot walls (with wood-fired flues) had given way to steam heating, hot water and eventually gas. Weekes' tubular boilers were introduced around the 1830–40s.

69 Blenheim Palace Muniments, Cash Ledger 1877–81, f. 361. William Crump and his wife Mary (a Hampshire woman seven years older than him) had two daughters, Mary and Lucy, both born at Blenheim.

70 A.L. Rouse, *The Later Churchills*, 1958, 233; W.S. Churchill, *Lord Randolph Churchill*, Vol 1, 75.

71 W. Eccles, *A New Guide to Blenheim*, 1870, 52.

72 *Gardeners' Magazine*, 1909, 292; *Proceedings of the Royal Horticultural Society*, 1880, xcviii.

73 Carters' Catalogue 1882, 18–9.

74 *Journal of Horticulture and Cottage Gardener*, 1874, 363–4.

75 Blenheim Palace Muniments, Cash Ledger 1877–81, f. 376.

76 Arthur Veitch ran the Royal Exotic Nursery on the King's Road, Chelsea. Blenheim Palace Muniments, Cash Ledger 1877–81, ff. 363–4, 369, 372–3, 376.

77 Blenheim Palace Muniments, Cash Ledger 1877–81, f. 368; *Gardeners' Chronicle*, 21 March 1964, 250. Orchid peat was supplied to Blenheim by Epps & Co.

78 Blenheim Palace Muniments, A/4/1883–5, f. 351.

79 F. Sander, *Reichenbachia, Orchids Illustrated and Described*, 1888, Vol. I, 35, Tab.15; A. Swinson, *Frederick Sander: The Orchid King*, 1970, 30; The Journal of the RHS, Vol. VII, No. 1, 78–9.

80 Block Plan of Additions, The Rent Guarantee Society, April 1885. The cost of building these structures was nothing compared to the value of the plants displayed inside.

81 Blenheim Palace Muniments, Cash Ledger 1871–5, f. 259. New pit houses had been built in October 1872 by Bolton & Co.

82 There were three Bothies at Blenheim. In the 1890s the main Bothy was occupied by seven men – Samuel Barker (aged 24), William Gordon (22), William Beckensale (16), Alfred Simeson (20), John Hedges (20), Alfred Chown (23) and Frank Jones (25). The second Bothy lodged four men (Albert Hubbard (aged 25), Henry Kerp (18), Thomas England (35) and Frederick Tyrell (21). Two women, both widows, were employed to cook and clean – E. White (aged 37) worked in the main Bothy, Maria Thornton (aged 70) in the second Bothy. (The second Bothy was destroyed in a gas explosion in the early 1990s.) The third Bothy was a cottage where the gardener John Coles lived with his wife and young son.

83 At 7 am, the bell called the men to work, at 8.30 am it rang to allow half an hour for breakfast, 1 pm was the call for lunch, 2 pm the return from lunch and finally at 5 pm it signalled the end of the working day. The bell was recast in 1878.

84 In the 1870s a series of wet summers had ruined harvests in England and ushered in an agricultural depression.

85 Jeri Bapasola, *Faces of Fame and Fortune: The Marlborough Family Portraits at Blenheim Palace*, 2006, 7–11.

86 *Birmingham Mail*, 9 November 1892.

9 Recreating Grandeur

1 Kathleen Lawrence, Where's Waldo? The Disturbing Disappearance of the Gilded Age Anglo-American Sculptor Waldo Story, *Sculpture Journal*, 18.1, 2009, 69–87. I am indebted to Professor Lawrence for generously sharing her research before publication.

2 Pierre de Nolhac, *Les Jardins de Versailles*, 1906, 74; M. Fouquier & A. Duchêne, *Des Divers Styles de Jardins, Modeles de Grandes et Petites Residences, Sur L'Art Decoratif des Jardins*, 1914, 122, illustrating a similar fountain by Le Brun for Versailles '*des tritons supportent des coquilles surmontees d'un lys epanoui*'.

3 I am grateful to Peter de Brant for access to the records in his ownership and kindly permitting reproduction.

4 Waldo shared a studio with his father at 9 Via S Martino e Macao.

5 Professor Lawrence's attribution.

6 Blenheim Palace Muniments, E/A/196, 62.

7 *The Gardeners' Chronicle*, Vol. XXVII, 6 January 1900, 10. The engineering work on site was carried out by J. K. Cooper and Sons (Blenheim Palace Muniments, E/A/196, 135).

8 Thomas Whillans was born in Scotland. Aged 41, he came to Blenheim with his wife Hannah, two sons (Walter and Sydney) and two daughters (Isabel and Maud). Another son, Ralph, was born when the family was at Blenheim.

9 *Journal of Horticulture and Cottage Gardener*, 9 March 1899, 192–4; Blenheim Palace Muniments E/A/196, 11.

10 *The Gardeners' Chronicle*, Vol. XXVII, 10.

11 Blenheim Palace Muniments, E/A/196, 15, 92, 180–1.

12 *New York Times*, 21 October 1888; *Journal of Horticulture and Cottage Gardener*, 9 March 1899, 194.

13 Blenheim Palace Muniments, C/4/ Orchid Stock Book.

14 *Journal of Horticulture and Cottage Gardener*, 9 March 1899, 194.

15 Blenheim Palace Muniments, E/A/196, 17; *New York Times*, 13 June 1900.

16 W.H. Taunt, *Blenheim and Woodstock*, 1909, 27; *Country Life Illustrated*, 10 June 1899, 723.

17 *Country Life Illustrated*, 10 June 1899, 723; H. Vickers, *Gladys, Duchess of Marlborough*, 1979, 191–2.

18 The exedra was established by 1876. W.H. Taunt, *Blenheim and Woodstock*, 1909, 27.

19 W.H. Taunt, *Ibid*, 1909, 27–28.

20 Bodleian Library, G. A. Top. Oxon. a. 79, *The Builder*, 6 January 1900; Blenheim Palace Muniments, E/A/196, 39, 41, 124, 127. The birds were brought out in certain seasons and kept at the farm the rest of the time. An eaglery and pheasantry established in Victorian times near the Temple of Health was removed by 1898. The rustic pavilion in the Arcade Flower Garden had also been demolished by then.

21 *Journal of Horticulture and Cottage Gardener*, 9 March 1899, 194.

22 *The Gardeners' Chronicle*, Vol. XXVII, 10; Alden, *Illustrated Guide to Blenheim and Woodstock, c.1922*, 26.

23 *Country Life Illustrated*, 10 June 1899, 723.

24 Garrett's annual wage (£150) was lower than Whillans', Blenheim Palace Muniments, E/A/196, 178.

25 Henri Duchêne worked in the town-planning office in Paris. His landscape gardening business was founded in 1877.

26 RHS Report of the Conference on Garden Planning, 1929, 21–2.

27 C. Frange (Ed.), *Le Style Duchêne*, 1998, 168, 180.

28 For £40,000, O. Bradbury, *The Lost Mansions of Mayfair*, 2008, 210. Adjacent leasehold properties in East and West Chapel Streets and Market Street were also acquired to provide a large enough plot of ground. The architects W.H. Romayne-Walker and F.W. Besant were commissioned to build a new house, initially called Blandford House, but renamed Sunderland House on completion, Post Office Papers, London Telephone Service Exchange installation record, 1904. The names Blandford and Sunderland are associated with secondary titles within the Dukedom of Marlborough. The Duke's eldest (or eldest surviving) son bears the title of Marquis of Blandford, while the eldest grandson is known as the Earl of Sunderland. The 9th Duke, nicknamed 'Sunny' from his early days as Earl of Sunderland, might have chosen to rebrand the new house as a mark of his personal association.

29 Blenheim Palace Muniments, Summary Account /WKV.

30 The principal contractors were M/s. Cormish and Gaymer, while the decorative work was undertaken by a French contractor, P. Lefebvre.

31 J.C. Loudon, *The Gardeners' Magazine*, Vol. iv, 1828, No. 14, 89.

32 Bodleian Library, Ms. Top. Oxon. a.37 f. 120v; Blenheim Palace Muniments, Maps and Plans; Duchêne Corr., Letter from Achille Duchêne, Paris, 1 June 1907. From this document it appears that Duchêne received the commission in 1902.

33 RHS Report of the Conference on Garden Planning, 1929, 22.

34 Duchêne Corr., 18 January 1904.

35 The equipment was supplied by Palmer's Travelling Cradles. Workmen employed by A. Dreyfus, a stone-restoration contractor, fixed the mock-up into place. I am grateful to William Palmer for these records.

36 Duchêne Corr., Letter from E. Dresse, 12 August 1905.

37 Supported on a metal armature. These statues were removed from the roof in stages from 1997, restored, and placed in niches on the exterior of the building at *piano nobile* level in February 2007. Cast stone replicas, formed in moulds taken from the originals were erected onto the parapet instead.

38 Blenheim Palace Muniments, E/A/227, 64, 645; Duchêne Corr., Letter from Achille Duchêne, 1 June 1907; A. Dreyfus & Co. correspondence. Dreyfus's men fixed the statues by the end of the year.

39 The steam rollers were sent by the Oxfordshire Steam Ploughing Company. Founded in Cowley in 1868, the firm was later taken over, operating as John Allen & Sons.

40 L. Lang & Fils, 3 June 1904.

41 Blenheim Palace Muniments, Letter to Angas 6 June 1904; 12 May 1904; L. Lang & Fils, 3 June 1904.

42 The final consignment of 5,500 setts was ordered from Lang in May 1907.

43 Roper was contracted to supply York stone paving, sawn on both sides, 2½ in. thick, three ft wide by at least four ft long (6.35 x 91.5 x 122 cm).

44 Peak Dt. Mines Historical Society Ltd., Tables compiled by Frank M. Wardell, HM Inspector for Yorkshire and Lincolnshire 1896. Roper ran six different quarries near Bradford. Robert Roper & Son, Quotation 1 July 1903; Misc. correspondence 1904–6. These records were used for all the information that follows.

45 Through the Great Northern Railway's heavy goods service directly to the Blenheim and Woodstock station. Because of delays and damage to the initial deliveries, subsequent truckloads were consigned through the Great Central Railway Company (GCR) which also operated from Leeds.

46 The wet weather in August put a stop to all outdoor work in the quarries. The requirement for stone became so urgent that Roper was subsequently instructed to send two truckloads at a time when deliveries resumed. A request was also made to the railway company to lower carriage charges and, after months of deliberation, GCR marginally reduced their rates to 11s:8d per ton. But carriage costs remained enough of a concern for Mr Angas to make enquiries with canal carriers experienced in transporting stone – John Griffiths, a Bedworth canal carrier was contacted in February 1905.

47 Robert Roper & Son Ltd., the Radfield Quarries and Estate at Eccleshill were acquired by Oddy & Booth in July 1906.

48 Blenheim Palace Muniments, E/A/227, 64, 642.

49 Taynton had been part-owned by the master mason Edward Strong, and Guiting belonged to Henry Banks, the stonemason responsible for building the colonnades to the east and west of the great court. D. Green, *Blenheim Palace*, 1951, 61, 237–8, 260. Strong's partner at Taynton was Edmund Bray.

50 Supplied in March–April, August–September 1904 at the rate of 17s:6d per ton, reduced from £1 per ton. I am grateful to Henry Groves for allowing access to records.

51 Colonial Office letters, 9 March 1904.

52 The construction of this feature was straightforward as the courtyard was founded on bedrock. Blenheim Palace Muniments, A/4/1886–8, f. 281. The initial ha-ha was sunk in 1886, the bastion shape created later; Duchêne Corr., 17 April 1925, 2.

53 The materials for this part of the construction were mostly supplied by the end of March 1904.

54 L. Bergeotte, Avenue de la Grande Armée, Paris. I am grateful to P. Chemineau for access to these records.

55 Bodleian Library, Ms. Top. Oxon. A.50, 1a, b; Gough Maps 26, 50b; British Library, OSD 162,9; Ordnance Survey Maps, 1st & 2nd eds.

56 The main planting periods – 822 elms in 1896, 1,179 in 1901–2 and 292 in 1904–5, Blenheim Palace Muniments, E/A/193; Centre for Oxfordshire Studies, 1961 Fairey series, D270056a, showing the avenue with the diamond shape.

57 Blenheim Palace Muniments, E/A/193, f. 27. Destroyed in the late 1970s by Dutch elm disease, the avenue has been replanted with limes.

58 The tree plantations on the wider estate included Bladon Heath, Morton Heath, Sturt Wood, Pinsley Wood, Abel Wood, Campsfield Farm, Combe Cliff, plantations adjoining Hanborough Station, Hordley Farm, Sansomes Farm, Wootton Farm, Combe Manor Farms, Dornford Park Farm, Upper Dornford Farm, Hardwick Plantation, Withy Clumps, Knot Oaks, Kings Wood, Burleigh Wood, Mill Wood, Ardley Wood, Gretna Hill and Stockey in Stonefield.

59 Blenheim Palace Muniments, Duchêne Papers, letter 30 December 1925. All references from this source are labelled Duchêne Papers or Duchêne Plans.

60 H.W. Taunt, *Blenheim Palace and Woodstock Illustrated*, 1907, 2.

61 Blenheim Palace Muniments, E/A/196, 234.

62 H.W. Taunt, *Blenheim and Woodstock*, 1909, 26.

63 Consuelo Balsan, *The Glitter and the Gold*, 1953, 33.

64 *Country Life*, 29 May 1909, 787–92.

65 The move was made by October 1906. A. Mackenzie Stuart, *Consuelo and Alva*, 2005, 270.

66 *The Victoria History of the County of Oxford*, Vol. XII, 1990, 460; W. Eccles, *A New Guide to Blenheim*, 1852, 72; D. Green, *Blenheim Palace*, 1951, 231.

67 July 2, 1934, quoted in D. Green, *Ibid*, 1951, 205.

68 S.J. Reid, *John and Sarah Duke and Duchess of Marlborough*, 1914, xlii.

69 Blenheim Palace Muniments, Duchêne Plans.

70 Charged at four shillings per cubic yard.

71 Duchêne Papers, 14 December; 19 December 1925, 4.

72 Contracts would have been signed with Maxwell Hart for work to begin in September but for a clash between Hart's manager, Mr Clark, and the Duke's new Agent, Mr Harbert. Within the week, discussions were hurried along with another firm, Aubrey Watson Ltd. Duchêne Papers, correspondence between the Duke and Maxwell M. Hart, July to September 1925.

73 Duchêne Papers, 10 March 1927.

74 Duchêne Papers, 30 December 1925.

75 Duchêne Papers, 30 December 1925.

76 Duchêne Papers, 30 December 1925.

77 Duchêne Papers, 22 December 1925.

78 Duchêne Papers, 19 December 1925; 22 December 1925.

79 Duchêne Papers, 22 July 1926.

80 Duchêne Papers, 30 December 1925.

81 Old stone from the demolition of Hensington House. (Designed by William Chambers, Hensington House was built by the 4th Duke of Marlborough for his Agent. In the 1840s it became the home of the Marquis of Blandford, later 7th Duke. It was subsequently tenanted and in the late nineteenth century, occupied by a school. By the early twentieth century, the building was the worse for wear and was demolished by the late 1920s.) Duchêne Papers, 14 January 1926; 15 January 1926.

82 Duchêne Papers, 20 January 1926.

83 Duchêne Papers, 30 December 1925.

84 Duchêne Papers, 31 December 1925; 19 December 1925.

85 Duchêne Plans, Cases 1–8; Duchêne Papers, 20 January 1926; 22 March 1926.

86 Duchêne Papers, 20 January 1926. However, it did remain a part of his scheme for some time.

87 Duchêne Papers, 20 January 1926.

88 C. Frange, Ed., *Le Style Duchêne*, 1998, 180.

89 The original design echoed an earlier scheme at Versailles. Duchêne Papers, 20 February 1926; 22 March 1926.

90 M. Fouquier & A. Duchêne, *Des Divers Styles de Jardins, Modeles de Grandes et Petites Residences, Sur L'Art Decoratif des Jardins*, 1914, 115.

91 Duchêne Papers, 20 February 1926.

92 Duchêne Papers, 22 March 1926; 5 June 1926.

93 Duchêne Papers, 4 November 1926.

94 Duchêne Papers, 17 December 1926.

95 Duchêne Papers, 2 March 1926; 29 June 1926; 16 July 1926.

96 Duchêne Papers, 22 July 1926; 24 July 1926; 30 July 1926; 31 July 1926; Vedovelli estimate FF 415,000 17 December 1926; Vedovelli estimate 21 March 1928; 12 August 1926. In August 1926, a new dynamo was installed for the terrace hydraulic system. Electric and gas supply was brought to the neighbourhood around the turn of the century. In 1906 the Woodstock Gas-Light, Coke and Coal Company (later known as the Mid-Oxfordshire Gas-Light, Coke and Coal Company) laid gas mains across the Park from Woodstock to Bladon, linking the gardeners' cottages and the Bothy to a piped supply.

97 Duchêne Papers, 24 July 1926; 2 November 1926; 30 July 1926; 4 November 1926.

98 A large cedar was felled and a large cork-oak was pollarded. Duchêne Papers, 20 February 1926; 5 July 1926; 16 August 1927.

99 Extra hands were brought in from June to August, with the entire workforce accommodated in tents on the grassy stable bank while the rooms over the stable block were cleaned and whitewashed. Duchêne Papers, 22, 25, 26, 29 March 1926.

100 Duchêne Papers, 5 March 1926. The staircase leading down from Terrace 1 to 2 was founded on limestone bedrock, 12 August 1926.

101 Duchêne Papers, 20 January 1926. He conceived the idea of niches in January when his six terrace scheme had run into trouble.

102 Duchêne Papers, 22 March 1926.

103 Duchêne Papers, 20 February 1926; 22 March 1926.

104 Duchêne Plans Cases 1–8; Duchêne Papers, 22 March 1926.

105 Duchêne Papers, Numerotage des Plans, 16 June 1926.

106 H. Vickers, *Gladys, Duchess of Marlborough*, 1979, 204; Repairs to the Rock Garden had previously been undertaken in 1886, Blenheim Palace Muniments, A/4/1886–8, 282.

107 I am most grateful to Hugo Vickers for access to his collection and for permitting publication. Duchêne Papers, 30 December 1926; 31 May 1929.

108 Duchêne Papers, 17 December 1926; 10 March 1926.

109 Duchêne Papers, 30 December 1926.

110 Duchêne Papers, 22 March 1926.

111 Duchêne Papers, 30 December 1926.

112 Duchêne Papers, 17 April 1925; 23 October 1925; 22 March 1926; 16 December 1926; 10 March 1927; 9 March 1931.

113 Duchêne Papers, 30 December 1926.

114 Duchêne Papers, 9 August 1926; 18 October 1926; Account prepared 21 October 1926 – total £7,109 (Aubrey Watson £6,009 + Kingerlee £1,100); 2 November 1926 enclosing cheque for £700.

115 Duchêne Papers, 24 July 1926.

116 A big chimney in one of these outhouses was taken down by February 1927, removing a considerable eyesore.

117 Duchêne Papers, 30 December 1926.

118 Duchêne Papers, 10 March 1927.

119 Duchêne Papers, 10 March 1927; 31 May 1929.

120 Duchêne Papers, 26 January 1931; 6 February 1931.

121 Duchêne Papers, 17 May 1929.

122 Duchêne Papers, 6 February 1931; the final drawings were received from the architect in March, 9 March 1931.

123 Duchêne Papers, 9 March 1931.

124 Duchêne Papers, 17 May 1929.

125 The Townley Venus was the Venus of Ostia. Although the Medici Venus is the most notable representation of the goddess, the 9th Duke had already placed a bronze copy of this statue (made in 1711 by Massimiliano Soldani Benzi) in the Italian Garden.

126 Duchêne Papers, 19 December 1925.

127 Duchêne Papers, 20 February 1926.

128 Duchêne Papers, [?] February 1927.

129 Duchêne Papers, 10 March 1927.

130 RHS Report of the Conference on Garden Planning, 1929, 23.

131 Duchêne Papers, 7 January 1928.

132 Duchêne Papers, 9 July 1927.

133 Staircases completed around Christmas 1927; Duchêne Papers, 16 August 1927; 25 May 1929; finally rejected 26 January 1931 and benches placed on the landings instead *'cela suffira largement pour eviter l'effet desagreable du vide'*.

134 Duchêne Papers, 25 May 1929.

135 Duchêne Papers, 16 August 1927, the Victories were made in England.

136 Duchêne Papers, 16 August 1927.

137 Duchêne Papers, 9 July 1927.

138 Duchêne Papers, 16 August 1927; 7 January 1928.

139 Duchêne Papers, 7 January 1928.

140 Duchêne Papers, 20 February 1926.

141 Duchêne Papers, 7 January 1928; 16 June 1928.

142 Duchêne Papers, 7 January 1928.

143 The French firm of Perret Frères agreed to supply the formula for an appropriate cement mix so that they could be made in England, but the work was eventually undertaken in France. Duchêne Papers, 6 June 1928.

144 Duchêne Papers, 6 July 1928.

145 Duchêne Papers, 10 November 1928.

146 Duchêne Papers, 30 October 1928; 24 November 1928.

147 By 16 June 1928. The plaster model was reproduced in the first niche on the left with its two flanking caryatids.

148 Duchêne Papers, 10 November 1928; 16 June 1928; C. Frange (Ed.), *Le Style Duchêne*, 1998, 118.

149 Duchêne Papers, 6 July 1928; 10 November 1928 – by making only two models, a saving of FF 9,000 was achieved.

150 As the most expensive part of the scheme, the carving had to be done last.

151 Duchêne Papers, 28 December 1928.

152 Duchêne Papers, 25 May 1929, dispatched from Paris in June 1929.

153 Duchêne Papers, 27 May 1929; 30 May 1929; 6 July 1928 – board and lodging for the sculptor was provided by the Duke plus a payment of FF 1,000 for incidental expenditure; 16 August 1927.

154 Duchêne Papers, 25 October 1928.

155 A. Duchêne, *Les Jardins de L'Avenir, Hier, Aujourd'hui, Demain*, 1935, quoted by C. Frange (Ed.), *Le Style Duchêne*, 1998, 180.

10 Changing Gardens

1   Winston S. Churchill to *The Times*, 1 July 1934.

2   *The Victoria History of the County of Oxford*, Vol. XII, 1990, 459.

3   D. Green, *Blenheim Palace*, 1951, 223.

4   H. Montgomery-Massingberd, *Blenheim Revisited*, 1985, 184.

5   Fon was the nickname of Alfonso Hollis who lived at Eagle Lodge. His brother Fred was a footman in the Palace.

6   H. Montgomery-Massingberd, *Ibid*, 1985, 176.

7   In 1962 after a bumper crop, 40 lbs (18 kg) of plums and 60 lbs (27 kg) of runner beans were sent up for freezing.

8   The beds around Gladys's grotto were dug over in February 1962.

9   H. Montgomery-Massingberd, *Ibid*, 1985, 196.

10 H. Montgomery-Massingberd, *Ibid*, 1985, 191.

11 R. Bisgrove, *The Gardens of Britain*, 1978, 37.

12 Blenheim Palace Newsletter – 1960s. I am grateful to Philip Druce for this information.

13 *New Oxford Guide*, 1759, 80–1.

14 N. Pevsner & J. Sherwood, *The Buildings of England – Oxfordshire*, 1974, 475. Richard Hayward (1728–1800) was a London-based sculptor.

15 Blenheim Palace Muniments, E/A/193. 465,037 trees were planted and transplanted in the park and the estate.

16 Model Railway Club, August 1960, Mr Wren (President), Mr Woodward (Treasurer), and Mr Cleaver (Secretary) officiated at the opening ceremony.

17 In August 1968, Jack Hirst, the Palace engineer, erected mock-ups for the fountains before they were installed.

18 Blenheim Palace Muniments, *Son-et-Lumière Programme* 1969; on 7 August 1970 the show was delayed by 50 minutes after a gardener cut a cable while mowing the grass.

19 The work was supervised by Thomas Rayson, the Palace's Oxford-based architect.

20 The original jets arching between the dolphins at the lowest level of the fountain were eliminated in the course of these works.

21 The gravel is still renewed every April, with 89 tons (90 tonnes) of it spread annually.

22 By the 1980s there were two large launches operating on the lake, but this service was discontinued in the late 1990s.

23 I am grateful to Mrs Anne Illingworth for this information.

24 The trophies were carved in Clipsham stone by Michael Groser. I am grateful to Christopher Rayson (retained architect until December 2003) for kindly permitting access to records. Much of the information on repair work is derived from this source.

25 The Temple restoration was begun in 1974 and completed in 1976 with new iron railings being installed to enclose the Temple (in order to put a stop to graffiti and protect the restored structure).

26 These repairs were not a scheduled part of the ongoing restoration plan but had been urgently pushed up the agenda when the bridge was vandalised and two balusters completely destroyed.

27 Carried out by J. Dawson & Sons.

28 The plan was published in July 2006, after public consultation.

29 J. Bond & K. Tiller (Eds.), *Ibid*, 1987, 127, 134.

30 The butterfly house and an adventure playground were in place before the maze was established. When the butterfly house first opened in 1985, the butterflies were supplied by the Guernsey Butterfly Farm. Today they are sourced from the Butterfly Farm at Stratford-upon-Avon. Deliveries of pupa are received once a week from February to October. The herb and lavender garden was planned and laid out in 1992–3.

31 Planned to coincide with the 300th anniversary of the maze at Hampton Court. Besides the Marlborough Maze, a number of other new hedge mazes were opened in 1991 – the Russborough Maze (Co. Wicklow, Ireland), the Italianate Maze (Capel Manor, Hertfordshire), the Alice-in-Wonderland Maze (Merrytown House, Dorset), and the Britannia Maze (Wolseley Garden Park, Staffordshire).

32 The consultants were Minotaur Maze Designs. Designers Adrian Fisher and Randoll Coates were assisted by the landscape architect Graham Burgess.

33 The remaining unplanted parts were left fallow, the soil turned twice a year to control weeds.

34 The world's largest (unsymbolic) hedge maze is at Longleat (62,000 square ft/5760 m^2); the oldest is at Hampton Court (planted in 1690).

35 Around five to eight years depending on the hedging used – beech, holly, yew, hornbeam and box are the most common.

36 *The Oxford Times*, 18 November 1988.

37 The hedge planting, using 18 in. (45 cm) high yews, was carried out by the estate forestry staff.

38 The railway linked the Palace to a plant centre which was run from the Kitchen Garden. In 1975 the engine was steam powered, converted to diesel afterwards.

39 In 1991 the house and maze were open daily from mid-March to end October (10.30 am to 5.30 pm). Entrance to the Palace cost £5.50, the maze £1.00 per person. *British Maze News*, Newsletter of the Maze Society, 20 September 1991. In 1994, the route through the maze was modified to eliminate design weaknesses and allow better transit through the entire structure by making the puzzle more difficult to solve.

40 Winston Churchill, a grandson of the 7th Duke of Marlborough, was born at Blenheim Palace on 30 November 1874.

41 International Council on Monuments and Sites; Blenheim Palace and Park nominated for inclusion on the World Heritage List on 23 December 1986.

42 ICOMOS World Heritage Convention, May 1987; UNESCO Cultural Properties UK, 11 December 1987.

43 The garden was completed in just nine months from September 2003. Trevor and Hilary Wood were also responsible for setting up and opening a new display of antique garden tools and machinery (called 'Blenheim Bygones') in early 2005.

INDEX